SCHOLASTIC

D1369703

Nonfiction Writing
From the Inside Out

BY LAURA ROBB

New York • Toronto • London • Auckland • Sydney
Mexico City • New Delhi • Hong Kong • Buenos Aires

Teaching
Resources

DEDICATION

For my grandson, Lucas Benjamin Hustick—with love

For all my students who teach me—my deepest thanks

CREDITS

excerpts from *The Diary of a Young Girl* by Anne Frank, Otto H. Frank and Mirjam Pressler, editors, translated by Susan Massotty. Copyright (c) 1995 by Doubleday, a division of Random House, Inc. Used by permission.

"A French Cat" by Jean Brody is reprinted by permission of Jean Brody. Copyright © 1997 by Jean Brody.

The review of Russell Freedman's book: From *The Horn Book Magazine*, Sept/Oct 2003. Reprinted by permission of The Horn Book, Inc., Boston, MA, www.hbook.com

The review of Jeanne DuPrau's book: From *The Horn Book Magazine*, May/June 2003. Reprinted by permission of The Horn Book, Inc., Boston, MA, www.hbook.com

excerpt from Rachel's Journey, *The Story of a Pioneer Girl* by Marissa Moss. Copyright © 1998 by Marissa Moss, reprinted by permission of Harcourt Inc.

"Jackie Robinson" from *Lives of the Athletes: Thrills, Spills (and What the Neighbors Thought)*. Copyright © 1997 by Kathleen Krull, reprinted by permission of Harcourt Inc.

From *Common Nonsense* by Andy Rooney. Copyright © 2002 by Andy Rooney. Reprinted by permission of Public Affairs, a member of Perseus Books, LLC.

Cover design by Maria Lilja
Interior design by LDL Designs
Cover and interior photos by Bonnie Forstrum Jacobs

ISBN 0-439-51368-5
Copyright ©2004 by Laura Robb
All rights reserved. Published by Scholastic Inc.
Printed in the U.S.A.
1 2 3 4 5 6 7 8 9 10   23   10 09 08 07 06 05 04

TABLE OF CONTENTS

Acknowledgments

Some books, like baby elephants, have long gestation periods. They require time for the ideas to develop and ripen. *Nonfiction Writing From the Inside Out* enjoyed the gift of time. I knew I wanted to write a book for teachers about how I teach the art of expository writing. And I knew I wanted the advice of published writers to inform it. It took time to marry these two ideas in a manner that would make the writers' experiences integral to the teaching of nonfiction writing.

Both my editor at Scholastic, Wendy Murray, and my agent, Ann Tobias, listened patiently to my evolving notions, which often tugged at my thoughts as I was writing *Teaching Reading in Social Studies, Science, and Math* (Scholastic, 2003). My thanks to both of these women for their confidence in me and their suggestions for selecting contributing authors.

Wendy, I treasure your editing. Your suggestions always drove me back to the text to make it ever more useful to teachers.

My sincere thanks to Terry Cooper, editor-in-chief of Scholastic Teaching Resources, who believed in a book that differed in concept from traditional professional texts for teachers. To Ray Coutu, editor of Theory and Practice books, thanks for your guidance with framing the interview questions.

My thanks to Margery Rosnick, Acquisitions Editor for Theory and Practice, for carving out time to read every phase of this book. I truly appreciate your support and belief in the book.

Deepest thanks go to every writer who set aside time to be interviewed on the telephone or to respond to my questions via e-mail. You are the foundation of this book and have provided many insights into writing that teachers can share with students.

To those who read and reviewed my book—Adam Berkin, Jean Gillet, and Kathy Jongsma—your candid comments provided me with many revision ideas. Rewriting is an opportunity to make a book the best it can be, and all of you helped me clarify ideas.

To my husband, Lloyd—how I appreciate your understanding during the long hours I spent writing in my office away from you and the family.

Finally, to all my students, thanks for your feedback and writing!

FOREWORD

"Nonfiction is utilitarian—like underwear and hot water heaters—the kinds of things you have to buy when you'd really like caviar and cruisers. Librarians have to buy nonfiction so kids can do reports."

This is how Margery Facklam, a great proponent of nonfiction, explains the relationship many of us have with any form of informational writing. I must confess that as a child I probably liked hot water heaters (and certainly underwear!) better than nonfiction. This sad attitude was to a great degree inculcated in me by my experiences with those sorts of reading materials in school. However, I loved fiction with a somewhat cloying passion. It was fiction our teachers read to us after lunch (if they read at all). And it was fiction my parents shared with me at night before bed. But nonfiction only surfaced in my life as dreaded report fodder, to be avoided with the age-old revulsion described by Shakespeare in *Romeo and Juliet*: "Love goes toward love, as schoolboys from their books."

Some say that children's nonfiction wasn't much good in the 1950s and '60s when I was a kid. However, there have always been fascinating informational offerings in books, magazine articles, essays, and so on, but young readers were rarely steered in that direction. Today there is little argument that current nonfiction materials are a genuine treasure trove, and this is, in part, Laura Robb's message. She celebrates writing that can so enliven every facet of our amazing universe that even history—pegged by students as dull and their most disliked subject in school—is jump-started. "Dear Mr. Freedman," writes a young boy, "I read your biography of Abraham Lincoln and liked it very much. Did you take the photographs yourself?" How invigorated by *Lincoln: A Photobiography* was this youngster? Enough to feel as if Lincoln was so real and approachable that he might have lived, as Russell Freedman himself puts it, "the day before yesterday."

However, Laura—the consummate teacher—leads us beyond a nonfiction reading celebration to the place I wish I had been led during my days at West Park Elementary School. She teaches us not only that nonfiction is worth reading—yes, just for fun—but that you can write it, too! Not the soporific, plagiarized reports so common in schools, but the very same sort of eye-opening selections found in print—selections that attract and hold an audience.

Extending the concepts of "Writers' Workshop," Laura has strengthened the reading-writing connection in the writing process, refining and referring to it as "reading with a writer's eye." This is perhaps the key to what her outstanding book offers, for she reminds us that the best writing instructors are the published authors we love to read. Therefore, learning to "read with a writer's eye" can reveal the secrets of their craft. In the following chapters, all we need do is open ourselves to what Bruce Brooks, Russell Freedman, James Cross Giblin, Joyce Hansen, Kathleen Krull, Kathryn Lasky, Walter Dean Myers, and a host of others have to say. Then let Laura help us guide our students toward recognizing and applying these secrets to their own writing. The biggest surprise? Why, they really aren't secrets at all! The "league of writers" isn't an exclusive fellowship—everyone is welcome.

T.H. Bell, former U.S. Secretary of Education, once said that there are three things that would cure all our educational ills, if we could somehow institute them into our public education system: (1) motivation, (2) motivation, (3) motivation. Motivation is sparked by personal intrinsic reward. In other words, I must to some degree value a thing if I'm to give honest time and effort to achieving it, whether it is a facility for basketball, knitting, auto mechanics, or reading and writing. Authors often give this advice to fledgling writers: Read, read, read. Write, write, write. But students will not sincerely pursue either reading or writing without finding them personally rewarding. Therefore, I am most impressed with Laura's truly democratic approach to writing education. There is nothing more motivating than personal choice—the freedom to follow one's interests. In writing, it is what unearths an individual's true voice. In this volume, we find that Laura Robb has turned expository writing into an honest-to-goodness adventure of discovery.

At a time when political pressures are demanding a one-size-fits-all system for "educating" our children, Laura Robb is a much-needed ray of sunshine in a darkened landscape. Good books and good guidance from a skilled and wise teacher can and will create good writers and good learners—skilled, avid, and superbly distinct from one another. In these pages, Laura shows us the way.

Michael O. Tunnell
Orem, Utah

Nonfiction Writing From the Inside Out

INTRODUCTION

In 1993 I interviewed more than a dozen writers of children's books, including Jean Craighead George, Bruce Brooks, and Lois Lowry. I knew I had a treasure chest laden with wisdom that could help teachers teach writing, but I didn't quite know what to do with it all. I also interviewed children's book editors—Dianne Hesse, Janet Chenary, and Andrea Davis Pinkney—with the notion that teachers could integrate editors' ideas into their writing classes and build similar nurturing relationships with their students.

For several years, the idea for this book floated, shadowlike, in my consciousness like some giant squid. Its form finally came into full view when a sixth grader made a comment that forced me to see my teaching of nonfiction writing for what it was—pretty much a failure. "Gosh, Mrs. Robb," Kenny blurted out during class, "can't you see how much we *hate* writing informative paragraphs? It's as boring as reading our history textbook."

Kenny was right. It was boring for them—and boring for me to read. Their pieces were fact after fact after fact, much like those textbooks, which I would never hold up as models of good writing.

Up to that time, I had always emphasized writing fiction and poetry more than nonfiction. They were a strong part of my background, and were types of writing that I was more at home with. Students and I enthusiastically shared and discussed novels, short stories, myths, legends, and poems. I felt comfortable supporting my students as they wrote narrative and poetry. Even the majority of my students' choice reading was fiction. In a class of twenty-four sixth graders, only three students included biography and information chapter books in their reading logs. Clearly, my preferences were affecting their tastes and abilities in reading and writing.

At home that night, I thought more about Kenny's challenge. Without quite knowing what I was after, I pulled the file of author and editor interviews out of the file cabinet. I began to reread the transcriptions. Read, read, read, Jean Craighead George and Lois Lowry both advised.

Read. That was it! My students found writing nonfiction tedious because I had never really encouraged them to read all the riveting, outstanding nonfiction there was out there, and to see these works as models to emulate.

Once this light bulb blinked on, there was no stopping me. I brought into class biographies and autobiographies, magazine articles, informational picture books and chapter books, newspaper editorials, and essays, and my students and I began to learn what made these pieces of writing tick. In the evenings and on weekends, I read books on the craft of nonfiction, including works by Donald Murray, William Zinsser, and Peter Elbow.

For the next several years, I learned about nonfiction writing alongside my students. Together we would analyze parts of texts, articulating for each other why the text grabbed our attention or bored us. We evaluated leads, word choice, organization, and use of simile and metaphor. My students came to call this work "reading with a writer's eye," feeling that this term better described what they were doing than the phrase "reading-writing connection" which struck us as awfully general. *Writer's eye* was apt because we had our eyes on the end goal: to grab these precious nuts and bolts and use them to put together our own writing.

The more students and I read and analyzed nonfiction, the more I recognized that a variety of nonfiction should be a part of every subject, from elementary school through high school. Why? Because nonfiction brings the world to students in ways that fiction can't do all on its own. Through nonfiction our students can learn about other cultures and countries, the natural world, machines and technology—virtually any topic—and this wide reading can inform and improve students' writing.

Writing nonfiction texts, I came to discover, helps children hone their thinking and cement their understandings in unique ways, too. Whether writing a comparison of two Civil War battles or an editorial about a current event, each nonfiction structure challenges students to connect concepts, to organize ideas, and to discover what they understand about a topic or idea.

THE TIME IS NOW

I began to write this book in earnest when I looked out my window a year or so ago and saw the cloud of high-stakes testing blowing in from D.C. to Winchester, Virginia, and wafting all across the country. I wanted to put out a book to offer teachers a better route to achieving high scores on the writing tests. In 2003 the Commission on Writing in America's Schools and Colleges, a panel of 18 educators organized by the College Board, emphatically stated that writing is one of the most important skills students can learn (*The New York Times*, April 26, 2003). Yet as this book goes to press, teachers across the country spend much of their instructional time preparing students to pass a standardized test. This is a sad state of affairs, because test prep perpetuates a kind of writing that doesn't carry much weight in the real world, such as writing a paragraph or an essay in response to a prompt.

I think teachers of writing are especially discouraged because we seem to have moved backwards from where we were in the '80s and '90s, when many teachers across the country embraced writing workshop, an instructional model based on the research of Lucy Calkins (1983, 1994, 1996), Donald Graves (1983, 2003), and Donald Murray (1982, 1984). These researchers had discovered that children can use and benefit from professional writers' habits and techniques. They helped teachers see writing as a process of thinking, talking, brainstorming, planning, drafting, conferring, and revising. They pointed out that as writers write, they move back and forth through these various acts of composing in what Donald Murray described as recursive motions (1982).

Researchers' studies of how professional writers compose, along with their studies of students' composing, led to classroom practice that is now known as process writing. According to Calkins, Graves, and Murray, the best setting to develop students' writing process is a workshop that meets daily or at least four times a week and includes choice of topic and genre, craft lessons, and time to think, brainstorm, plan, draft, revise, and confer.

Writing workshop—and all the authentic practices that go with it—lives on in many classrooms, thankfully, but too often I visit schools and see that formulaic writing has replaced the research-based model that linked the process professional writers use for instruction in school. Students might receive a topic such as "My Winter Break" or "My Favorite Season" and are then expected to compose a final draft in 40 to 45 minutes. For students who spent their break in an ordinary way or who have never experienced four seasons, completing the essay is a struggle because they don't have the experiences or background knowledge to write well. Forget about *choice* and the energy that it gives writing; forget the notion of revising. The assumption is that 45 minutes is all the time students require to pump out a perfect piece. When I visit schools, students mutter comments such as: "Borrrr–ring. Not another paragraph. Same thing every day." Even if they *can* jump through this artificial hoop, they do so with increasing indifference.

Employing recipes such as "one topic sentence that states the subject, three facts to support the topic sentence, and a conclusion that repeats the topic sentence" will surely create a nation of stunted writers whose experiences have been limited to formulaic paragraphs and essays. As adults, these writers will find it much harder to bring voice, passion, energy, depth, and personal commitment to their writing.

Macrorie (1985) described this kind of "school writing" beautifully, dubbing it "Engfish," dull, impersonal writing, such as the five-paragraph essay, that students practice continually.

Our job, then, is to have faith in teaching the writing process in a manner that reflects how actual writers practice writing. With this book, I aim to share instructional practices that can develop young writers who understand their own writing process well enough to write an article, editorial, how-to text, or essay with voice and enthusiasm. Over the years, I have observed that those who write well *do* pass the tests.

So as the drums for high test scores rumbled in the media and in the hallways of schools, I sat in my third-floor office and dialed up David Quammen, Kathryn Lasky, Patricia McKissack, and Donald Graves. "Tell me how you do what you do. We've got to help students everywhere catch your passion for writing." This was in essence how I began the conversations. The generous replies of these writers, in phone interviews and in e-mails, were an incredible salve for me. The love these writers have for their work, the advice they gave, and their commitment to children reminded me that as teachers, we simply need to learn from those who write well for a living and from the children we teach.

With this book, we *can* learn from them—about writing biography, essay, memoir, informational picture books and chapter books, diaries, interviews, book reviews, and more. This book is 100 pages longer than originally planned because I wanted a large amount of the writers' thinking and advice delivered to you verbatim. I wanted their process, their research and writing habits, and their techniques to support my own lessons in this book in a comprehensive way. So in addition to quotes woven throughout the text, I start each chapter with a section called "In Their Own Words," where you can hear these writers speak to the topic of the chapter.

I encourage you to share these excerpts with your students. Post on chart paper or construction paper passages that speak to you. Invite students to discuss these quotes and connect professional writers' words to their own process.

In each chapter, I've linked the authors' quotes to lessons, because advice alone from professional writers, no matter how detailed and eloquent, is not enough to teach writing. Our children need to see the writing techniques and habits modeled by you, and they need guidance as they practice them on their own. In addition, many of the lessons use excerpts from these nonfiction writers' books, so that students can see precisely the end result they're after. The unique power of this book, I think, is in this fusion of author advice, lessons, and book excerpts that remind us to *read widely in order to write well.*

I hope this book will inspire you and your students to write nonfiction by interpreting data and connecting information to students' lives, their communities, and world issues (Kingsolver, 1995; Yolen, 1983). I want it to help you build an authentic writing program where writing at school matches, as much as possible, writing in the real world. We must help our student writers find their voices and approach nonfiction writing as an exciting craft they will want to fine-tune throughout their lives. — *Laura Robb*

CHAPTER ONE

WRITING ABOUT THE WORLD

Frameworks That Support the Teaching of Creative Nonfiction

In Their Own Words

Why are you drawn to nonfiction writing?

Russell Freedman

As an aspiring writer, I tried my hand at various forms. I wrote short stories for school magazines and at college I won the James Phelan Prize for poetry, a cash award that was the first money I ever earned for something I had written. But it was as a reporter for the Associated Press in San Francisco that I found my true writer's voice. I discovered that while I enjoyed the act of writing, no matter what the subject or form, I felt most at home, most gratified, when I was writing about real people and events. So that's what I've been doing ever since. The best thing about my work as a writer of nonfiction is that it gives me the opportunity to explore just about any subject that interests me.

~~~~~~~~~~~~~~~~~~

Jean Craighead George

The human must "learn." The other animals "inherit" knowledge. A wild turkey chick, raised without being instructed by a parent, suddenly at about one month of age, knows the difference between poisonous and nonpoisonous spiders. The human child must be told or read such information. My joy as a writer is to make knowledge, particularly in biology, available through mammal, bird, or reptilian protagonists. In all my nonfiction, I carry a narrative thread. Stories are still the best way to learn, even for adults.

~~~~~~~~~~~~~~~~~~

James Cross Giblin

I've always been curious about people and events in history, and writing about them enables me to satisfy my own curiosity first of all. I often say that every one of my nonfiction books for children has been like an adult-education course for me!

~~~~~~~~~~~~~~~~~~

Joyce Hansen

I wasn't drawn to nonfiction at first. I'd just finished writing a piece of historical fiction based on the Civil War and my publisher asked me to write a non-fiction book about black soldiers in the Civil War. I was tentative and unsure at first about how to really make the book alive and interesting. After several dry drafts, and helpful advice from my editor, as well as reading successful nonfiction written for young people, I began to understand how fictional techniques, images and a distinct voice, are all important elements in nonfiction. I also began to see how wonderfully creative nonfiction can be.

Kathryn Lasky

I never read nonfiction as a kid because it was all so dry—like textbook writing. It lacked a human element. There was this authoritarian voice telling you what to think. I was drawn to it as an adult when there was a great popularizing of nonfiction. Carl Sagan and Stephen J. Gould had an enormous influence on me because they seemed to make it a more human endeavor; it had a human drama I expected to find in fiction and things debatable. There can be voice in nonfiction. That I could find a voice in nonfiction drew me to it.

Patricia McKissack

I'm drawn to nonfiction because I really see nonfiction as a way of telling the stories that have been worth knowing. When I was a teacher, twenty-five years ago, there weren't a lot of worthwhile nonfiction materials. There weren't a lot of materials available about African-American heroes and there was a need for them. That drew me to nonfiction. I love fiction as well, but I felt that nonfiction was so necessary. I wanted to bring the real stories about people and history to readers.

Walter Dean Myers

Nonfiction allows me to satisfy my personal curiosity about a subject. Sometimes I want to know what happened at a particular time or place, but more often I want to be able to "feel" the subject, to imagine how people felt during a particular event.

Including Authors' Insights in Instruction

WHEN I ASKED THE CHILDREN'S WRITERS I interviewed for this book, "Why are you drawn to nonfiction writing?" their responses revealed an intense drive to explore the world—to understand nature, science, history, the lives of famous people, and cultures that intrigue them.

In writing for children, these authors work to make true stories and information as compelling for young readers as they are for them. In my conversations with them, they often uttered words like *wonder* and *fascinate* and *curiosity*. Their excited stance, their engagement with the world, and love of living is what they want to transmit to their readers. And this is of course what every teacher wants for each student: a hunger to know the world.

Share the quotes from In Their Own Words with your students. Discuss with them why these writers have gravitated to writing nonfiction. Notice the ideas these writers have in common—that nonfiction has drama, story, and voice; satisfies their curiosity; and shares understandings about the world. These are the core attributes of outstanding nonfiction that you will explore in this book, and as your students read nonfiction by these authors and others, these attributes will begin to show up in students' writing. Why? Because nonfiction literature can awaken the latent researcher in every child, stirring young minds to wonder about people, plants, animals, birds, sea creatures, and virtually anything else. Inspired to know and to share what they've learned with others, they then have the reason to gather the details and ideas to write nonfiction in creative ways.

But of course, reading nonfiction is only a part of the whole. As with any craft, learning to write nonfiction is a multifaceted endeavor, and to teach it you need a full menu of strategies, which you'll gain in the course of this book.

In this chapter I help you build a foundation for teaching nonfiction writing. I'll define *creative nonfiction* and some other terms, and then explain eight teaching practices that support student writers. So as you implement the ideas in this book, you'll know the philosophical framework of each one.

I think there is a unique power to be found in good nonfiction—the power to illuminate facts and make learning about the world delicious. That's what draws me to it as both a reader and a writer. However, it is a challenge to write a nonfiction account in a manner that truly breathes life into the subject.

— Michael O. Tunnell

Each morning I race out the back door, shove open the stubborn gate, charge to my car, and toss my book bag, water bottle, and pocketbook onto the back seat. A minute later, I'm turning the car onto Braddock Street in Winchester, Virginia, heading to Powhatan School, the independent K–8 school where I teach reading-writing workshop and coach teachers. As I drive through the city streets, I check the clock and make my decision: When I'm running late I take the highway because it is faster. Most days, however, I'm on time, and I navigate the country road, relishing every twist and curve, and glad the speed limit is 25 to 40 miles per hour, for it gives me the opportunity to notice. In spring, magenta buds bloom on the branches of Virginia red-bud trees, and I drink in the green of unfurling leaves. If I'm lucky, I might spot a bluebird, or a barn owl, with wings like an airplane, as it flies across the road.

Every once in a while I have to set the car's hazard lights blinking and stop to let a family of deer cross, or wait for two box turtles wending their way across the asphalt. In spring and autumn, horses nod to me, their heads leaning over weathered wooden fences. Once, two cows who'd escaped from a hole in their fenced pasture, led the way to school. There was no passing them as they trotted in tandem along the road. Periodically, both stopped to sniff the May air or munch some grass sprouting on the road's shoulder.

A line of cars grew behind me and my Holstein escorts. Several drivers blared their horns or sounded them in bursts of syncopated rhythms to announce their irritation. Oblivious to these noisy cues, the cows continued ambling until a farmer arrived on horseback, and with a long stick shooed them into a field. I loved every minute of the unexpected traffic jam. How silly to get irritated at cows! Even on mornings of less drama, I treasure this time, for it allows me to experience a part of my world.

Nonfiction writers delve into the ancient past, travel to study endangered species, attempt to know the universe millions of miles above. They take on larger pieces of the world than I do on my daily commute, but our stance is the same—we're receptive to the world. I share the story of the two cows to underscore one essential thing I want you to keep in mind as you read this book: to write *creative nonfiction*, our students need to be guided to perceive with their senses in order to understand the very heart of a place, person, invention, period in history, or whatever it is they're examining.

CREATIVE NONFICTION: WHAT IT IS

"What I want is Facts. Teach these boys and girls nothing but Facts. Facts alone are wanted in life. Plant nothing else, and root out everything else," declared Thomas Gradgrind in Charles Dickens's novel *Hard Times*. Poor Thomas. If he only knew that readers of every age reject such writing. Bobby, an eighth grader, said it best with, "When I read the science textbook, it's like a huge garbage truck has compressed thousands of facts about protists, then dumped them into a few pages."

Jane Yolen and Myra Zarnowski distinguish "nothing-but-the-facts" nonfiction from creative nonfiction this way: The nonfiction writer, according to Yolen (1983) and Zarnowski (1998), takes data and transforms them into information—*information that conveys what the data say and mean* [italics mine]. In other words, it's an interpretive process. Sharing what the raw facts "say and mean" is really a form of storytelling. Patricia McKissack reminds us that "nonfiction is a way of telling stories that have been worth knowing."

William Zinsser makes the points that the writer's story—the writer's self—is a mysterious part of the text as well:

> *Ultimately the product that any writer has to sell is not the subject being written about, but who he or she is . . . This is the personal transaction that's at the heart of good nonfiction writing. Out of it come two of the most important qualities that this book [Zinsser's] will go in search of: humanity and warmth. Good writing has an aliveness that keeps the reader reading from one paragraph to the next, and it's not a question of gimmicks to "personalize the author." It's a question of using the English language in a way that will achieve the greatest clarity and strength.*
>
> — From *On Writing Well: The Classic Guide to Writing Nonfiction*,
> by William Zinsser, pp. 5–6

To see this humanity at work, let's look at two examples of creative nonfiction, one by Jean Craighead George and the other by Barbara Kingsolver, and each of which I set against a World Book encyclopedia entry about the same topics. I think you'll agree that Craighead George and Kingsolver have what Zinsser calls an "aliveness" and what Walter Dean Myers describes as "feeling the subject," whereas the encyclopedia entry delivers data because that is the goal of this genre.

Craighead George describes an owl searching for a mate, while Kingsolver chronicles how she and her daughter came to love the hermit crab they mistakenly brought home to Arizona from a vacation in the Bahamas.

Of the typical owls, the great horned owl lives in many places throughout North America....The eyes are very large. These eyes point forward, unlike the eyes of most birds. For this reason, owls can watch an object with both eyes at the same time. They have binocular vision like man.

— From *The World Book Encyclopedia* (Field Enterprises Educational Corporation), vol. 14, p. 674

The owl, who stood almost two feet high, stared into the sunless forest. To him there was no darkness. The pale light from the moon and stars, and their reflections off the snow and clouds, fell onto mirrorlike cells on the retina of his eyes. The cells magnified the dim light, and he could see even though it was dark. He saw a snowflake on his great hooked beak. He saw a twig fall from the pine. Through these eyes, and his unique ear, the night is day.

—From *The Moon of the Owls,* by Jean Craighead George, illustrated by Wendell Minor, HarperCollins, 1993, p. 10

Hermit crabs live in empty seashells and close them tightly using one claw as a door. The color, form, and texture of claws, legs, and bodies run through many shades and shapes, from smooth to rough and spiny.

—From *The World Book Encyclopedia* (Field Enterprises Educational Corporation), vol. 4, p. 895

We've also learned to give him [a hermit crab] a continually changing assortment of seashells, which he tries on and casts off like Cinderella's stepsisters preening for the ball. He'll sometimes try to squeeze into ludicrous outfits too small to contain him (who can't relate?). In other moods, he will disappear into a conch the size of my two fists and sit for a day, immobilized by the weight of upward mobility. He is in every way the perfect houseman: quiet, entertaining, and willing to eat up the trash.

— From *High Tide in Tucson* by Barbara Kingsolver, HarperPerennial, 1996, p. 3

CREATIVE NONFICTION: QUALITIES IT SHARES WITH FICTION

Writers of creative nonfiction:

• are receptive to the world around them.

• use their senses as they research and write.

• tell stories.

• show, don't tell.

• allow humanity and warmth to infuse their prose.

Wow! That sounds a lot like what fiction writers do—and with good reason. The best nonfiction writers deliberately borrow fictional techniques to satisfy the human need for story. During her interview with me, writer Sue Bartoletti put it this way:

> Nonfiction writers often utilize devices of fiction (character, dialogue, setting, "hooks" to draw in the reader, and vivid writing).
>
> The only caveat is that the nonfiction writer can't make anything up . . . . Even dialogue must be authentic. Every detail must be verifiable.

As you will discover in the chapters that follow, many of the mini-lessons I share are just about identical to ones I present when teaching fiction and poetry, covering such topics as using strong verbs and specific nouns and writing enticing leads. Indeed, these lessons have a lot of "reach," helping your students write in any genre with greater creativity and precision. In the box at left, I've outlined some of these shared elements. However, I don't want to set up a good/bad dichotomy in your mind, where intensely fact-based writing is bad and imaginative writing is good. My focus in this book is on teaching children about creative nonfiction, but I feel compelled to state that of course there are times in life when *all* we want are the facts. Maybe when we are listening to the news, or reading an article on aging or the common cold, or collecting data from an encyclopedia, facts alone satisfy. So suffice it to say, I believe that factual or technical writing is as important as creative nonfiction.

SOME ELEMENTS OF FICTION AND POETRY NONFICTION WRITERS USE

• character

• dialogue

• first-person point of view

• figurative language: metaphor, simile, alliteration

• details that help readers envision a place or event

• strong verbs

• specific nouns

• narrative thread

• leads that create a mood, use dialogue, or stir emotions to hook readers

IS NONFICTION A GENRE?: DEFINING OUR TERMS

In addition to the term *creative nonfiction*, there are terms that will crop up throughout this book and that I want to define now: *nonfiction, genre, nonfiction features*, and *nonfiction structures*. Keep in mind that these terms are used somewhat differently by various linguists and professors of English.

Nonfiction includes a wide range of genres—but it is not a literary genre in and of itself. Think of nonfiction as an umbrella arcing over a variety of genres that include biography, autobiography, informational chapter and picture books, photo essays, interviews, personal, informative, and persuasive essays, magazine and newspaper articles, how-to books, book reviews, cook books, and question/answer books. These specific kinds of nonfiction are each literary genres. Genres have different purposes. For example, the purpose of a biography is to recount significant events of all or a part of a person's life, whereas the purpose of an essay can be to persuade or inform, and the purpose of an interview can be to reveal a person's childhood, career, beliefs, inventions, and so on (Duke & Bennett-Armistead, 2003; Kletzien & Dreher, 2003; Bamford & Kristo, 1998).

Increasingly, the lines of genre have become blurred (Laminack and Bell, 2004). Marilyn Nelson stretches the term *biography* in her book *Carver: A Life in Poems* (Front Street, 2001). Charles R. Smith, Jr., uses poems to present twelve female basketball players in *Hoop Queens* (Candlewick, 2003).

A newer type of literature that combines nonfiction and fiction, called faction, has been accepted as a genre by some countries (Tomlinson and Lynch-Brown, 2002). Faction is nonfiction that includes fictional elements such as recreated dialogue, first-person point of view, and a story line based on careful research. Examples of this kind of literature are *Cathedral* by David MacCaulay (Houghton, 1973) and *My Place in Space* by Robin and Sally Hirst, illustrated by Roland Harvey and Joe Levine (Orchard, 1988).

The primary purpose of nonfiction is to inform readers by using documented fact (Tomlinson & Lynch-Brown, 2002). To enhance and extend the information and ideas, nonfiction writers use features such as sidebars, photographs and captions, letters, quotes from diaries, primary documents, eyewitness accounts, charts, and diagrams (see pages 45–52 for a more on nonfiction features).

Nonfiction writers use six basic structures to inform, show, describe, and explain information (Alvermann and Phelps, 1998; Harvey, 1998; Robb, 2003; Vacca and Vacca, 2000).

The six structural patterns are:

- sequence,
- compare/contrast,
- cause/effect,
- question/answer,
- problem/solution, and
- description.

Authors rarely use one structure exclusively throughout a text. Instead, authors intuitively shift from structure to structure depending on their content, and their changing purposes as they write. For example, a writer might use description to paint a picture of a rain forest at dawn, then slide into sequence for a few paragraphs as she describes her day studying howler monkeys, and so forth. Generally, I teach these structures as paragraph structures, but I point out to students that nonfiction writers often craft paragraphs that are a blend of a couple of them, and that they then string these hybrids together in a way that makes sense. (In Chapter 5 you will explore ways to use reading to heighten students' awareness of these structures.)

DEFINING OUR SCOPE

Now, let's define the parameters of this book. Just as I wouldn't want a student to attempt to write an account of the Civil War, but would instead encourage her to narrow her focus, my editor smiled and said, "An 800-page, book, huh?" when, after handing in a first draft, I said I wanted to add a chapter on writing workshop, one on assessment, a lesson on every nonfiction genre, and so on and so on. She assured me that my original instincts were correct, that no one professional book can be a completely comprehensive guide to nonfiction writing—nor should it be, as it would be an overwhelming door stopper of a resource. In framing the book, I considered middle- and high-school teachers' schedules and the number of students they work with each year. I took the following into account:

- For middle- and high-school teachers, English period can be as little as 40 minutes a day, or as much as a 90-minute block three times a week. During this time teachers must cover reading, writing, spelling, vocabulary development, and grammar—a tall teaching order even in a 90-minute block.
- English and content teachers work with 125 to 140 students each school year. Finding the time to prepare lessons, keep abreast of theory and practice by reading journals and

professional books, confer with students about their nonfiction pieces, and grade stacks of papers are issues I appreciate and understand, for they are part of my teaching life.

In this book I focus on several genres that my students relish, such as conducting and writing up interviews and writing short biographies, articles, diaries, and book reviews. To meet basic nonfiction writing requirements of school districts, I've also included lessons on writing paragraphs and developing these into personal, persuasive, and analytical essays. Several lessons are devoted to writing techniques and usage, and all of them are presented with an eye to writing creative nonfiction rather than traditional research reports.

I've included scaffolding ideas to help you differentiate your instruction, and address assessment, mainly in Chapter 7, providing you with a few examples of how I evaluate pieces to improve students' writing and inform my teaching.

DEFINING OUR GOALS

Any lesson or activity you do with your students needs to be anchored in a harbor of beliefs about teaching and learning writing. This harbor contains all the lessons, all the writing projects you do. Students grow as writers when they write within an environment that has clearly defined rituals and practices. Whether you call it a workshop, writing time, or whatever, the important thing is that it has a predictable flow and that during that time, children think of themselves as writers.

I'd like to define a handful of practices that create such an environment. These eight practices inform all the lessons you will explore in subsequent chapters. I hope you'll hold these eight practices dear and make them integral to your writing classes. Without them, teaching and learning nonfiction writing, or indeed any writing, won't have enough oxygen flowing through it to become creative and alive. They are:

1. Present mini-lessons.
2. Build in time for discussion.
3. Read and analyze nonfiction.
4. Use writing guidelines.
5. Help students view writing as an act of discovery.
6. Let students choose their writing topics.
7. Give your students time to write.
8. Teach students the writers' process.

1. Present Mini-Lessons

Over the course of the year, you'll want to cover nonfiction features, structure, craft techniques, and writing conventions. Most mini-lessons take from five to fifteen minutes. Keeping mini-lessons focused is key when you have a 40- to 45-minute period. Some days I present two 5-minute mini-lessons in one class. For example, I might present one on understanding the use and purpose of sidebars, and another on crafting a lead that grabs readers' attention. On subsequent days, I might review a mini-lesson I've presented on using strong verbs or repairing run-on sentences. I take my cues from my students' writing and from how much they know about specific nonfiction genres we're studying. The point to remember is that before inviting students to write in a nonfiction genre, you need to present mini-lessons that deepen students' understandings of how the genre works (see more about mini-lessons in Chapter 2).

> ### WRITING CONVENTIONS
>
> What are writing conventions? Commonly agreed upon elements that make writing readable, including capitalization, punctuation, paragraphing, spelling, sentence structure, and usage.

2. Build in Time for Discussion

I integrate discussions in my writing classes for these purposes:

- to browse through nonfiction texts
- to examine a genre
- to examine the features of nonfiction texts
- to explore ideas for topics
- to raise questions that help students search for more details
- to discover what students already know about a topic or genre
- to review our brainstorming
- to share drafts
- to analyze texts from a writer's point of view
- to debrief on a mini-lesson
- to peer-edit
- to confer and provide feedback on a draft
- to make sense of and better understand research
- to connect ideas to self and other issues

In my classes, students sit at tables in groups of four. Discussions usually occur after mini-lessons, before and during writing, and in peer conferences. Students usually begin discussing in groups of two. Once they've conferred, I frequently have partners share their ideas with members of their table and then with the entire class. I note key ideas on large chart paper and the chart becomes a student resource. The all-class share is important because it brings a wealth of ideas and background knowledge to every student. This three-step discussion strategy works well with 20 to 24 students. If you teach classes of 25 or more students, it can be too chaotic to organize students into small groups, so have them discuss with partners only.

Generally, I keep discussions brief, two to five minutes. Limiting each phase of discussion to short bursts of time helps students stay on task, especially students in grades four and up. And they can accomplish a lot in that amount of time.

Their discussions teach me what kinds of mini-lessons students need; for example, if students discuss using strong verbs in their writing, I'll do a mini-lesson on using the thesaurus, or a mini-lesson on working with a partner to generate lists of alternate verbs.

Another benefit of splicing brief discussions into your writing class is that it develops writers' abilities to hold internal one-on-one conversations as they read (Rosenblatt, 1978), as they observe, and as they mull over facts and ideas while they draft. When students talk about what they are learning, they can discover what they understand (Alvermann, Dillon, and O'Brien, 1987; Freeman & Person, 1998; Mazzoni and Gambrell, 1996). As students link facts to their experiences and knowledge, and as they ask questions, they can discover the meanings behind the facts (Evans, 2001; Gambrell, 1996).

3. Read and Analyze Nonfiction

Reading and enjoying a variety of nonfiction texts ought to be a staple in students' reading diet, and an integral part of nonfiction writing instruction. Through their reading, I want students to discover that "learning about the world is delicious," as Michael O. Tunnell has said.

After students have enjoyed a nonfiction text, whether a read aloud, instructional, or independent reading book, you can select passages for students to study and analyze with a

TALKING CORNER

Place pillows or a few comfortable chairs in a corner of your classroom so that students who need to converse can do so. This allows other students to concentrate on reading, planning, or drafting away from the quiet chatting.

writer's eye. (We'll explore this activity thoroughly in Chapter 2.) Choose selections from different nonfiction genres—diaries; editorials; magazine and newspaper articles; and informative, persuasive, and analytical essays.

When students learn about craft through reading, they gain dozens of mentors who can support them as they compose or struggle to figure out a problem with organization and find the perfect example or word to shape an idea. Reading texts and thinking about what the writers' choices and intentions may have been helps students become aware of genre features, structures, and other techniques (Graves, 1983, 1994, 2003; Portalupi & Fletcher, 2001; Ray, 1999). When students write, their knowledge of how genres work helps them choose the genre that best suits their topic.

4. Use Writing Guidelines

Clear writing guidelines are integral to students' composing a successful piece of writing. I've found that when I establish writing criteria with students, usually as they are beginning to draft their piece, they appreciate my being clear about what I expect. The guidelines, which include content, style and organization, usage, and mechanics, should mirror what students know and what they are learning—in mini-lessons and conferences, by studying published writing, and by reading and discussing one another's pieces. Ultimately, guidelines make for effective teacher, peer, and self-evaluations because students understand the purposes for reading a piece and can measure the writing against the guidelines. When I present and discuss samples of students' writing in later chapters, I will provide examples of the guidelines students and I negotiated. (See pages 260–261.)

5. Help Students View Writing as an Act of Discovery

The poet Robert Frost captured the notion of writing as discovery when he said, "For me, the initial delight is in the surprise of remembering something I didn't know I knew." Because writers continually think, recall, read, and reflect before and during writing, they often uncover buried ideas, information, and thoughts, and connect these ideas in ways that surprise them.

Share with students what professional writers say about writing as an act of thinking and discovery. Encourage paired or small-group discussions by inviting students to connect quotes to their experiences. Post author quotations on chart paper or on small pieces of construction paper and display these in your classroom. Here are four of my favorites:

We write to taste life twice, in the moment, and in retrospection. —Anais Nin

There is in writing the constant joy of sudden discovery. —H. L. Mencken

Good writing is full of surprises and novelties, moving in a direction you don't expect.

—Iris Murdoch

Many new insights and understandings will come to you as you engage in this writing on the voyage out, but don't demand them or struggle for them. If you want to end up with new insights, you have to allow yourself to lose sight of your topic during much of the voyage out.

—Peter Elbow

6. Let Students Choose Their Writing Topics

When students write about their passions and life experiences, when they can make an informed decision about the genre that works for their topic, they willingly invest time and energy in their writing. In contrast, assigning writing topics prevents students from discovering and exploring experiences and topics they truly care about—topics that can result in writing that absorbs readers (Calkins, 1994; Calkins & Harwayne, 1991; Graves, 1983, 2003, 1994; Harwayne, 2000; Murray, 1984; Zinsser, 2001). Moreover, when students rarely have the choice of topic and genre, they become dependent on teacher-made prompts. And those who rebel against prompts, like me, end up in trouble.

When I was a sixth grader, Ms. Weeks, my teacher, never offered choice in writing. She printed on the chalkboard either a title or the first two or three sentences of a piece we were to complete. Because I refused to write using prompts and chose my own topics instead, printed on my report card were these words: "Needs improvement in writing."

Just before the reporting period closed, I won first place in a local writing contest. My story, called "Racer," was about my pretend Shetland pony who lived in our cramped three-room apartment in the Bronx in New York City. Even though Ms. Weeks erased her comments, I knew she was serious about my need for improvement. She had pressed her words so deeply on lines under the heading "Second Marking Period Comments" that the indentations remained even after she erased the pencil marks.

Maybe I needed improvement in cooperation instead of in writing. I loved to write and spent hours at home filling notebooks with pictures, observations, and stories. Even though she never knew this, the lesson Ms. Weeks taught me at an early age was that choice matters. Choice, for writers, holds the potential of the writer connecting ideas to her life experiences—and that's what published writers do.

GIVE CHOICE TO STUDENTS IN ALL SUBJECTS

English and content-area teachers can offer writing topics that are broad enough to allow students to choose an aspect that interests them. Hopefully, students can make a powerful connection between the selected topic and their lives. The examples that follow illustrate how broad writing topics offer students choices within the context of what's being studied in required curriculum.

English
- Interview a shopkeeper, a firefighter, or another community person.
- Write about something you love doing outside of school.
- Write a biography about a friend.

History
- Choose an explorer for a biographical sketch.
- Plan a piece on one aspect of daily life in ancient Rome, ancient Greece, the Renaissance, the Great Depression, the American colonies, etc.
- Choose a Civil War general and plan a piece that discusses his military strategy, its effectiveness, and how and why you might have changed it.

Science
- Choose one of the single-celled plants or animals we've studied and write about its habitat and how it reproduces; include a labeled diagram.
- Plan and write about the formation of igneous, sedimentary, or metamorphic rock.
- Pick an inventor and his or her invention. Create an illustrated, informative card that fourth graders could use.

WRITING A LIFE

How do life experiences affect your writing?

My life experiences are woven throughout—it's like a tapestry. Behind the stories are the shadows of my life, and stories are coming out of and connecting to my own experiences. For example, my interest in Mary McLeod Bethune and some civil rights leaders came from my childhood. I was a little girl at the time of the Supreme Court's decision on civil rights legislation. When I'm writing people's stories, I'm not writing out of a void. I'm writing out of my own life, my own joy, my own uncertainty.

—*Patricia McKissack,*
Interview, February 2003

7. Give Your Students Time to Write

Teachers often ask me, "How do you schedule time for students to write when there are so many things to teach?" It isn't easy, but it's very important to build in enough time for students to move deeply into a subject or topic that has aroused their curiosity. Here are some scheduling ideas that will help you accomplish this.

Scheduling Time For Nonfiction Writing: Options for Daily 40- to 45-Minute English Classes

Alternate Your Reading and Writing Classes:
Think of scheduling in terms of two-week blocks. For example:
> **Week One:** Reserve three periods for reading and two periods for writing, spelling, and writing conventions.
> **Week Two:** Set aside three periods for writing and two periods for reading.

Teach in Two-Week Blocks
> **First Two Weeks:** Schedule reading daily.
> **Next Two Weeks:** Schedule writing daily.
> **Adjustments:** For some nonfiction writing tasks, you might need to add a few days or an entire week to the writing cycle.

To maintain writing momentum and interest, students can continue to write at home during the two-week reading block. Reserve independent work times during both learning blocks, and let students choose whether to read or write during them.

8. Teach Students the Writers' Process

When I ask myself, "What kind of writing could I produce without thinking, planning, drafting, revising, conferring, and editing?," the answer is: *very poor writing*. And that's just the kind of writing our students will produce if we don't help them understand and use the writing process that all professional writers use. Whether you have a short class period or a long block, your students can learn to write creative nonfiction texts by applying the writers' process to their own composing.

In the section that follows, I will review the writing process writers use so you can bring this creative process to your students' nonfiction writing. If you need more than the brief refresher this section offers, then read some of the professional books listed in the box that follows. They will deepen your knowledge of the writing process and assist you in setting up a workshop environment in your classroom.

Selected Books on Teaching Writing

Directing the Writing Workshop: An Elementary Teacher's Handbook by Jean Wallace Gillet and Lynn Beverly (Guilford, 2001).

In the Middle: New Understanding About Writing, Reading, and Learning by Nancie Atwell (Heinemann, 1987).

6 + 1 Traits of Writing by Ruth Culham (Scholastic, 2002).

What You Know by Heart: How to Develop Curriculum for Your Writing Workshop by Katie Wood Ray (Heinemann, 2002).

Write to Learn by Donald Murray (Holt, Rinehart & Winston, 1984).

Writing: Teachers & Children at Work by Donald H. Graves (Heinemann, 1983).

Writing Workshop: The Essential Guide by Ralph Fletcher and JoAnn Portalupi (Heinemann, 2001).

The Writing Process: An Overview

Donald Murray offers an apt visual image of the writing process when he likens it to tangled, cooked spaghetti, with coils and twists that meet and touch one another (1984). The strands—of thinking, collecting, focusing, planning and organizing, drafting, and revising—intermingle. Writers continually shift among these strands as they compose.

THINKING AND COLLECTING

This stage of the process is also called *rehearsal* or *prewriting*. Writers think and perhaps talk to others in order to reclaim sensory memories and information. They may brainstorm orally or in writing to freely generate ideas, with the goal being to discover topics and ideas that interest them.

STRATEGIES TO TRY: Use some of the strategies that follow to encourage students' thinking and collecting of ideas:

- whole-class discussion
- writing lists
- making charts
- drawing
- free-writing, letting ideas flow
- interviewing others

- reading through journals or notebooks
- paired or small-group discussions
- posing questions about an idea
- browsing through books and magazines
- brainstorming

FOCUSING

"What do I want to write about?" and "What am I trying to say?" These are daunting questions for any writer; for young writers, the prospect of settling on a topic can make them slam down their pencils and declare, "I have nothing to write about." Strategies that help them focus an idea into something compelling *and* manageable in scope can help them past this I-give-up stance.

While collecting, writers gather more information and ideas than they will use. Some children seem to know exactly what their purpose is and quickly narrow their long list of ideas. Most don't. For them, pinpointing the topic can be as tough as grasping a slimy, wriggling trout. So it's helpful to demonstrate ways to focus their inventory of ideas.

STRATEGIES TO TRY: The list that follows represents some questions you can pose and activities you can model. Post the list in your classroom and continually add students' suggestions, since what works for one student might support another.

- Reread your list of ideas. Circle ideas you want to include in your piece.
- Discuss your list of ideas with a partner. Talking can help writers discover what they are trying to communicate.
- Ask your partner to read your list and pose questions. Thinking about questions can clarify ideas and purposes.
- Think of your audience and select ideas that will help these readers understand what you're trying to say.
- Jot down a list of questions you want your piece to answer. Return to your collection of ideas and circle those that answer the questions. Then decide if you need to collect additional information.

Managing a classroom
full of students engaged
in the writing process
isn't easy, and here's
why: By the end of your
second week of class
your students will be at
different points in the
process; some will be
planning, others collect-
ing ideas, and a few will
be drafting.

At the start of
every two or three
classes, you can note on
a chart where students
are in the process (see
Appendix page 326 for
sample chart). Nancie
Atwell calls this "taking
the status of the class"
(1987, 1999). You can
also negotiate, with stu-
dents, due dates for
drafts, revisions, and
publishable pieces, so
you keep a handle on
their progress. When
students are all focusing
on a specific nonfiction
genre, it's easier to
keep them on a single
schedule.

PLANNING AND ORGANIZING

Before drafting, most writers organize the information they've gathered and make a plan. Having a plan enables writers to imagine their piece as a whole, to see a final destination. They may use note cards, webs, numbered lists, outlines, and other techniques.

Writers know that the plan will probably change a bit during drafting and revising; that's as it should be.

In Chapter 3 we'll explore strategies for teaching students to plan in more detail. For now, just keep in mind that plans are fluid; resist any temptation to hold students to their original conception.

Be Flexible

I always ask students to try a technique, but I'm also aware of the fact that students' processes and needs differ. Some students, like eighth-grader Andy, spend a long time thinking and planning before picking up a pencil. While his classmates brainstorm lists, Andy stares at the ceiling or out the window. He might do this for two workshop classes. After jotting down a sketchy plan, Andy writes. "The words just pour like a steady rain," he explains. "It's all organized up here [he points to his head] and I have to write and write until it's out of me."

Students' writing processes will also vary depending upon the topic or genre. A student might draft a personal essay quickly because the ideas are in his memory. That same writer, writing about the monarch butterfly, may research, take a stack of notes, and jot down a plan before attempting a draft.

STRATEGIES TO TRY: Introduce students to various writing plans and expect that they will adapt plans to their needs. Model how to use some of the planning strategies that follow. Encourage students to share their plans with classmates so they teach one another. Here are the three kinds of plans I introduce:

- Note cards on which students write a main heading at the top and details underneath.
- Webs that invite students to place their topic in the center with four or five main points radiating from the topic.
- The Venn diagram, which is especially effective for planning compare-and-contrast essays

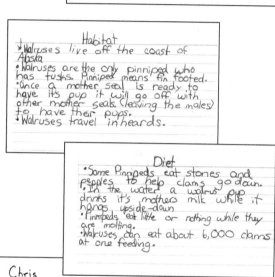

Apperance
- Walruses have 26 ribs altogether.
- Walruses pups are born in Spring or summer.
- A mother gives birth to only one pup at a time.
- Walruses have holes in there heads for ears.
- Walruses travel in heards. (20—600)
- Walruses spend most of their life sleeping.
- All pinnipeds are mammals.
- Walruses tusks can grow to be 39 inches long.
- Walruses grow all througout the walruses life

Habitat
- Walruses live off the coast of Alaska
- Walruses are the only pinniped who has tusks. Pinniped means fin footed.
- Once a mother seal is ready to have its pup it will go off with other mother seals (leaving the males) to have their pups.
- Walruses travel in heards.

Diet
- Some Pinnipeds eat stones and pebbles to help clams go down.
- In the water a walrus pup drinks it's mothers milk while it hangs upside-down
- Pinnipeds eat little or nothing while they are molting.
- Walruses can eat about 6,000 clams at one feeding.

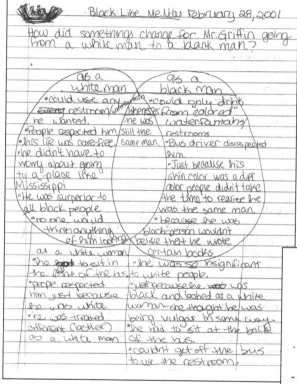

Black Like Me Nber February 28, 2001

How did something change for Mr. Griffin going from a white man to a black man?

As a white man
- could use any restroom he wanted.
- People respected him.
- his life was care-free
- he didn't have to worry about going to a place like Mississippi
- He was superior to all black people
- no one would think anything of him looking at a white woman
- he could sit in the front of the bus
- people respected him just because he was white
- he was treated different (better) as a white man

(middle) still the same man.

As a black man
- could only drink from "colored" waterfountains
- restrooms
- Bus driver disrespected him.
- Just because his skin color was a diff color people didn't take the time to realize he was the same man.
- because he was a black person wouldn't belive that he wrote certain books.
- he was so insignificant to white people.
- just because he was black and looked at a white woman-she thought he was being vulgar in some way.
- he had to sit at the back of the bus.
- couldn't get off the bus to use the restroom.

Students use the Venn diagram, note cards, and a web to plan their writing.

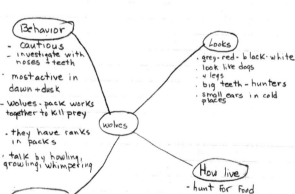

Chris

Behavior
- cautious
- investigate with noses & teeth
- most active in dawn + dusk
- wolves-pack works together to kill prey
- they have ranks in packs
- talk by howling, growling, whimpering

wolves

Looks
- grey-red-black-white
- look like dogs
- 4 legs
- big teeth - hunters
- small ears in cold places

How live
- hunt for food
- have babies in April, May
- dig dens for babies
- stay with babies until they want to go.

Great Facts
- heat comes out of ears
- eats up to 20 lb.
- unusual for a healthy wolf to attack and kill a person

By circulating around the room as students collect ideas, focus, and draft, you will identify students who need extra support. Sit side-by-side with them and start by asking questions about the topic—questions that start the student talking about his idea. After a rich flow of ideas, invite the student to jot these down on paper.

Sometimes, students have a rich list of ideas in their heads, but their insecurities about writing prevent them from noting it. I invite these students to dictate ideas, and we focus the material together. Often, I ask these students to dictate their first draft. Visible proof that they can create an excellent draft builds the confidence these students need to work independently.

DRAFTING

Donald Murray recommends that writers draft without using their notes (1989). Why, you might well wonder, put aside all the notes you've worked so hard to collect? If the moment is right for drafting, then the ideas will slip onto the page as easily as a greased pig slips out of one's hands at a county fair.

For me, I know I'm ready to write when all the information I've read begins to jell into *ideas* of my own. For example, let's say I've been interviewing farmers and taking notes for a piece on raising prize heifers. I'd know I was ready to start my first draft when the information was, as Russell Freedman put it, "seeping out of my pores," and the image of a cow proudly wearing a blue ribbon refused to leave my mind as a lead for my piece.

Help students to recognize this moment when the information they've gathered begins to jell into ideas—such as a point of view on a subject, an opening or other organizational idea, or a metaphor.

Some students plunge right into their first drafts and maintain this intense momentum throughout the drafting process. Every teacher fantasizes about having an entire class of students like this. However, if your classes are like mine, you have students who "can't write" during class time and some who chat with a friend to avoid writing.

Professional writers experience similar feelings. What motivates professionals can also motivate our students: establish a reasonable deadline. Deadlines can curtail avoidance. You will, however, have some students who need more than a deadline date to complete a writing project (see Scaffolding Ideas, at left).

STRATEGIES TO TRY: For free-choice writing, students and I negotiate the number of first drafts to be completed during a trimester. Here are some suggestions that can keep students focused on their writing:

- Post deadline dates in the classroom and review these weekly.
- Offer students the option of negotiating adjustments two to three days prior to the due date.
- Teach students, during a trimester or semester, about one or two nonfiction genres, such as how to write expository paragraphs and essays or conducting and planning an interview. The number of nonfiction genres you teach will depend on the amount of writing time you have.

REVISING

Revision. Let's slow the word down to appreciate its meaning: re-vision, a *re-seeing* of our ideas, and then a refining of them, as we get more command of what we are trying to say with a piece of writing. Revision offers writers a chance to adjust, add, and remove details and to reorganize parts; revision focuses writers on the content of a piece. In chapter 7 we are going to explore revision in much more detail. For now, however, the point I want to emphasize is that although for professional writers, revision is the be-all and end-all, a process they engage in with every piece they publish, for student writers, we have to keep in mind where they are developmentally and not push revision to the point at which it becomes counterproductive. I recommend that students only revise four to six pieces a year, depending on the length and complexity. Here are other strategies to help you make revision more effective and palatable for your students.

STRATEGIES TO TRY: When teachers don't provide revision strategies, students tend to rewrite their entire piece, which is frustrating and discourages finding joy in rewriting the individual parts that need it. In my class, revision materials are always available: staplers, tape, correction fluid, pencils, scrap paper, sticky notes, paper clips, and scissors. Here are two suggestions for supporting revision—suggestions that don't ask students to continually rewrite their entire piece. The first is the one most of my students use.

Seventh graders read a favorite book together.

- Have students number the section to be rewritten on the draft. Then, on a clean sheet of paper, students write the same number and complete the revision. The numbering tells a reader to stop, read the rewrite on a separate sheet of paper, then return to the draft and continue until he or she comes to the next number.
- Have students bracket off the passage on the draft that needs rewriting. Students then rewrite the section on a strip of paper or a sticky note and tape, staple, clip, or attach the piece of paper or sticky note over the part of the draft to be revised. When rereading, pause at the bracketed section, read the revision, then continue until the next passage to be rewritten.

Support students who are revising by circulating around the room and holding brief conferences (see Appendix pages 318–320).

EDITING

Editing pertains to correcting errors in punctuation, usage, spelling, and paragraphing. Editing also invites students to repair fragments and run-on sentences to make the meaning clear. I'll explore editing in more detail in Chapter 7, but for now, my advice is to limit what you expect children to edit at any one time.

It's tough for students to edit a piece scrutinizing several writing conventions in one reading. My students have also taught me that it's impossible for them to catch every writing convention error; they don't have the expertise to do this. I urge my students to read their pieces aloud, listening for one writing convention at a time: missing and misspelled words, punctuation, paragraph breaks, and so on. This means students will complete several rereadings. Some students catch more errors when they read the piece backwards, for they are less likely to gloss over things. Here are a few more ideas.

STRATEGIES TO TRY:
- Place a piece of your writing on an overhead transparency. Model how you edit for one element at a time. Then have students try the process themselves—in class, never for homework. This way you can circulate and support them.
- After their second reread and edit, have the class debrief, offering reactions and feedback. Success with spotting errors breeds enthusiasm for using this process. The more errors students correct, the more they learn about editing.

- Have students edit only for the guidelines set, and then read their work aloud *for one guideline item at a time.* So, if the criteria calls for paragraphing, complete sentences, and commas separating compound sentences, they will read a piece three times.
- Support students' editing beyond guidelines by using editing symbols in the margin (see

Appendix page 324). If a piece is to be published, then you will act as the editor in a publishing house and complete corrections for students.

Your students will not absorb the stages of process writing by moving through them once. It's crucial to continue coaching them as they use each stage of this recursive process. As students apply the writing process to their nonfiction pieces, they will adapt the stages to meet the needs of each topic.

Erica   Sputnik

As Sputnik soared into space Sonny listened anxiously to the radio, enraptured by what he was hearing. Deep in thought, Sonny had fallen in love with rockets he decided he would build one no matter how hard it was. This led to the farming of the BCMA or Big Creek Missle Agency because Sonny knew he could build rockets without his friends. Due to the BCMA's first rocket exploding, Sonny was pulled deeper and deeper into the rocket phenomina and he made a decision that would get him out of Coalwood. He wanted to be a rocket engineer at NASA againist his father's wishes. However, Sonny was determined to build a rocket and wouldn't be veered off course.

Editing symbols in the margin help Erica find errors.

CONTINUE TO THINK ABOUT

Take time to get in touch with your own writing process (Graves, 1990), so you can better understand its recursive nature and share your insights with students. You don't have to be a professional writer to teach writing well. Here are two things you can do to raise your awareness of your own process and enlarge your knowledge of nonfiction:

1. Write often. Write letters and notes; keep a personal diary; write journal narratives about your students.

2. Learn to read and analyze nonfiction with a writer's eye and deepen your understanding of nonfiction in its many forms.

The process of writing cannot be bound by a standard definition, a series of steps, or a formula; it is a creative process (Calkins, 1994; Graves, 1983, 2003; Murray, 1984). Therefore, teachers must help students find their way of working with ideas and words. Equally important is the lesson learned from professional writers: value nonfiction writing and help students learn to write in this genre. Who knows? Perhaps like Russell Freedman, students will find their voice and passion for writing by exploring subjects that interest them.

Eighth graders read each other's pop-up books they made in math class.

Nonfiction Writing From the Inside Out

CHAPTER TWO

NONFICTION FEATURES AND STRUCTURES

Mini-Lessons That Make These
Elements Accessible to Students

In Their Own Words

How do you use text features and structures in your books?

James Cross Giblin

I don't use sidebars in my nonfiction books, but I do make frequent use of back matter—time lines, glossaries, extracts from historical documents, and, of course, an index—to add to the scope and usefulness of the book.

Kathryn Lasky

I feel that every book has its own natural structure. I have to unearth that structure. It's a different decision with each book. In *The Man Who Makes Time Travel*, I pulled out some quotes in sidebars. I use sidebars when I think they can enlarge the text and make it interesting for a reader who might want to go a little further. It's important to remember that all of these features can be overdone.

Patricia McKissack

I like to include a picture of the person— kids like to see what a person looked like.

I love time lines. When I do a time line I try to show connections between music, art, books of the times, and the person's life. My husband and I did that in *Young, Black, and Determined: A Biography of Lorraine Hansberry*. As a teacher I loved having those connections. It gave me the opportunity to get kids thinking about these connections and move them beyond *me, my,* and *I*.

I also love sidebars. These are all through *Days of Jubilee: The End of Slavery in the United States*. Sidebars let the slaves tell their stories.

I imagine when you read the work of others, it influences your own writing. What do you read?

James Cross Giblin

I read a broad assortment of things, nonfiction and fiction, newspaper articles and columns, magazine pieces, and books. Recently, I've been delving into a collection of classic examples of journalism from the World War II years. I've also gone on a Michael Cunningham kick, reading not just *The Hours* but his two earlier novels. I think he's a master stylist.

Joyce Hansen

I read a lot of history, especially about the Civil War and Reconstruction. Why? I find these periods fascinating. We are still reliving these eras and as Americans are affected by them. The Civil War ended in 1865, yet the Confederate flag remains an issue in certain southern states. Segregation is itself rooted in the struggles over Reconstruction after the Civil War. While legal segregation has ended, de facto segregation has not.

Kathryn Lasky

I read more fiction than nonfiction. I get my nonfiction through the *Smithsonian*, the *New Yorker* and *The New York Times*. I loved the beautiful writing in *Seabiscuit*. I read Jane Austen repeatedly.

Donald Murray

I admire writers who can get out of the way and focus my attention on the page, not on them. I like writers who write with information that reveals detail and not with rhetoric. I am attracted to the music of writing—the author's voice tuned to the subject. I like writers who have a writer's eye that makes me see my world in a new way.

Walter Dean Myers

I read a lot of history. Currently I'm reading Thomas Paine. I'm drawn to books that reproduce original documents.

What advice do you have for young writers about reading?

Joyce Hansen

Give students examples of the best nonfiction and analyze with them the structure, showing the students how the writer formed the piece.

Walter Dean Myers

If you're serious about writing, you should be equally serious about reading. Read junk if you will, but also tackle the best books. After a while you will set internal standards for yourself.

INCLUDING AUTHORS' INSIGHTS IN INSTRUCTION

TEACHERS OFTEN ASK ME: "How do we best teach young writers nonfiction features and structures? Do we isolate structures such as question and answer or compare and contrast and invite students to practice these? Do we require students to incorporate specific features into their writing?" This chapter responds to these questions and also offers some tips for selecting nonfiction texts for your students and for use in your mini-lessons.

The authors I interviewed clearly read widely, and glean stylistic and structural ideas from what they read, but this takes place fairly subconsciously. They mention being attracted to a certain writer's style, or because he is a master stylist or uses a lot of primary source documents, all comments that suggest that reading for them is like listening to music. These authors may hope the cadences of others' writing will echo in their own prose, but they don't study other's writing in a deliberate way.

Similarly, when these authors write, they are not conscious of features and structures. For them, the topic determines the structures and features they employ. But students are novices; they need to have conscious, deliberate experiences with these devices. As teachers, then, we have to walk a fine line between giving students necessary, introductory *practice* with features and structures and isolating them in a way that is unnatural. In this chapter, I'll help you achieve this balance by showing you how to habituate students to notice the features authors have used to organize their information and ideas and engage their readers. I'll then show you mini-lessons that use sections of these authors' works to highlight six basic nonfiction structures. These lessons will help you underscore for students that these structures *can be put to use in an array of genres*. The goal is to deliver to our students a giant box of tools with which they can hammer out and hone their nonfiction writing.

Nonfiction Writing From the Inside Out

Approach my work from a literary point of view. Dissect it so as to allow the student to understand how my work was put together and what its deeper meaning might be. Look beyond a work's entertainment to plumb the author's mind as it might be revealed in his writing.

—Homer Hickam, Jr.

During one of our Wednesday morning meetings, teacher John Applin told me, "I'd like to do some nonfiction writing with my fourth-grade class. I figure I'll need two to three weeks for them to write a piece." This is John's first year at Powhatan, and I've been coaching him for a few months. John is a talented, enthusiastic young teacher, who often says to me and other colleagues, "I want to grow, and I want help." So I feel comfortable nudging him to rethink his notion of covering nonfiction in just a few weeks.

"You know, my sixth grade class just completed writing magazine articles," I say. "Exploring nonfiction features and structures, as well as finding topics, reading, researching, planning, and drafting took about fourteen weeks. Students completed all their work at school. We reserved three hours a week for this—some days we used the entire ninety minute block."

I pull out several sixth-grade student folders and invite John to read them, knowing that these pieces can show this young teacher why it's best to devote months, not a few weeks, to studying nonfiction. We decide to meet again the next day.

At our meeting, we talk about the sixth graders' work and how it reveals their knowledge of nonfiction features and structures. John is impressed by the sixth-graders' ability to write articles that use structures like question/answer, cause/effect and compare/contrast, as well as their facility with features like sidebars, diagrams, and photos with captions. He smiles and says he now figures his students will probably need the final twelve weeks of school for a nonfiction writing unit. He plans to give his students a choice of writing a nonfiction picture book or a short magazine article. Sounds great, I say, and we agree to meet twice each week. During these meetings I'll help John plan the mini-lessons he will offer students on features and structures of nonfiction.

Mini-Lessons: Spotlighting Techniques

From this chapter onward, you will explore mini-lessons dealing with many aspects of non-fiction writing. Because mini-lessons vary from teacher to teacher, here is a brief overview of how I conduct them:

These short and focused demonstrations take between 5 and 15 minutes. I usually begin my workshop by presenting a mini-lesson to the entire class. The purpose of these lessons is to model your use of the tools you want your students to use when they are ready to plan, draft, and revise their pieces. So in a sense, students don't begin to apply what you're modeling right away—but they absorb your modeling like sponges.

In each subsequent workshop, I repeat variations of the lesson using different examples until I see that students "get it." If there are still a few students who haven't gotten it or need extra support, I'll review the mini-lesson with a small group, a pair, or even one student.

The students who have a good grasp move into pairs or groups of four to discuss other examples of the specified nonfiction structure or technique that they find in magazines and nonfiction texts. I listen to these small-group discussions, gauging whether students are indeed ready to move on to a mini-lesson on a new topic the next day, or whether they need to see me model some more.

FOUR MINI-LESSON SHADES

For the purposes of this book, I've organized my mini-lessons into four types to help you see that I have slightly different intentions with each lesson I do. But of course, they are shades of the same color and all fall under the umbrella of teaching writing nonfiction.

1. The Writer's Craft Mini-Lesson. You share your process, brief examples of your own writing, and selections by professional and student writers in order to introduce or reinforce various elements of craft.

2. The Reading With a Writer's Eye Mini-Lesson. You use passages from student and professional writers to demonstrate the application of the writing mini-lessons. These text-based

---

MAKE A MINI-LESSON INDEX

So that my students and I can quickly find mini-lessons that have been presented, I use large sticky notes to label the topics and place them on the edge of the chart paper where I've written the lesson. Students love this system because they can find any mini-lesson with ease.

---

lessons are powerful for advancing students' knowledge of nonfiction features, structures, and how a writing technique works.

3. The Revision Mini-Lesson You model strategies that foster rewriting and improving the content and organization of a draft.

4. The Editing Mini-Lesson You respond to what students show they need in order to improve their knowledge of specific writing conventions.

Ways to Integrate the Mini-Lessons Into Your Writing Classes

1. Plan Your Mini-Lesson: Advance preparation enables you to record the mini-lesson on chart paper prior to class. I urge you not to reuse mini-lessons you presented and reviewed one year to a new group of students the next year. I find that my presentations change as I grow and change as a writer and teacher.

2. Conduct an Impromptu Mini-Lesson: Sometimes, as I'm circulating and briefly conferring, the need will arise for a mini-lesson that a few students will benefit from immediately. It's often a small matter, such as which details to put in a sidebar. I'll gather these students together and do a quick, on-the-spot lesson.

3. Review a Mini-Lesson: Throughout the year, periodically revisit mini-lesson charts with pairs or groups of students whom you detect could use additional scaffolding. Repetition deepens the understanding of how a technique works.

MINI-LESSON TOPICS: TAKE YOUR CUES FROM STUDENTS' WORK

Topics for mini-lessons are easy to identify while you read your students' writing. I keep a list of the students in each class. Each list has two columns: one for writing techniques, the other for writing conventions. Under each column I note the particular needs students show me through their work. Next, I reread the lists to set teaching priorities and offer individuals, small groups, or the entire class the needed mini-lessons.

So, while reading sixth graders' personal essays, I observe that half the class is writing dialogue incorrectly. The next day I present to a large group a mini-lesson on writing dialogue, then assign writing buddies so that students who are experts at writing dialogue can support their peers. In addition, your school might have a list of required writing conventions and nonfiction genres you have to teach.

So that you can develop your own mini-lessons—ones that meet your students' unique writing needs—I've included a planning guide in the Appendix on pages 316–317.

Think-Alouds: Making the Mysterious Visible

In their book *Verbal Protocols of Reading* (1995), Pressley and Afflerbach trace the use of think-alouds as far back as the time of Plato and Aristotle. Ancient philosophers used the think aloud to study and make visible to one another processes of thinking. Educators and researchers in recent years have championed the think-aloud as a technique for helping students "hear" each mental move you make as you engage in a process so that they can then internalize it for their own use in reading or any other thinking process (Baumann et al., 1993; Robb, 2001, 2003; Wilhelm, 2001).

I've found think-alouds effective for teaching nonfiction, especially nonfiction structures, because they construct for students a tangible mental model of ideas that are often elusive for them, such as organizing information into a compare/contrast structure. Think-alouds can be monologues, where teachers or students talk out loud alone while others listen. Think-alouds can also be dialogues, where partners talk out loud to one another.

Nonfiction Writing From the Inside Out

A PARTNER THINK-ALOUD IN ACTION: FOURTH GRADERS

Here is an example of a partner think-aloud.

John Applin and I organize fourth graders in pairs and invite partners to think-aloud in order to better understand a specific nonfiction feature. What follows is part of the shared think aloud between Georgi and Sara that helped them better understand how a nonfiction text can include more than one story line and many nonfiction features.

The girls skim through the book *Ms. Frizzle's Adventures: Ancient Egypt* by Joanna Cole, illustrated by Bruce Degen (Scholastic, 2001). Here's part of their think-aloud as they browse:

Georgi: There's so much to look at I don't know where to start. I think she [Cole] is trying to help us go to Egypt with Miss Frizzle's class and see what life was like then.

Sara: Here there's a part that says "Egypt in Modern Times" and on the next page "Egypt in Ancient Times." I think it's to help us know that today some Egyptians look like us and children go to school and learn English.

Georgi: This will be great to read. There's lots of stories. The main one in the white boxes and the balloons like comics and sidebars that tell about the ancient gods. And there's parts of the Miss Frizzle's students' diaries. I think she [Cole] does this so we read about Egypt like kids like us see it.

Sara: It's like she doesn't have to write it in a Venn diagram or a paragraph. The different stories show us. I like being with kids like me to learn about building the pyramids and farming and ancient parties.

As the girls think aloud they discover what they will read about and how Cole presents information. Notice how thinking aloud focuses each partner on a specific feature. The pair also offer reasons for features such as the diaries and sidebars. Their peers benefit from the think-aloud too, of course, and the assumption is that spotlighting authors' choices in this way will help children make similar choices as they write.

DISCOVERING FEATURES AND STRUCTURE THROUGH READING

Dr. Tom Estes, one of my teachers at The University of Virginia, said, "The richness of learning experiences depends on the background knowledge of the reader and listener." We don't all read a book the same way; our reading depends on what we bring to the book (Rosenblatt, 1978; Robb, 2000; Vaughan & Estes, 1986). Nor do we all hear and process information in the same way. And equally true, the way any of us writes nonfiction is colored by the amount of nonfiction reading we do, the information we have about a topic, and the writing experiences we bring to the topic (Graves, 1994; Ray, 1999; Zinsser, 2001).

I think it's fair to say that, in general, teachers tend to focus lessons and discussions of literature on reading strategies, or on why characters change in a novel, short story, or biography. Analyzing nonfiction texts gets short shrift. In this next section, I'll show you how to integrate more nonfiction instruction into your teaching.

BROWSING NONFICTION: A SIXTH GRADE SNAPSHOT

When teacher Cindy Potter and I plan a nonfiction study in sixth grade, we first comb our school library's shelves for books on animals, airplanes, sports, weather, machines, and so on. Our goal is to fill a two-tiered cart with fifty to sixty nonfiction picture and chapter books and dozens of magazines. The process is slow, because each time we find an intriguing book, we pause to share a photograph or diagram or read a sidebar, caption, or quote. It's a good lesson for us to remember—that it takes time to browse, gain insights, and process information. We both agree to offer the sixth-graders enough time to enjoy browsing and to think aloud about their discoveries with a partner or their group.

The first day, Cindy and I model the kind of browsing we expect from partners. We demonstrate how we look at the pages and pore over the photographs that intrigue us, reading some captions, quotes, and sidebars. We model pausing to share and discuss our discoveries.

Sixth graders browse through books in their classroom library.

The next day Cindy thinks aloud for students using a book and a *Science World* magazine (Dec. 11, 2000, vol. 57, no. 7). Here's what she says:

I learned so much from browsing through nonfiction magazines and books. Let me show you two structures I really enjoy. [Cindy opens the *Science World* magazine to a sidebar on page 9 and circulates among students so they can see it.] *Sidebars have extra information that doesn't seem to fit in the text of the article. Listen to what I learned about chimps: I learned that a primatologist is a scientist who studies primates. I learned that chimps are like humans because like humans, chimps pass on learned behaviors to their babies. We teach our children to eat with cutlery and chimps teach their offspring to eat with a stick.*

For several days, Cindy Potter opens each class with a mini-lesson and think aloud that introduces one or two nonfiction structures. After each demonstration she invites students to pose questions and comment on what they have seen and heard. Then partners select materials from the cart and classroom library to browse, share with each other, then share with the class.

MINI-LESSON

Browsing to Learn About Nonfiction Features

Purpose

To explore nonfiction magazines and books to gain insights into the various structures professional writers use

Materials

50-60 nonfiction picture or chapter books or a mixture of magazines and books; students' journals. (You can find materials in your school and public libraries. Bring in materials on a wide range of topics that contain a variety of nonfiction features so that students' browsing becomes a rich and memorable experience.)

Guidelines

Reserve 20 minutes a day until students can recognize and discuss each nonfiction feature.

1. Think aloud to model the browsing process. Then call for questions from students.
2. Have students head a journal page with their name, date, and the heading "Browsing Nonfiction."

3. Invite small groups of students to the cart to select two to three books for browsing.

4. Reserve about eight minutes for browsing. Have students note, in their journals or on sticky notes, what they learned about nonfiction. (Students store sticky notes on their journal page.)

5. Invite students to share what they have learned about nonfiction after each browsing session. Have them use materials they browsed through to illustrate each element. On chart paper, write what students notice. Post this list of features on the wall; students will refer to it and annotate it as they delve into nonfiction reading and writing.

Here's what sixth-graders discover and note in their journals over three days.

- Use of photographs with captions
- Use of different size type for headings
- Sidebars with facts that relate to the text
- Excerpt of an interview with a person
- Quotes by prominent people that relate to students' topics
- Excerpt of a newspaper article
- Table of contents
- Glossary of words—how to say and meanings
- Index
- Introduction
- Graphs
- Maps
- Boldface words
- More photos and sidebars on a page than the story
- Diagrams with labels
- Bubbles with words people say

By the end of the third browsing period, students beg to start reading. At this point I invite them to make a list of four to five topics they are burning to research, promising to bring in additional books from the school library. Students understand that if the school or public library does not have materials for their first choice, they will have to choose another topic from their list. Since students complete all reading and note-taking in class, losing library books is never an issue.

While students read to explore a topic and decide if it interests them enough to stick with it for ten to fourteen weeks, Cindy Potter and I engage them in reading to learn more about some of the nonfiction features students listed on the chart. First, Cindy presents a mini-lesson to demonstrate what we want students to accomplish.

MINI-LESSON

Examining Nonfiction Features

Purpose
To look at nonfiction features and understand their purposes

Materials
Books and magazines that contain an array of features

Teacher Preplanning
1. Use a planning period to complete this. You'll need enough materials so that pairs of students can work with a text together. It's fine to have pairs study the same features as each will offer some insights that are similar and some that differ.
2. Select books that have lots of examples of two features you want a pair of students to study. Jot the features on a sticky note and place it on the front cover.

Guidelines
Set aside 30 minutes in two or three classes.

On the First Day
1. Organize students into pairs.
2. Model, in a think-aloud, how you learn more about a specific nonfiction feature (first, read both pages of the text while walking around and showing the illustrations). Here's what I say to fourth graders, using pages 6 and 7 in *High in the Sky* by Steve Parker:

> *I notice the size of type on the page heading is different. "SHIPS IN THE SKY" is in caps, so I see it immediately. It must be important and when I read the text I discover why—these ships or airships are a combination of plane and balloon. There are numbers next to the sidebars at the bottom of both pages so I know the order to read them. I learn that sidebars have information that doesn't fit directly in with the text that describes how an airship flies and the location of the*

engines and passenger and pilot areas. With sidebars authors can add amazing facts, diagrams, or historical data that relate to a topic but don't belong in the main text.

3. Write on chart paper with large, boldface print what you have learned about sidebars and parts of a text. I invite fourth graders to help me compose each explanation (see chart on pages 50–51).

4. Give each pair a book or magazine and some sticky notes. Tell children they are going to jot down on sticky notes what they learn from a feature such as a diagram, and how it helps the reader.

5. Ask pairs to read the book or a magazine article silently or take turns reading parts aloud.

6. Have pairs study and discuss the nonfiction feature assigned to them, such as a sidebar. Then partners prepare an explanation of its function based on their reading and notes.

On Another Day

1. Hand out nonfiction materials that partners read.

2. Invite pairs to show their nonfiction feature to the class, then explain what they learned about it.

3. Print, on chart paper, students' explanations. Preserve their language.

4. Hang chart on a wall or bulletin board as a resource for students.

Fourth-Graders' Explanations of Features in Nonfiction Books and Magazine Articles

<u>Sidebars</u> are boxes on a page in a book or magazine. They have diagrams, photographs, quotes, part of an interview, a newspaper clipping, a letter, or fascinating facts about a topic. Sidebars give information that makes the book more amazing but the writer didn't think she could add it to the story and she wanted us to know these things.

Oversized Bold Type says, "Look at me." It's important stuff and it gets you thinking about what's on the page.

Photographs and Captions help you see an animal, an airplane, a planet, or a mountain. These help you know more about what the author says. They really help when you don't know much about the topic. Captions help too. They're words under a picture that explain it. But not all pictures have captions. They don't need words, the picture says it.

Quotes and Interviews can be in sidebars or on a part of a page that's not the story. Quotes help you hear the exact words of a slave or a scientist, or what someone saw on a trip down the Amazon River.

Maps show you where a place is. They're good because if you don't know a place, like the Galapagos Islands, you know where it is when you read.

The Introduction can tell lots of things: how the idea came to the author, why the author wanted to write it, or how other people helped the author write the book.

Table of Contents lets you know what the book has. You get the chapter titles and page numbers each start on, and it gives you ideas of what you'll read in the book. If you only want to read parts of a book, the table of contents will help you find these.

Glossaries list and explain hard or unusual words. Sometimes they show you how to say a word.

The Index is in a, b, c order. It lists the important topics and names of people and places in the book. It gives page numbers next to each item. When you see one page, it means not much information on that topic. If you see lots of pages (25 – 31) it means that book will help you. When you use the index, you know right away if a book has information you need.

A Time Line can be in tiny pictures or a line with dates and little bits of information. It lets you see an event or a person connected to other things happening at that time and in the past and future.

The Bibliography is at the end of the book. It lists the books and magazines the author used to get information for her book.

DISCOVERIES ABOUT NONFICTION: SIXTH GRADERS' COMMENTS

Here's what sixth-grade students noticed from browsing, reading, and discussing nonfiction text features that helped them make decisions about the articles they were planning to write. Remember, it's important to expose students to a wide array of choices for features—but equally important to assure them that just like published writers, they can choose to use only a few!

- Some books only have photographs and the story.
- Some pictures and photographs don't have captions.
- Magazines seem to have more sidebars than nonfiction books.
- Each book by the same author has different nonfiction structures in it.
- Some books have more pictures than writing.
- Even nonfiction chapter books had maps and labeled pictures.
- Not every book has a table of contents, index, or glossary.

Taking the time to ask students to first discuss with a partner, then share with the class what they have learned about the parts of nonfiction books and magazines lets you know how much information students have absorbed. If you gather a rich list, then you can move forward. If not, continue exploring, discussing, and sharing.

In other words, use your judgment about when to teach any of the mini-lessons in this book. Because writing is recursive, you may teach a mini-lesson you find in Chapter 3 or 4 before covering all the writing structure mini-lessons addressed below. That said, generally speaking, while students read, talk, and take notes on their topic, I introduce the six nonfiction writing structures in mini-lessons that invite students to read like writers.

> ## DAILY NONFICTION READING
>
> Tune your students' ears to the beauty of creative nonfiction by reading aloud short selections on a wide range of topics. Sometimes Cindy Potter and I reread a short selection twice and invite students to listen for and discuss an unusual simile or how the author created images with powerful verbs and specific nouns. Other times I read, pause, and think aloud to spotlight a technique. After reading from a book, place it in a plastic crate or a basket. During independent reading times, many students will gravitate to these books and read one that piqued their interest.

SUGGESTIONS FOR EVALUATING AND SELECTING NONFICTION

Your librarian is an excellent resource for helping you select high-quality nonfiction for mini-lessons and for your students to read. On appendix page 321, I've also included a list of resources you'll find in your school and local public libraries that review nonfiction literature.

Here are some guidelines to consider when choosing nonfiction trade books:

Information Contained in the Text Is Accurate

- Note when the book was written; this will tell you if the material is current or possibly outdated.
- Discover the author's experience in the field; this will help you determine her qualifications.
- Read the acknowledgments to learn about others in the field who have supported the author.
- Look for information at the back or in the introduction that explains the writer's research process.
- Check the bibliography and look for and evaluate a list of additional readings the author recommends.

Book to Try: *Attack on Pearl Harbor: The True Story of the Day America Entered World War II* by Shelley Tanaka, with paintings by David Craig, Hyperion, 2001.

Writing Style Is Clear and Easy to Understand

- Look for a writing style that is conversational, with a strong voice and varied sentences.
- Check out the writer's word choice; it should be interesting.

Book to Try: *Alvin Ailey* by Andrea Davis Pinkney, illustrated by Brian Pinkney, Hyperion, 1993.

Captions and Labels Are Informative

- Make sure that these short texts are clear and precise so that they can help readers understand the point of a photograph, chart, map, or diagram.
- Read to decide whether captions and labels extend or simply repeat information in the text.

Book to Try: *Give Me Liberty! The Story of the Declaration of Independence* by Russell Freedman, Holiday House, 2000.

The Author Clearly Differentiates Fact, Opinion, and Theory

- Included are qualifiers such as "maybe" or "perhaps" or "apparently" or "might be" or "can be inferred" or "we are told" to separate facts from the hunches authors offer.

Book to Try: *Around the World in a Hundred Years: From Henry the Navigator to Magellan* by Jean Fritz, illustrated by Anthony Bacon Venti, Putnam and Grosset Group, 1994.

The Visual Appeal Is Strong

- Browse for attractive covers, and intriguing photographs or illustrations, as well as a balance of text and visuals that grab readers' attention.
- Make sure that the visuals are appropriate to the content. Ask questions such as: Would photos be better than drawings? Are primary sources included to recreate an historical period?

Book to Try: *Through My Eyes* by Ruby Bridges, Scholastic, 1999.

The Topic Is Appropriate to the Age of the Readers

- Offer students books on subjects they can relish and enjoy.
- Avoid topics that are too difficult to comprehend or too upsetting, as such experiences can turn students away from nonfiction.

The Text and Visuals Don't Stereotype Groups

- Look to ensure that a book has positive and accurate images of various cultures and historical periods.

Book to Try: *The Blues Singers: Ten Who Rocked the World* by Julius Lester, illustrated by Lisa Cohen, Hyperion, 2001.

Six Expository Writing Structures: Putting Them in Perspective

Like the other writers quoted at the beginning of this chapter, writer Donald Murray is not big on emphasizing structure. He told me:

> *I am not particularly interested in structure as I write. It rather naturally evolves as I discover what I have to say. I was in school, forced to write in strict forms that contradicted*

An eighth grader works on a draft of an essay.

the good writing we were studying. Writers didn't do what teach-ers taught. I have to unteach these [expository structures] so the student can learn to see the organic or natural structures that arise as the piece is being written.

Murray elaborates on this idea of "unteaching" in his book, *Expecting the Unexpected* (1989) when he describes teaching a freshman English honors section.

They [college freshmen] could organize. They could follow—rigidly—the rules of usage and mechanics. They could say nothing, absolutely nothing, with enormous skill and correctness. Their detachment from their writing was terrifying (page 173).

Murray's words—"strict forms that contradicted the good writing we were studying" and "They could say nothing, absolutely nothing, with enormous skill and correctness" chal-lenge us to rethink the instructional underpinnings of teaching writing in elementary and middle school.

So how do we teach the big six? As I said at this chapter's outset, students need some explicit exposure to and practice with structures—we just can't overdo it or do it in isola-

---

TIME-SAVING TIPS

Examples Are Rarely Pure: Remember that in a paragraph, page, chap-ter, or two to three pages of a picture book, authors can inte-grate a few or even all six nonfiction text structures. Share this fact with students—and don't drive your-self crazy looking for short passages that are purely one structure.

Make Examples Visible: It's helpful to enlarge the example you are using to illus-trate a writing struc-ture and turn it into an overhead transparency. Each mini-lesson has two examples—one for you to think aloud with and one for your students to discuss.

---

tion. Here are three strategies that work well for me, which you'll see in action with the mini-lessons on pages 57–69.

1. **Brief mini-lessons.** First, students study models of expository writing structures, which you provide. Then pairs of students search for examples in books they are reading. This simple strategy can easily function as the mainstay of your writing instruction. In addition to examples in this chapter, mine books by the best nonfiction authors to help students read with a writer's eye. You can also use magazine articles (see Appendix page 322 for a list of outstanding nonfiction magazines).

2. **Collaborative writing.** Students work together—as a class or in small groups—to practice a specific structure. Collaborative writing can provide students with enough insights to understand and absorb the structure so they can incorporate it into their writing. Just like professional writers, students will integrate more than one structure into their group composition because the topic influences the form. Writing together spotlights the thinking process of many students, offering everyone additional mentors. I have included part or all of a piece of collaborative writing for the mini-lessons on sequencing and cause and effect so you can see the benefits of group composing.

3. **Discussion after mini-lessons.** Follow-up discussions foster reflection and inquiry, and ultimately enable students to better understand the craft of writing nonfiction.

Scaffolding Idea: Knowing When to Collaborate

Continue sharing and analyzing selections from books and magazines until students demonstrate their ability to analyze selections. Most classes will have a few students who remain silent during these discussions, making it tough for you to evaluate what they know.

You can work with these students one-on-one and discover what they have absorbed. With classes of thirty-plus students, however, this strategy becomes difficult. In larger classes collaborative composing that the teacher records on chart paper is an ideal scaffold for students who need a bit more practice, because it allows them to observe their peers' thinking. The chart becomes a resource, offering a concrete model for them to reread. There's no magic figure for the number of collaborative pieces students compose. Your observations will enable you to decide when they can work independently.

Nonfiction Writing From the Inside Out

Structure: Chronological Order

The writer uses this structure when it strikes him that the topic, idea, or story at hand lends itself to a sequence or time order.

MINI-LESSON

Using a Think-Aloud to Clarify Sequencing

Purpose

To illustrate that authors sequence events and ideas both with and without signal words

Materials

A section from a trade book or magazine article

Examples

From *Wilma Unlimited* by Kathleen Krull, illustrated by David Diaz, Harcourt, 1996.

> Wilma Rudolph was walking. Row by row, heads turned toward her as she walked alone down the aisle. Her large family, all her family's friends, everyone from school—each person stared wide-eyed. The singing never stopped; it seemed to burst right through the walls and into the trees. Finally, Wilma reached a seat in the front and began singing too, her smile triumphant (unpaged picture book).

From *Tooth and Claw* by Ted Lewin, HarperCollins, 2003.

> The male chimps organized the hunt as if they were generals in a campaign. First, they chased the terrified red colobus troop through the treetops. The female chimps stayed on the ground, screaming madly to confuse the monkeys. The colobus males turned back and confronted the chimps to allow their females and young to flee. They put up a fierce fight with chimps that were many times their size. Finally trapped, they were overwhelmed and killed (page 46).

Signal Words That Help You Write a Sequence

until	before	after	next	finally
now	first/last	then	on (date)	at (time)

Guidelines

1. Read aloud the first example or another passage you've chosen.

2. Think aloud using the passage you've just read. Here's what I say for the selection from *Wilma Unlimited*:

   > Even though the only key sequencing word the author uses is "finally," in the last sentence, she creates a clear chronology by helping the reader observe what Wilma sees as she walks down the church aisle. This section also contains cause and effect—the results of family and friends seeing Wilma walking. Krull also includes description that shows the energy and joy of the singing. The author helps me connect Wilma's triumphant smile to the song that becomes triumphant as the melody "bursts right through the walls and into the trees."

3. Call for student comments and reactions. Here are points that seventh-graders shared:
   - There are two structures—time order and cause and effect.
   - Heads turning show the impact Wilma had by walking.
   - Lots of descriptive details that put you in the church: rows, school friends, wide eyes, continuing to sing.

4. Invite pairs to use the selection from *Tooth and Claw* or one you choose and to think aloud, commenting on sequencing and other structures. Here's a summary of what sixth-grade partners noted:
   - "First" and "finally" were clues to putting ideas in order.
   - There's lots of description like "screaming madly to confuse."
   - The order is clear even with only two key words from the list.
   - There's also cause and effect—like after the colobus males confronted the chimps there was a fight and then the chimps killed the colobus males.
   - The simile comparing male chimps to generals in a campaign helps me see how tough and in charge they are and wanting to win.
   - One paragraph blended three structures. The author used structures to make his point and keep me interested.
   - Why do textbooks use so many signal words?

5. Have pairs search for examples of sequencing in books they are reading. Then ask two

Nonfiction Writing From the Inside Out

sets of pairs to share with each other. Circulate through the room and listen to their conversations. Invite one or two pairs to share their discussions.

6. Ask students to suggest a topic for a short, collaborative piece. Here's what seventh-graders composed after brainstorming about grooming a cat. Students noted that they included cause and effect and descriptive details.

> Yesterday, my cat vomited a hairball mingled with chewed pellets of dry food. Watching wave after wave of muscle contractions and hearing gagging noises forced me to vow that I'd brush her daily. Early every morning, before I walk to the corner to catch the school bus, I gather the wire brush, an old towel, and place these on the kitchen floor. Cat in hand, I sit on the floor, legs crossed as if I'm ready to meditate, and towel under cat. First, I pet her until she purrs. Then gently, I brush her head, back, legs, and stomach. By the third week, she enjoys the ritual as much as a bowl of tuna, and jumps into my lap, sits silently, waiting for the stroking and brushing to begin.

Structure: Compare and Contrast

A writer uses this structure to describe how two or more topics, ideas, people, events are alike and/or different. Generally speaking, the writer aims to show how two or more things are distinct from each other.

Examples:

From *Shadows in the Dawn: The Lemurs of Madagascar* by Kathryn Lasky, photographs by Christopher G. Knight.

> Like humans, lemurs are primates, mammals that share certain common traits, such as hands that are good at grasping, brains that are large in comparison to body size, and eyes that face forward to allow good depth perception. Millions and millions of years ago primates were very similar. But as with all living things, both plants and animals, life-forms change over time. This slow change is called evolution (page 10).

From *When Plague Strikes: The Black Death, Smallpox, AIDS* by James Cross Giblin, woodcuts by David Frampton, HarperCollins, 1995. In this passage, Giblin compares the different kinds of medical care in the early fourteenth century when the Black Death raged through western Europe.

> Surgeons usually had some medical training in a university. They were regarded as skilled craftsmen, able to close wounds, set broken bones, and perform simple operations.
>
> Most barber-surgeons were illiterate men whose only training came from serving as apprentices to surgeons. As their name implies, they cut hair as well as setting simple fractures and bandaging wounds (pages 24–25).

Words That Help You Write Compare and Contrast

on the other hand	however	other than	differently
and yet	similar to	like	different from
similarly	but	nevertheless	as opposed to
likewise	while	either . . . or	neither . . . nor
least	most	less than	more than
unlike	not only . . .	but also	difference
same as			

Mini-Lesson

Using a Think-Aloud to Clarify Compare and Contrast

Purpose
To show that writers use this structure to explore how two events, conflicts, characters, or terms are alike or different; to show that contrasts can be implied

Materials
A passage from a nonfiction book or a magazine article

Guidelines
1. Read aloud the first example, or another passage you've chosen, from the transparency.

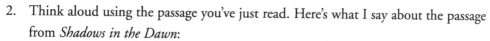

2. Think aloud using the passage you've just read. Here's what I say about the passage from *Shadows in the Dawn*:

> *Lasky clearly shows what humans and lemurs have in common. By starting with the words "like humans" she lets us know that shared traits will follow. However, she does not explicitly state how lemurs and humans differ. She leaves the contrasting to the reader, who can use photographs, text, and his own experiences to draw these conclusions.*
>
> *Lasky helps by pointing out that long ago primates were more alike than they presently are, because they changed over millions of years. It's important to understand that although history and science textbooks often make their comparisons and contrasts very explicit, writers of creative nonfiction don't. I notice Lasky uses a sequence structure with her definition of evolution.*

3. Call for comments and reactions from students. Here are points that sixth-graders shared:
   - It's fun to have to think about how lemurs and humans are alike. The passage makes you do that.
   - The part that starts you thinking is that animals change over time. Instead of just a list of common traits, she pushes us to think of the uncommon and that makes me want to read more.
   - She uses "such as" and I know examples are coming.

   Repeat steps 4, 5, and 6 from the mini-lesson on Sequencing on pages 58–59.

Structure: Cause and Effect

A writer uses this structure when he wants to express the reasons and/or consequences of events and actions.

Examples

From *The Greatest: Muhammad Ali* by Walter Dean Myers, Scholastic, 2001.

> Within weeks of Muhammad Ali's conviction [for refusal to be drafted] and the removal of his championship status, each state revoked his boxing license. Sportswriters, athletes, politicians, and entertainers joined in condemning Ali. He was called a coward, a traitor, and a racist. His lawyers appealed the case, but

if he lost the appeal Ali would have to serve the five years in jail. His character was suddenly considered not good enough for professional boxing (page 66).

From *Safari Journal* by Hudson Talbott, Harcourt, 2003.

Just picture it: A lioness quietly drags an animal twice her size over the huge wall of thorns, and feasts nearby with her pals. Then the jackals grab the leftovers and the vultures polish the bones. Old Bossy was a skeleton by daybreak.

Words That Help You Write Cause and Effect

since	therefore	this led to	due to
so that	for this reason	consequently	as a result
because	thus	nevertheless	if . . . then
then	so		

MINI-LESSON

Using a Think-Aloud to Clarify Cause and Effect

Purpose

To deepen students' understanding of how authors embed cause-and-effect relationships in their writing; to point out that biographies are rich in cause-and-effect relationships

Materials

A passage from a nonfiction book, a biography, or a magazine article. Give students any background they would need to appreciate the piece; for example, for the passage from *The Greatest*, I'd tell students that Muhammad Ali was convicted for refusing to be drafted into the military during the Vietnam War, which he did for religious reasons.

Guidelines

1. Read aloud the first example, or another passage you have chosen, from the transparency.
2. Think aloud using the passage you've just read. Here's what I say about the passage from *The Greatest: Muhammad Ali*:

    Though Walter Dean Myers chose not to include any signal words, the cause–and–effect relationship of the events is obvious. The cause is Ali's conviction. The effects include his losing his

Nonfiction Writing From the Inside Out

championship status and boxing license, and his subsequent condemnation by people in the sports press as well as celebrities. When the author mentions that lawyers appeal the case I can view this as an effect of his conviction as well as an embedded cause with the effect being a conviction and jail sentence. Often one cause leads to another cause which in this case helps us understand how Ali's appeal, a natural outcome of losing his license, could further hurt the boxer.

3. Call for comments and reactions from students. Here are points and queries eighth-graders shared:

    • I like the way Myers builds cause and effect without using signal words.
    • Most nonfiction writers we've looked at use signal words sparingly. I think if you use too many, cause and effect is in your face.
    • I think the last sentence sets you up for more effects.

    Repeat steps 4, 5, and 6 from the mini-lesson on sequencing on page 58–59.

7. Eighth-graders brainstormed and collaborated to write a piece that includes cause and effect, using as their topic a storm that left more than three feet of snow on the ground. Students made an effort not to use signal words. Here is a passage that illustrates cause and effect but also includes description and compare and contrast.

    Like early morning fog, the falling snow became a white screen. Spinning car wheels stuck on the unplowed streets could be heard, but not seen. When the radio announcer said, "All public and private area schools will be closed tomorrow," his voice mirrored my excitement. No school. Sledding, building a snow fort, and making snow angels rocketed to the top of my agenda. Mom's voice ended my snow-day fantasy. "Here's an e-mail for you from your teacher," she said. Thoughts of a day of pure fun faded as I read the homework assignment that ended with a cheery, "Just wanted to make sure you had something to do."

> ### HOWARD FAST'S TAKE ON READING
>
> Read the writers you admire most, unravel the net of words that they spin, and let them be your teachers. You can learn a great deal about the mechanism of writing in school, but the real picture lies in your understanding of the human heart. No school can teach you that. Only your own ears and eyes (*Chicken Soup for the Writer's Soul*, page 137).

Structure: Description

The writer provides detailed information about a topic, concept, event, person, idea, or object by describing attributes, features, facts, details, traits, and characteristics.

Examples:

From *Black Cowboy Wild Horses: A True Story* by Julius Lester, illustrated by Jerry Pinkney, Dial, 1998.

> Bob Lemmons rode his horse slowly up the rise. When he reached the top, he stopped at the edge of the bluff. He looked down at the corral where the other cowboys were beginning the morning chores, then turned away and stared at the land stretching as wide as love in every direction. The sky was curved as if it were a lap on which the earth lay napping like a curled cat. High above, a hawk was suspended on cold threads of unseen winds. Far, far away, at what looked to be the edge of the world, land and sky kissed (first page of an unpaged picture book).

From *Give Me Liberty!* by Russell Freedman, Holiday House, 2000.

> Rowing quietly, Revere and his comrades set out across the river. They stayed well downstream from the looming hulk of the sixty-four gun British warship Somerset, whose great hempen anchor cable was creaking and groaning like a ghost in the night. On the far shore, other Patriots waited with a swift mare named Brown Beauty. By the time Revere joined them, they had seen two signal lanterns glimmer in the distant church steeple. The British troops were already on their way across Back Bay (page 35).

Words That Help You Write Description

for example	such as	some characteristics are
look at	like, as	by observing

Nonfiction Writing From the Inside Out

Using a Think-Aloud to Clarify Description

Purpose

To show how authors create compelling descriptions by using strong verbs, specific nouns, and figurative language, and by showing, not telling.

Materials

A passage from a nonfiction trade book or magazine

Guidelines

1. Read aloud the first example, or another passage you've chosen, from the transparency.

2. Think aloud using the passage you've just read. Here's what I say about the passage from *Black Cowboy Wild Horses*:

    > *Lester quickly takes us to the edge of the bluff. He uses specific nouns such as* corral, cowboys, morning chores. *He uses simile and compares the concrete frontier with abstract love—"stretching as wide as love"—to paint an image of a vast frontier. Lester continues to use similes to show and not tell: he compares the curve of the sky to the earth "napping like a curled cat." The strong verb* suspended *enables me to picture the hawk hovering on wind currents. Narrative elements are also part of the description as Lester takes readers up the rise to the bluff.*

3. Invite students to react to your think-aloud and to the passage. Here's what fifth-graders said:

    *   I like the way he says "land and sky kissed" to describe the earth and sky meeting.
    *   He never says the land is vast—you know it. That's showing.
    *   I can close my eyes and see what Lemmons saw. Do you think Lester tried to do that?

    Repeat steps 4, 5, and 6 from the mini-lesson on sequencing on pages 58–59.

Structure: Question and Answer

Authors can use this structure to organize an entire book, or they can weave questions and their answers into the heart of the text.

Examples:

From *The Joke's on George* by Michael O. Tunnell, pictures by Kathy Osborn, Tambourine, 1993.

> For instance, when his first pocket watch stopped working, did he [Charles Willson Peale] take it to someone to be repaired? Certainly not. Charles just pulled his watch apart, studied how it worked, and fixed it himself. And when he saw portraits painted by Mr. Frazier from Norfolk, which he thought were terrible, Charles was convinced he could do a better job. Did it matter that he had never painted? Of course not. By the time Charles joined the American Revolution, a few years later, he had become one of America's best portrait painters (unpaged picture book).

From *Now Is Your Time! The African-American Struggle for Freedom* by Walter Dean Myers, HarperCollins, 1991.

> What was it like to be called a slave? What was it like to be "owned" by someone? There is no single answer to these questions. There is the common experience of being considered inferior, of being bought and sold as if one were a horse or household furniture. Many people who sold Africans would often add a few household items to the sale so that they would not appear to be "slave dealers." Most plantation owners did not seem to realize that the Africans hated the very idea of not being free. (George Washington, in August of 1761, complained that his Africans ran away without cause.) But the best way to find out what it was like to spend a lifetime in bondage is to read the documents from those days (page 71).

Words and Phrases That Help You Write Question and Answer

how	when	what	where
why	who	how many	it could be that
it's possible	to conclude		

Nonfiction Writing From the Inside Out

Using a Think-Aloud to Clarify Question and Answer

Purpose

To show how a question-and-answer structure can format an entire book or be embedded in parts of a text

Materials

A passage from a nonfiction trade book or a magazine

Guidelines

1. Read aloud the first example, or another passage you've chosen, from the transparency.

2. Think aloud using the passage you've just read. Here's what I say about the passage from *The Joke's on George*:

    Tunnell uses questions to paint character. His questions make us see what a determined risk-taker Peale was as well as a dedicated worker. Asking questions and giving a short reply both times lets us know that Peale was unstoppable once he made a decision. The questions also draw the reader into the book because they make you feel as if you are the questioner. Tunnell also uses problem and solution here. Peale creates his problems and solves the first by pulling the watch apart and the second by practicing painting.

3. Ask students to react to your think-aloud about the passage. Here's what seventh-graders shared:

    *   The questions were what popped into my mind. It's like the author brought me into the book.
    *   He used questions and problem and solution to show us Peale's character. He never had to tell us what Peale was like.
    *   This has changed my view of question-and-answer to a more complex way of using it. It's not as simple, like in my science textbook.

    Repeat steps 4, 5, and 6 from the mini-lesson on sequencing on pages 58–59.

Structure: Problem and Solution

With this structure, the writer presents a problem, states its causes, and then describes one or more solutions.

Examples:

From *Rose's Journal: The Story of a Girl in the Great Depression* by Marissa Moss, Harcourt, 2001.

That's how it is for us, all the time—dust just everywhere. Mother used to wash the whole house thoroughly every day, but now she's given up. What's the point of cleaning, when the dust comes back no matter what?

Floyd and I still try to keep things as clean as we can. Otherwise we'd go crazy! We've figured out little tricks to fight the dust—like if we coat our lips and nostrils with Vaseline, then the dust sticks to the Vaseline, and we don't breathe or swallow as much grit (unpaged journal).

From *Be Seated: A Book About Chairs* by James Cross Giblin, HarperCollins, 1993.

Indoor plumbing was unknown in the eighteenth century, so many wing chairs contained removable chamber pots beneath their seat cushions. For people whose feet ached from gout, a common disease at the time, craftsmen made upholstered "gouty stools" to accompany their wing chairs (page 66).

Words And Phrases That Help You Write Problem and Solution

one reason is	a solution	a problem	solved by
outcome is	issues are		

MINI-LESSON

Using a Think-Aloud to Clarify Problem and Solution

Purpose

To show how writers use a problem-and-solution structure to organize information and advance their ideas

Materials

A selection from a nonfiction book or a magazine article

Guidelines

1. Read aloud the first example, or another passage you've chosen, from the transparency.

2. Think aloud using the passage you've just read. Here's what I say about the passage from *Rose's Journal*:

> Dust storms were a problem for the whole family. The children figured out a solution—to place Vaseline in their noses—so that breathing and swallowing became more bearable. This paragraph also contains descriptive details and can be thought of as cause and effect. The dust storms are the cause, the effects are what the dust does to the house and family. I find three writing structures in just one part of a journal entry.

3. Ask students to respond to your think-aloud and the passage. Here's what eighth graders shared:

   - *None of the signal words were in this passage.*
   - *I think we should try to use as few signal words as possible so the writing flows more.*
   - *I think knowing signal words gives us a choice when we revise a piece.*
   - *Is problem and solution connected to cause and effect?*

Repeat steps 4, 5, and 6 from the mini-lesson on sequencing on pages 58–59.

Repeat steps 4, 5, and 6 from the mini-lesson on sequencing on pages 58–59.

LOIS LOWRY ON READING LIKE A WRITER

This summer I did an all-day workshop for education graduate students at Bowling Green State University. The afternoon part centered around doing writing in class. In the morning, I read a published piece of my writing and then went through phrase by phrase and analyzed, by thinking aloud, the technique of how and why I did things. This really helped them.

—Interview, August 1994

Continue to Think About

To deepen students' understanding of nonfiction, it's beneficial to study the work of published writers. Once students understand nonfiction features and structure, they can allow their topic to shape the structure of their piece and the features they include.

For such deep absorption to occur, you need to build layers of reading to understand writing. During a read aloud, pause to comment on something you noticed the writer did. Continue helping students read with their writers' eyes through mini-lessons. Set aside time for students to share what they've learned and extend one another's understanding. The point of all of this to help your students become unconscious of structure as they draft. They should swim, and dive down deep in the content of their topic, and the exciting challenge of bringing a fresh view of it—their view of it—to their readers.

And finally, motivate your students to read widely, with an insatiable appetite. Author Julius Lester's statement on reading sums up what we teachers need to do:

> An unfortunate fact of American life is that most people stop reading once they finish high school. Thus, their knowledge base stops at the level of an eighteen-year-old. Reading increases the quality of one's information, challenges one to think and rethink ideas. Reading provides one with the knowledge to continue to grow and mature and have something to say as a writer. If one does not read, he or she is in danger of remaining an eternal adolescent.
>
> — *Interview, April 2003*

CHAPTER THREE

WHAT WRITERS DO

Helping Students Select Topics,
Research, Plan, and Draft

In Their Own Words

How do you choose your topics?

Jean Craighead George

I read; I mull. I talk to people; I mull. I go to the mountains; I mull. I go to the city; I mull—and finally a very simple theme occurs to me.

Kathryn Lasky

The topic selects me. I rarely start out with a topic and then do research. With the butterfly book, I read this article in *The New York Times* about the migration of monarchs. When I finished the article, I thought, what a great idea for a book. There's drama—endangered groves, and people trying to pass a bond issue to buy the groves.

Joyce Hansen

I enjoy history so I like writing about historical figures and events. Often a topic finds me, though. When I'm reading history, I'll come across an interesting passage or person that sparks my imagination. I cannot write a book unless I am interested in and excited by the subject.

Julius Lester

I sometimes feel that subjects choose me . . . . I generally write about experiences I want to know more about, or I have a question and I write to find answers. Certainly, my books on slavery came from a sense of feeling chosen by dead slaves to tell the stories they had never been able to tell about their lives.

How do your life experiences affect your writing?

Russell Freedman

No one writes in a vacuum. Whether you're working on an article, a biography, a history, or whatever, your world view, your personal set of values, the sum total of all your life's experiences, affect your perception of the material, your judgments, your decisions about what to include and what to leave out and what to emphasize. If a work is not informed by the writer's own values and beliefs, then it will lack a point of view, it will have no cutting edge. It will be as flaccid and noncommittal as a textbook written by a committee.

Patricia McKissack

Stories are coming out of my own life experiences. For example, I was a little girl at the time of the Supreme Court's decisions on civil rights. I can remember my mother telling me about this great woman singer, Marian Anderson. I can remember having heard her sing. I can remember her struggles to get a hotel room, find a restaurant to eat in, or travel by train. When I'm writing nonfiction, I'm not writing out of a void. I'm writing out of my own life, my own joy, my own uncertainty.

If there was one piece of advice you could offer young writers, what would it be?

Russell Freedman

The best advice I can offer an aspiring nonfiction writer is to write only about what interests you most, really interests you, and to soak yourself in your research until it is seeping out of your pores. At some point the material begins to speak to you. As you work, a picture begins to develop in your mind. How do you know when you've done enough research? I think it's when you can't stand

doing any more research and you've just got to get started writing. But of course, you're never finished with the research. You keep going back to find out where the holes are and how to fill them in.

Patricia McKissack

Show, don't tell. A lot of people think that nonfiction is simply listing facts. Spewing facts and numbers gets boring. But when you go in and tell a story, that's good writing. For example, the poet Laurence Dunbar walked to school with Orville and Wilbur Wright. Now that's a story. It's also a fact, but it's a good story for a writer to wonder about. What did they talk about? How did they get to be friends? Were they in the same class? Asking questions helps writers find stories in facts.

Walter Dean Myers

Every piece of nonfiction that I do begins with a question. I work very hard to come up with the right question, one that will allow me to explore the subject in depth and make it come alive for my readers. The question format also gives me direction.

Including Authors'
Insights in Instruction

As these authors state, there are many roads to writing well, but perhaps the most direct and smoothly paved is for a writer to choose a topic that fascinates him. Riveting topics don't land in the middle of a writer's living room while he passively sits in an armchair—instead, they're discovered because of a writer's openness to ideas and sensory information. Whether reading the paper in a local diner or by traveling in a foreign place, these writers read between the lines of life, always wondering, mulling, sniffing out the interesting drama of nature or people. In this chapter, I'll share strategies for bringing out children's natural receptiveness to information and ideas.

Another point the authors make, which we'll also explore in this chapter, is that even though a writer may feel he knows a great deal about a topic he's been happily steeped in, he will also have to do research to clarify thoughts and collect new information. Some of the writers I interviewed love research, others resist it, and virtually all of them go about it a little differently.

With this in mind, in this chapter I describe lessons that reflect the authors' insights about winnowing their ideas and then performing the juggling act that is research, planning, and drafting. We'll then explore strategies that guide students to transform those dogeared, jam-packed journal pages and rough drafts into nonfiction pieces that are alive with students' voices and their passion.

The child is more important than the writing. I think a lot of teachers have forgotten that. It is the writing I want to make parallel to where the kid wants to go in life. If I can sneak the writing into the kid's goals, then the writing will take off.

— Donald Graves

It's September. My sixth- and eighth-grade students are learning the routines of workshop: the format of mini-lessons, listening and responding to teacher Read Alouds, keeping a writing journal, and so forth. Establishing routines builds structure into the workshop and teaches students to work independently and seek support from peers, freeing me to confer with small groups and individuals.

In the midst of introducing all these routines, I have begun preparing students to study nonfiction by reading aloud short biographies, magazine articles, informational picture books, and excerpts from informational chapter books. I lace the mini-lessons I described in chapter two into the mix. Students are also spending part of workshop time reading and browsing through nonfiction texts in our classroom library. My hope is that books and magazine articles on a wide range of topics will spark an interest in each student that he or she will want to pursue as a focus for a nonfiction piece. Between this initial browsing and the completion of a final work of nonfiction are several exploratory phases, including additional reading, discussion with peers, perhaps interviewing an expert in the field. The phases are exploratory, because as Donald Graves says, the child is more important than the writing, so as my students explore, I let them know that they have to be keen on the topic they choose. If they're not, it's okay to abandon their topic and look for another one.

Strategies for Guiding Students to Find Topics

When your students study nonfiction texts as preparation for doing their own nonfiction writing, you'll want to reserve about 12 to 15 minutes of several workshops for pairs to brainstorm and discuss ideas that interest them. During the last five minutes of this time, I collect students' ideas on chart paper and post the class list. Nudge students to be specific. If one says "sports," ask "Which one?" The more specific a topic, the easier it is to focus it. Here's a list generated by sixth graders.

Possible Topics We Can Write About

- in-line skating
- basketball
- being a goalie
- pony club
- raising a cow, pig, lamb
- instant messaging best friend
- my pen pal
- breaking a leg, arm, etc.
- my best friend
- riding my dirt bike
- killing roaches on vacation

- skiing
- playing the guitar
- waterskiing
- winning at the county fair
- the telephone
- training for cross country
- losing my grandpa
- first visit to emergency room
- hating homework
- snowboarding

Every four to five weeks, reread the posted list, invite partners to chat for a few minutes, then add new ideas. When students hear the list read aloud periodically, it generates new ideas, which I then add, and it keeps the excitement of ideas in the air. In addition to a class list, I have students keep a personal list of possible topics in their writing folders.

Sixth grader Colleen's personal writing list reflects her many passions. Talking with her about her list helps me get to know her, which in turn improves my teaching. Says Donald Graves, "Above all get to know your students—get to know what they know."

Colleen

- basketball
- dancer jazz, tap, modern, ballet, pointe,
- drawing
- lacrosse
- field hockey
- summer/spring
- piano
- singing
- family - cousins, family gathering
- situations/events
- school - teachers, class, interests in school
- flowers
- friends
- ocean
- Body
- Babysitting
- braces
- gossip
- fights - argueing

Colleen's list of writing topics becomes the focus of conference conversations with me.

Nonfiction Writing From the Inside Out

WALKABOUTS: BUILD SENSORY EXPERIENCES

Kathryn Lasky, Julius Lester, and Patricia McKissack all mentioned that topics for writing non-fiction frequently "find them." For these writers, daily events, conversations, and reading connects them to a topic they had never considered. Sensitive to their surroundings, these writers look deeply and listen carefully. We teachers can heighten students' powers of observation by engaging them in learning experiences that raise their awareness of their environment. When we do, students can experience this same satisfying phenomenon of a topic "finding" them.

Attune children to their world by inviting them outside to observe trees, a meadow, a stream, the sky, or a city street. Take them on observation and listening walks on or close to school grounds where they can study a tree in different seasons, observe the insects in a rotting log or a patch of ground, or collect rocks to identify and study. Place a bird feeder outside your window so students can observe the behaviors and eating habits of feathered visitors.

Extend these firsthand experiences by building collections of nonfiction books into classroom and school libraries, and encouraging students to read magazines such as *National Geographic, Ranger Rick, Cobblestone,* and *Zoobook* (see Appendix page 322 for annotated list of magazines).

A Woodpecker Told Me: How Two Authors Found Their Topic

STEPHEN R. SWINBURNE:

My book *Unbeatable Beaks* taught me to keep my "ears and eyes open" since you never know when you will get an idea for a book. One day, a few years ago, I was coming out of my house when I heard *tap, tap, tap, tap, tap!* I looked up at the old apple tree out back and saw a woodpecker pecking away at the bark trying to uncover some bugs. While watching this woodpecker work away for its breakfast, I started thinking how much its beak was like a hammer or chisel. I then thought how beaks are really pretty unbeatable tools. That's when I went upstairs and began my poem *Unbeatable Beaks.*

PATRICIA McKISSACK:

Topics are everywhere. Sometimes they beckon to you and say "Come and look at my story." I remember walking through an airport and seeing an artist painting a mural. I asked him what it was. He said it was about the Tuskegee Air Base of World War II. I said I want to know more about it, and he gave me the name of a contact to interview in St. Louis. Out of that encounter came *Red-Tail Angels.* Sometimes ideas come to me from odd places at odd times. I do not go looking for them; they find me.

JOURNALS: GIVE STUDENT WRITERS A PLACE TO GO

My students use journals for many purposes. In their **class journal** they record their responses to books, magazines and newspaper articles, either before or after they've discussed them with peers. For several weeks, students also use their journals to write letters to me and/or one another about the nonfiction books they are reading (Atwell, 1987, 1999). I also have them record in their class journals notes from their research and their reactions to nonfiction read-alouds and guest speakers. I want their journals to be an elaborate weave of material for them to reread and reflect on, as rich in detail as a medieval tapestry.

Nonfiction topics can "pop out" from this rereading, but I always introduce a more deliberate method of collecting ideas by inviting students to try keeping a **writer's journal**, in which they write brief "bursts" of text frequently. Students can purchase a separate notebook for this purpose or use a section of their class journal.

Some writers, like Donald Graves, Donald Murray, and Stephen R. Swinburne write daily in a diary or journal. Others, like Jean Craighead George, keep detailed notebooks while researching a topic.

Keep a journal in which you put down on paper what's happening in your life. Shape the account as if you were writing it for a wide audience, even if the only reader is you. Try to bring out the humor and drama in the events you describe, and above all, make them interesting. Just as daily physical exercise helps to keep your body in good shape, so a journal will help you to develop your writing skills.

I require that all students keep a writer's journal during class for at least three weeks so they can determine for themselves whether or not it's beneficial. If they choose not to maintain one outside of school, I respect their decision. Occasionally I invite students to choose and read part or all of an entry to the class. This strategy broadens possibilities of what to write about for everyone. I only read some entries if a student needs help finding a topic.

On at least two occasions, invite partners to discuss how writer's journals support them—or why they dislike using them. Then ask students to share their thoughts with the entire class. Such debriefings permit students to air their feelings as well as discover benefits they might not have considered.

When you invite students to generate ideas, spelling and punctuation should not be an issue, especially when exploring content is the primary goal. Never mark corrections in writer's journals—or any other student journals—for doing this can discourage them from pouring out ideas.

Nonfiction Writing From the Inside Out

WRITER'S JOURNALS: A PLACE TO TRY WRITERLY MOVES

In a journal, students might describe an experience, or they might closely observe a place, an animal, or a person. They might record some of the day's activities without much editorializing or use the journal as a place to pour out feelings about a person or a conflict in their life. A journal may hold lists, rough drafts, the tiniest kernels of a writing idea—all are rehearsals for writing (Murray, 1984).

Below are some ideas to share with students that may give their journal writing variety. Model for students how you do each one (see "Scaffolding Ideas" on page 81). Their entries will be richer after observing you and then discussing the process.

- **Lists:** Create wish lists, idea lists, to-do lists, gift lists, party lists, and lists of data on a topic of interest.
- **Unsent Letter:** Write a letter to express anger, disappointment, disagreement with an actual event, but don't mail it.
- **Dear Diary:** Pretend your diary has a name and write your deepest feelings about friends, a memory, a pet, a class, homework, school and home rules, etc., to your pretend friend.
- **Descriptions:** Describe places so that others can picture them.
- **Day's Events:** Record the day's key events or focus on one or two events that sparked your interest.
- **What I Saw:** Write a first-hand account of what you observed, saw, or were part of.
- **Wish Writing:** Write about something you truly want—a pet, a bike, a trip, and explain why it's so important to you.
- **Admiration Notes:** Tell why you admire an historical figure, an adult, or a friend.
- **If I Could Be . . . :** Write about who you'd like to be and why.
- **Respond to Information You Read or Heard:** React to information you learned from reading an informational chapter or picture book, a magazine or newspaper article, or an historical document.

STEPHEN R. SWINBURNE ON JOURNALS

I've kept a diary or journal nearly all my life. It started when I was twelve. I remember going to bed and pulling the sheets over my head and reaching under my pillow for my flashlight, diary, and pen. Here's an entry from February, 1964: "It was a very cold Monday and nothing really happened." Isn't that great? Actually, it's pretty bad. But every night I'd pop that flashlight and write in my diary. And you know what? My writing got better, and it began an interest in writing.

When you write in your journal you can keep it as simple as recording the day's weather or you can use it as a place to record events and feelings. Most of all it's a place to begin a love of words.

I would like others to understand that yes, I am thin, but no, I am NOT anorexic. It seems that because I do have a thin body, people who don't know me either don't think I eat or I make myself throw up. It's rediculous. I didn't ask to be this skinny, but I am, and thats ok. So, to all of those people who talk smack about me behind my back, thanks for making me the center of your world.

Two different entries by eighth graders. Above, Sara confides thoughts about her figure; at the right, Jeanette spills out feelings about child labor.

English Scope Issue

I almost cried when I read about 15 year old Kaushalya Kumari, who said, "Why can't a poor person's child dream of becoming a doctor?" We, at Powhatan, simply take for granted that we will have the money to go to college, & become whatever we want to be. To children such as Kaushalya, their dreams are simple dreams, though for us, who have never worked an hour of hard work in our life, is probably a reality. This article shows how corrupt the world is. Even in the U.S., Canada, & developed European nations, there is illegal child labor. These children's childhoods are literally being stolen from them. I completely agree that something has to be done. I think I will try to get the Social Responsibility Club to support a fund toward child labor. I hadn't realized how blind I was until I read this article. I thought child labor only existed in small amounts in 3rd world developing countries. I had no idea so many children were suffering. The other article also spoke to me of stolen childhoods, though in a different way. People that become involved in drugs are literally stealing their own childhoods. I also agree that more funds need to support addicted children & sponsor them to go to rehabilitation centers.

BRAINSTORMING AND FAST-WRITES

Once students choose a topic you can help them discover what they know about it—and what else they need to learn—by modeling brainstorming and fast-writes. Later in this chapter, on pages 90, 93, and 94, you'll see how students can use these two techniques again as they begin to plan and draft.

Brainstorming is a free flow of ideas, feelings, and information related to a topic, conducted orally or in writing. The goal is to have students write words and phrases without censoring each idea. Bruce Brooks notes the importance of brainstorming ideas for nonfiction:

> Ideas for nonfiction lead to investigation, but these ideas can start with writing. I might write ahead of the facts, based on what I know about a topic or an idea that interests me. While writing, I'm using my imagination to take me beyond what I know. Then I check my imagination's accuracy. In this way the process is often reversed, for people think that the research comes first and then the writing begins. —Interview, 1993

Nonfiction Writing From the Inside Out

A Fast Write, completed after an eighth-grade trip to the Holocaust Museum in Washington, D.C.

Fast-Writes help writers swiftly reclaim memories, feelings, experiences, and knowledge—and most of all, to take that crucial step of getting something down on paper. To fast-write, ask students to take two to four minutes to write everything they think they know and feel about a topic. With a fast-write, it's important to not stop writing—to always keep pencil and paper connected. If ideas stop flowing, simply write "I'm stuck" or rewrite the last word again and again until a new thought surfaces.

> Fast Write
> Holocaust
>
> The Holocaust Museum was um um.. so sad, and and depressing. It is a very dim um depressing place to visit, because you see all these pictures of dead people. Um — Um... Um... It was educational but very, very scary. I'm glad I had my friends in my group. Um... hummm no. You saw lots of children died and we also saw pictures of people that died before the war.... Um Um — Um... Um. It made me uneasy seeing all of that. My stomach didn't feel good, niether did my friends' smotachs. Um um Um... Um... um... Um. It was like being dehumanated which is really sad. They would put number Tatoos so that they didn't have to remember names. Um... Um... Also they humiliated then made them feel like nothing.

Scaffolding Ideas: Modeling Makes a Difference

Whether you invite students to brainstorm, fast-write, or try one of the journaling techniques on page 79, reserve time to model each one by writing and thinking aloud on chart paper in front of students. I find that when I model and students observe and react, their work contains more details.

After modeling, set aside two to three minutes for students to chat with a partner about their observations. Then field questions to clarify students' understanding. The next day, pair your struggling writers and invite them to choose a topic and discuss it for two to three minutes. Partners can select a topic from the chart of nonfiction ideas the class generated (page 76) or select a different topic. Then have pairs try one of the journaling ideas listed on page 79. Once partners show you they can generate a list of ideas after talking about their topic, have students work independently.

Strategies for Guiding Students Into Their Research

Some of the best student nonfiction I read tends to come from a student's careful observations about things he/she experiences *combined with* research about the topic. But how many sources should we expect students to use, how much time should we allow for their research, and how can we structure our class time to make this phase of the writing fruitful for students? These are a few of the issues we'll look at now. As the following authors express, research requires time and "eight arms" in action at once.

Stephen R. Swinburne: I have what I call an "octopus" or "multi-armed" approach to research. I get in lots of field time [for observing]. I read books and magazines. I check references in the library. I surf the Internet. I telephone experts and scientists. I interview people. I rely on all these sources to give me a foundation of fact on my subject.

Marissa Moss: I spend about six months doing research before I start writing the historical books. Generally, I read around a hundred books that get condensed down into my one.

Hudson Talbott: Sometimes I feel that I create books so I can do research. I fall in love with a subject and can become obsessive about learning "all there is to know" about it. I do a fair bit of research now on the Internet but don't find it nearly as satisfying as sitting with several open books, going back and forth, linking bits of information so I gain a more comprehensive understanding of my subject.

David Quammen: I read, read, read, and I go into the field, and walk miles through the mud with tropical ecologists. I visit remote places, ask questions, and observe carefully. I take abundant notes in an old-fashioned notebook.

I recommend that once students have a topic, you set aside ten to fourteen weeks for research, drafting, and revising to be completed in class. Some days students work for half of my 90-minute block; other days they use most of the time.

Like the writing process, the research process is recursive, not a sequence of steps. Students move back and forth from browsing to reading to talking to observing to interview-

Nonfiction Writing From the Inside Out

ing to taking notes to reading and browsing again to drafting and to rereading and learning more information. That said, there are three basic practices my students keep looping through each class during the research phase: 1. reading; 2. retelling to a peer what they've learned; 3. writing notes in their journals based on the reading and the peer conversation.

1. **Reading: *20 to 30 minutes*.** During each class students read books, magazine and newspaper articles. It's important to ensure that you have enough materials that students can read independently. In my classroom, students have access to books on a wide range of reading levels from the class and school libraries and the local public library. (Students also do research outside of school, which can include more reading, conducting an interview, using the Internet, and so on.)

2. **Retelling to a Peer: *7 to 10 minutes*.** After they read, students pair up and, by turn, tell each other about their reading. Retelling what they have learned from reading enables students to clarify new information and deepen their understanding of the topic. When talk precedes writing it stimulates thinking, allowing students to generate more detailed lists of information and ideas and discover what they know about a topic (Calkins, 1986, 1994; Graves, 1983, 2003). The goal I have for students is to draft without notes after *several* reading, discussing, and note-taking experiences, then select and organize notes into a plan.

    The listener's role is to raise questions about things that confuse him, which often points out to the researcher fuzzy spots in his own knowledge of his topic.

    Here, sixth-grader Ethan retells to a partner what he's just read about optical illusions. During the retelling, Ethan refers to photographs and diagrams in his books to further clarify points for William and himself. This is fine as long as the book becomes a reference and not a crutch used to skim and retell or read and retell.

ETHAN: I learned that drawings are only one kind of optical illusion. Trick photography is what I read about today.

WILLIAM: What makes the photograph a trick?

ETHAN: It's when the people or things in the photo aren't really what you see.

WILLIAM: Would you show me a trick photo to help me see what you mean?

ETHAN: [Opens book] See these two people? They look like they're standing on another man's hands. If you thought this was real, then the photo fooled you.

WILLIAM: How did the photographer do this?

ETHAN: [Closes book] This happened on a hill. The photographer had the big man stand far away in back of the hill—just where it starts to go down. The two smaller people are standing close to the front part of the top of the hill. It looks like the man is holding the two but he just has his palms up.

WILLIAM: Cool! Are there people known for optical illusions?

ETHAN: Houdini was one. Escher made drawings that are optical illusions.

Note the number of questions William asks—questions that compel Ethan to offer more exact details. Such exchanges help students make new information their own. You can also have each student retell to the entire class. Listeners can raise two or three questions. Although this takes more time than partner retellings, whole-class sharing has benefits. "Kids became interested in topics they would not have considered researching by listening to the excitement in a peer's voice," says teacher John Applin.

3. **Writing Notes in a Journal: 8 to 10 minutes.** After paired discussion and questioning, most students can jot down detailed notes without referring to the materials read. Instruct your students to make notes using their own words, and to sketch labeled diagrams. To replicate a diagram, students often have to refer to the resource for accuracy, and that's fine. But other than

Fourth grader Meg takes notes on seals.

> ## Scaffolding Ideas: When Students Have a Tough Time Retelling
>
> When students can't retell what they've read, it's time for me to discover why, especially if I have tried to locate materials they can read independently. In a conference corner, I meet with these students one-on-one and ask why the retelling is not going well. Answers might include, "I can't remember what I read," or "I don't like this topic," or "The words are hard." You can use your school or local public library or the Internet to find accessible materials when the reading becomes frustrating. If students discover they dislike a topic, then encourage them to change it at this point. Even if time is tight, once the topic interests a student, the research will flow. Remember Russell Freedman's words: "The best advice I can offer an aspiring nonfiction writer is to write only about what interests you most . . . . "

that, research materials should be put away. With books open, most cannot resist the temptation to copy chunks from the text. Copying discourages reflection and learning.

Invite students to reread their notes from time to time during their research process. This helps them continue to build the background knowledge needed for them to connect to new ideas and information in order to construct new understandings (Alvermann and Phelps, 1998; Gillet and Temple, 2000; Robb, 2003; Vacca and Vacca, 2000).

COACHING YOUNG RESEARCHERS: THE TEACHER'S ROLE

All the time that students are reading, retelling, and jotting down notes, I'm circulating around the room, ready to provide support. For example, if I see a student struggling to read a resource, I might read the material to him. I listen to pairs retell what they learned and scan notes as students write. My observations help me decide when groups or the entire class is ready to use what they've learned to further focus their topic. I can also identify students who need extra help. From a teaching standpoint, these weeks of research can make great demands on your time as you try to reach every student. I find I can pair strong students and have them support one another; this frees me to help weaker readers and writers by conferring with them individually or in small groups (see Appendix pages 318–320 for more on conferences).

NARROWING TOPICS: SEVEN STRATEGIES

Some student writers find a focus before they start browsing through books. Fifth-grader Jordan knows exactly what she wants to research: how the ancient Egyptians made mummies. But a majority of students begin with a topic that's far too broad. "I want to write about Tasmanian devils," fourth-grader Ellie tells me as I kneel next to her desk.

"What about them interests you?" I ask.

"Everything!" says Ellie enthusiastically. Ellie is typical of students who have a great passion for a topic. With mini-lessons and conferences, I continually help children narrow a broad topic to a manageable idea and then to decide what elements to include in a topic.

Here are seven ways to help students like Ellie focus their subject. Have your students:

1. **Read about a topic until they have absorbed information and have several journal pages of notes.** Absorption means students can discuss the topic without rereading research materials and notes.

2. **Reread their journal notes and star, check, or circle ideas that interest them.** Donald Murray points out that while rereading journal notes, "certain ideas will keep coming up, sort of like a whale

> can start to be seen.
> 1. 12 weeks – 1½ inches, they have fur, eyes open, ears erect, long whiskers, can make noise and open mouth
> 2. 15 weeks – 3 inches long, ½ pound, and they are fully developed.
> 3. During the first fifteen weeks the little devils are called pouch embryos.
> 4. Embryos is a word for unborn babies but it describes a half formed marsupial in the pouch.
> 5. The pouch opening is controlled by a ring of muscles similar to our lips.
> 6. The second birth takes place in August to September the beginning of spring.
> 7. The 2nd birth is when the devils leave the pouch.
> 8. Devils are good swimmers
> 9. Since they don't sweat they get in water to cool off.
> 10. If a mother has babies in her pouch she closes it tight so they don't drown.
> 11. When they're seven months old they're on their own.

Note how Ellie stars and checks *all* of her notes. This occurs when students have not yet focused their topics and are unsure of how to zoom in on a single aspect.

Nonfiction Writing From the Inside Out

that surfaces from time to time. When I spot that recurring information or thought it may become the focus for the piece I'm going to write" (*Write to Learn*, page 84).

3. **Consider their audience and what they might already know about the topic** (Fletcher, 1992; Graves, 1983, 2000). This was the key that enabled Ellie to discover her focus. "My audience," she says, "knows nothing about Tasmanian devils. I have to give them the basics."

   If a writer's audience knows the basics, then he can quickly review these and dive into other aspects of a topic. For example, Kevin, a sixth grader, quickly reviewed basic basketball positions. Then he engaged his audience with descriptions of slam dunks, rebound shots, faking, and creative dribbling.

4. **Think of four to five categories they'll need to cover to meet their audience's needs.** Ellie rereads her notes and quickly writes: "Attitude, Reproduction, Appearance, and Habitat." Not all students will identify these categories so easily. I reread their notes and discuss these with them. Then I ask, "tell me your audience." Sometimes I have to provide one or two categories before students can think of the rest.

Ellie's final draft for her article on Tasmanian devils.

Tasmanian Devils may look fuzzy, cute, and cuddly but they are really mangy, bloodthirsty, and very dangerous. Here is an article on them.

The mother devil has 50 babies at a time. They are born from the cloaca. The devils pouch is near the tail and the babies come in and out to suckle on the nipples.

Newborn: 1/4 an inch long, 1/2000 of a pound, and they're blind deaf and have hairless pink skin.

4 weeks: 1/2 inch long and their eyes lips and ears are beginning to form.

8 weeks: 1 inch they have black skin but no hair tiny eyelashes and whiskers begin to form.

12 weeks: 11/2 inches they get fur, eyes open, ears erect, whiskers form, and they can make noise.

15 weeks: 3 inches 1/2 pound and they are fully developed.

During the first 15 weeks the little devils are called pouch embryos. The pouch opening is controlled by a ring of muscles, similar to our lips. They are as small as a grain of rice when born. All of the above takes place in the first birth, which is from April to May, and the whole process takes 5 minuets while being totally ignored by the mother. The second birth takes place in August to September (The beginning of spring). This is when the devils leave the pouch. Babies, use their littermates for practicing in developing skills they will need to survive on

their own. When they're 7 months old they're on their own at last.

Devils are marsupials they get their name from the word "marsupian" which means, "pouch". They have pouches just like their relatives even though they look nothing like their relatives. Their forelegs have 5 toes and their hind legs have 4 toes. Devils have the 3rd strongest jaw out of all the animals in the world. The 1st is the Great White Shark the 2nd is the hyena. The male devil rarely weighs 20 pounds the females usually weigh 12 pounds. They got the name "sarcophilus" which means "meat lover" because they are so oriented to food. Devils love to lay in the sun, but it is hard to tell whether they're asleep or in an energy conserving torpor.

They have knobby soles for good traction. They have long claws to help dig. They're black with a white spot on their chest or side. Their nose is 100 more times sensitive than ours. They are described as Ugly, Mangy, Dangerous, Scary, Smelly, and Bloodthirsty.

Devils are experts at conserving energy. Devils may look like great hunters and runners but they are really clumsy. They can climb trees and are great swimmers. Since they don't sweat they get in the water to cool off. If a mother is carrying babies in her pouch she will tightly close it so they don't drown. The number 1 killer of baby devils is other devils. The winner of the fight eats the loser of the fight. They are cannibals.

Devils live in Cradle Mountain National Park Tasmania Australia if you ever want to visit them.

In Tasmania devils live freely. I hope you have enjoyed and learned more in this article.

5. **Use 3 x 5 note cards.** Have students write one category heading on each note card. Ellie writes "Attitude" on one card, "Reproductions" on a second card, and so on. She jots down ideas that relate to a specific heading. Often, students will use two or more index cards to cover all the notes they have for a specific heading.

> #1   Attitude
> • Devils are experts at conserving energy
> • But sometimes when they look like great hunters or runners they really are very clumsy.
> • Devils can climb trees and they are good swimmers.
> • Since they don't sweat they get in the water to cool off
> • If a mother has babies in her pouch she closes it tight so they don't drown

One of Ellie's note cards for her article on Tasmanian devils.

What Ellie now has is a plan for four paragraphs for the two-page article she will start to draft (see pages 31, 91–96, and Chapter 5 for more about writing plans).

6. **Raise questions readers might ask about their topic.** Have students select the four most important questions to address in their piece. Fourth-grader Margaret poses these questions to focus her research on kit foxes: What do they look like? Where do they live? What do they eat? How do they survive?

7. **Talk to a classmate about information on the note cards.** Have students share the different features they plan to use in their nonfiction pieces. They can then add ideas that their conversations spark.

WILLIAM ZINSSER ON NARROWING TOPICS

Every writing project must be reduced before you start to write.

Therefore think small. Decide what corner of your subject you're going to bite off, and be content to cover it well and stop (*On Writing Well*, page 52).

BRIEF CONFERENCES: HELPING STUDENTS NARROW TOPICS

Most students will find their focus after they've engaged with a few of these seven strategies. However, some students will need to confer with you to narrow their topic. Perhaps more to the point, in these conferences I often find that students are in a sense asking for our blessing to limit what they cover. Through their research they've learned so much; they need reassurance from us that it's okay that they don't share all.

Sixth-grader Katie asked me for a conference about her three-page article on ballet. She couldn't find an angle to commit herself to. "I like everything about ballet—lessons, making up dances, watching ballet, the costumes, and the history—I learned a lot about the history. I can't choose what to use in my piece."

"Tell me what you think of when you say *ballet*," I suggest.

[long pause] "Mainly my pointe class."

"That's a good focus. I never took ballet and I'd love to know what you do."

"But I want to do more," Katie insists. "I know so much."

"Could you put some of that extra information in sidebars?" I ask. Immediately, Katie walks to a computer and types up drafts of two sidebars that allow her to share what she loves about ballet but that do not directly relate to her pointe classes—the focus of her piece.

Sidebar One
Did You Know...?
1. That Pointe shoes take well over twelve hours to make!
2. That Ballets five basic positions were created in the eighteenth century by Pierre Beauchamps, the ballet master of King Louis XIV of France.
3. And that Pointe shoes are handmade. Their toe boxes are 'blocked' or painted with glue, then baked in ovens to strengthen and stiffen them. Some professional dancers can go through twenty pairs of Pointe shoes a week; In fact, some can wear a pair of them out in one hour!!!!

Katie's sidebars for her article on pointe class.

Sidebar Two
Here are some pictures of Pointe and Ballet shoes:

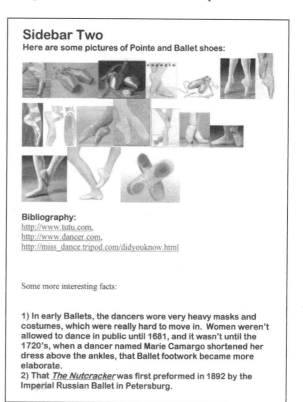

Bibliography:
http://www.tutu.com,
http://www.dancer.com,
http://miss_dance.tripod.com/didyouknow.html

Some more interesting facts:

1) In early Ballets, the dancers wore very heavy masks and costumes, which were really hard to move in. Women weren't allowed to dance in public until 1681, and it wasn't until the 1720's, when a dancer named Marie Camargo shortened her dress above the ankles, that Ballet footwork became more elaborate.
2) That *The Nutcracker* was first preformed in 1892 by the Imperial Russian Ballet in Petersburg.

On the next page is a reproducible for students that may help them focus their topic, though it works best for students who already have a manageable angle.

Some students will continue to waver about their topics for so long that unless they choose one, they will not be able to meet the established deadline for a draft. That's when I'm forced to choose one for a student. Doing this is always a last option, and I'm careful to say something like, "Deciding has been tough for you. Based on our conversations and the materials you have, I think you should work on the bald eagle. Save your notes on chimps and electric eels. You can use them in other pieces." Even though I have made the decision, I let the student know that she can still use her other topics.

Getting Ready to Draft: Tips for Students

- Decide on your audience. Is it your peers? Younger children? Teachers and other adults? People who know little about your topic? People who know a lot about it? Answering these questions will help you decide whether to include only very basic information about your topic or move beyond the basics.

- Reread your brainstorm list and/or fast-write. Circle information you think your audience needs to know. List additional ideas you want to include.

- Make a list of what you need to learn from research. Your list will help you find books and magazines in your school library. It will also help you decide whether you can find an expert to interview. For example, you might list that you need to discover more about the habitat, diet, and social interactions among wolves.

- Think about page limits. If your teacher has limited the length of your piece, you need to use that information to help you decide what's important to include.

- Share with a peer. Read all of your notes to a peer and gather suggestions or more information.

- Create a writing plan before drafting. You can web, use note cards, or make lists of what to include under each category.

There's some overlap between the phases of narrowing a topic and making a writing plan. For example, in choosing five or so categories to write on note cards, students simultaneously narrow their topic and end up with an initial plan of sorts.

But there's more planning to do, of course. Once they've got their details organized onto the cards, they need to consider the form their writing will take: Will it be an essay? An article? A series of journal entries? In Chapters 5 and 6 we'll look closely at a wide range of nonfiction genres to introduce to students, for they must understand a genre's structure before they attempt to write in it. But for now, let's look at some strategies for teaching students to use writing plans that help them organize their information regardless of the genre they select.

SOME SAMPLE STUDENT PLANS

A plan needn't involve formal outlining with Roman numerals and alphabet numbers. I don't know any writers who plan that way. A good working outline might be a marked-up fast-write, a list, or a web. For the first couple of months of school I require rather detailed plans, but once I know students, I'm flexible. For example, if students are writing an essay from personal experience, I may tell them that doing a fast-write before drafting will suffice.

Whether highly detailed or brief, a plan makes a big difference in the quality of students' drafts. Let's look now at some student plans.

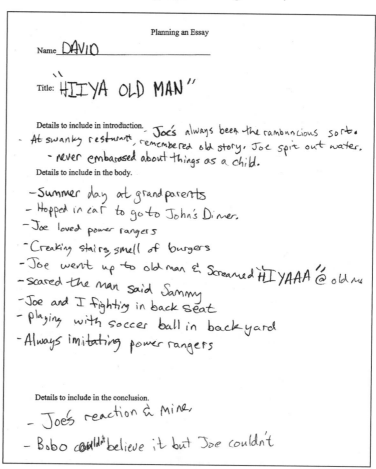

Planning an Essay

Name DAVID

Title: "HIIYA OLD MAN"

Details to include in introduction. — Joe's always been the rambunctious sort.
- At swanky resturant, remembered old story. Joe spit out water.
- never embarassed about things as a child.

Details to include in the body.
- Summer day at grandparents
- Hopped in car to go to John's Diner.
- Joe loved power rangers
- Creaking stairs, smell of burgers
- Joe went up to old man & screamed HIYAAA @ old m
- scared the man said Sammy
- Joe and I fighting in back seat
- playing with soccer ball in backyard
- Always imitating power rangers

Details to include in the conclusion.
- Joe's reaction & mine.
- Bobo could believe it but Joe couldn't

Eighth-grader David likes to write detailed plans prior to drafting. "The plan makes me feel secure," David explains. "I go back to it if I'm stuck or if I want more details. It kind of frees me to write."

When sixth grader Katie did research for her article called "A Cat Guide," she read four books about cats; observed her own cat; and interviewed friends, classmates, her mom, and the owner of a local pet store. "I knew so much," said Katie. "It was easy to make a plan to decide what to include."

MODELING THE PLANNING PROCESS

Okay, I'll admit it: there is great resistance among my students to the planning process. "I don't need to plan; it's all in my head," or "A couple of words is all I need, the rest is in my head," are typical comments. Their resistance is natural, of course, but at times it signals that a student does not have a solid idea of what her piece is about. Earlier in my career I was more inclined to let students write without a plan. Invariably though, for these writers the lack of a plan resulted in dozens of "false starts." They began drafting with enthusiasm, but then halfway down the first page, they crumpled the paper and tossed it in the trash can, muttering "It's not working."

So what to do, given this resistance? The key to helping students develop plans is for you to model your own process. Tell students that their plans aren't set in stone—they can depart from them down the line. Then model your own complete writing process. Start by

Nonfiction Writing From the Inside Out

thinking aloud about how you consider your audience, brainstorm lists, and generate fast-writes, then organize these into a plan. Here's how it might go:

Think Aloud and Model

[I say aloud] *The audience for this opinion or persuasive piece will be teachers and the principal and assistant principal. My topic is No Written Homework on Weekends.*

Remember how you did fast-writes when you were beginning to choose your topic? I am going to use that technique here, because it's great for creating a writing plan, too.

I will write continually until all my ideas are on paper. If I have no thoughts, I'll repeat the last word I wrote. Fast-writes are ideal for reclaiming memories and making connections between ideas.

Fast-Write

Next, I fast-write on chart paper as students observe and jot down all the questions that enter their minds. I deliberately work with a topic of high interest to my students.

[I write] *No written homework means that I can spend time with friends on the weekends. I can see a movie, take long walks, and cook, which I really enjoy. No written homework, homework, homework means I can read. I love to read but I always have to take notes for history and science and do lots of math work. It's good to do different kinds of work on the weekends. It refreshes your mind and lets you follow your interests. You also have time to be with friends and cousins and go to a museum or a concert. Do things that you learn from only they're not school assignments.*

Reread it Aloud and Add Notes

[I continue writing] *What I want to do is what my parents get to do on weekends. Have choices, read, and do things they love to do.*

Debrief

Next, debrief so that students can share what they noticed, ask questions, and express their feelings about the strategy. Here's what sixth graders notice:

- You got stuck and repeated "homework."
- You never stopped writing.
- Your ideas aren't organized. I guess you can fix that.
- You reread and got another idea.

On another day I review the fast-write with students and show them how I create a plan for the short essay. I model how I bullet ideas on my fast-write page, and circle specific examples I want to include. If students have suggestions, I include them. Here's what I write:

Title: Learning for Life

Lead: Two choices: outline history chapter or listen to uncle tell stories about his African safari. Question—which can you learn from more? End with statement that calls for no weekend homework.

Body: Include these points: Discuss alternate ways to learn on weekends and show what you learn from these: see a movie, show, concert; visit relatives, friends; build model airplane; read; spend time thinking and talking to parents. Include anecdotes about bird watching and Air and Space Museum—show what these taught you.

Conclusion: Learning is not just for school—but it should prepare us for adult life. That's why we should do things grown-ups do on weekends.

Display the plan to refresh students' memory of your process.

GIVING STUDENTS FEEDBACK ON THEIR PLANS

When you meet with students about their plans, you want to help them gain clarity. Here are some samples of the kinds of comments I've made that help the young writers continue to refine their ideas. In general, posing questions is the most powerful kind of feedback, as it compels the writer to articulate—and clarify—her thoughts on a topic.

- Can you tell me what your audience needs? Are these points part of your plan? Let's talk about additional information you can include.

- What else have you learned about your topic? You know a great deal about training dogs. How about including details about grooming and the kinds of rewards you offer so that your dog follows commands?

- This plan has terrific questions that your piece will answer. How can you gather more details for the last two? Do you need to reread your notes? I recall so many more details because you shared them with me.

- Your list is shaping up, but you need more details and examples before drafting. Check your notes first, then skim some of the nonfiction texts you read to refresh your memory. Sometimes, facts and details that didn't pop off the page will speak to you now that you have background information.

- It might be helpful for you to talk to Riley, an eighth grader. He plays the drums and knows firsthand about drumming in a band.

- This plan has excellent details and anecdotes. You might want to call a pediatrician for some quotes that you can use to support your point that middle-school students need a snack as much as younger students. Here's the telephone number of Dr. X. I know he will help you.

A sixth grader discusses her research with me.

Scaffolding Ideas: Helping Students Who Struggle With Planning

Even with modeling and several brief conferences, a few students will struggle with planning. At this point, I sit side by side with them and ask questions such as: How would you like to open your piece? What will you include in the body? As students talk, I write down what they say.

Then I ask the student to reread her dictation and tell me details to add. Finally, I ask, "What do you think you might include in the ending?" Here is the dictated plan of a fifth grader who was writing about how to prevent hair balls in a cat.

> Jenny, my tabby throws up every evening. Mom makes me clean up the mess. Mom says, "Maria, Jenny is your cat. It's your job to help Jenny. You need to brush her and put oil in her food. Now I brush Jenny in the morning and evening. She loves the brushing. Most times Jenny purrs. I scoop out gobs of cat hair that Jenny would have swallowed. I put a drop of oil in Jenny's food two times a week. She hardly throws up now.

Once a student's ideas begin to flow during dictation, gradually release the scaffold. First, invite the student to talk while you write part of the piece. Then have the student talk and write, explaining that you will remember the ideas for her. Increase the amount the student talks and writes until she has the confidence and experience to work independently.

SAMPLE PLAN AND DRAFT

As the following student samples illustrate, planning before drafting is worth the effort:

John Kent   English

1. Bio of his life
2. First illusion
3. Reflective ball work
4. hand drawing a hand
5. Mobius strip
6. Personal Favorite illusion
7. That he drew everything by hand
8. Real Name
9. PowerPoint Presentation   Original occupation
10. My favorite artist
11. QQ notes

ESCHER SURVEY

Did you know that Escher failed 4 courses in college?

Escher didn't start school until he was 14

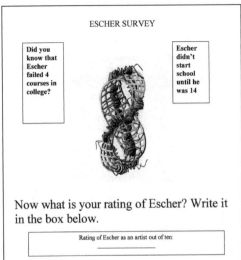

Now what is your rating of Escher? Write it in the box below.

Rating of Escher as an artist out of ten:

_____

The Art and Life of M.C. Escher

Metamorphose. Written up, down, and across. The words form squares, and the squares form lizards. The lizards become the cells of a beehive. Out of the beehive bees fly, changing into a background for fish. The fish and the background blend and form three different birds of different colors. They fuse and create a town with a tower in the water. That tower becomes the rook on a chess board. The squares on the board continue on, and eventually become Metamorphose again. This is Escher's Metamorphosis II.

Maurits Cornelius Escher was born in Holland in 1898. He was born in a house that became a museum. He went to school in Arnhem and in Delft. Escher also went to an art institute in Haarlem. Escher made his first piece of artwork while in school. It was an image of his father.

Escher was married in Rome to Jetta Umiker. She and Escher had two sons, George and Arthur. He moved to Switzerland soon after, and in 1940, he was forced to move to the Netherlands due to German occupation. The following year Escher returned to his homeland of Holland, where he lived for the rest of his life.

In 1955, Escher became a knight. He made his final work, Snakes, in 1969. Shortly afterward, in 1972, he died. But Escher's work still lives on. His illusions have bewildered many, and his art remains unequaled. He has probably created more tessellations than any other human being, ever. He spent his life working on art that would amaze people for many generations. He devoted most of his time studying geometric patterns for a picture, planning the layout of his next work, or illustrating the incredible drawings, woodcuts, and carvings that will be legendary in the hearts of many for long years to come.

Escher's work has convinced me that he was the greatest artist of all time. He wasn't the smartest person, but anything he lacked in intelligence he made up for twice over in hard work and perseverance. That kind of work ethic has made a lasting impression on me. See the survey sheet and rate him for yourself!

Nonfiction Writing From the Inside Out

DRAFTING

A friend told me, "I always write when I take long showers. I let my mind go and the words and ideas pour out. Then I wrap myself in the towel and grab pencil and paper. I'm impatient to write and discover thoughts I wasn't aware of." For my friend and many professional writers, thinking is writing, too. It's what Jean Craighead George means when she says, "I mull."

This mulling is often likened to a cow chewing its cud. For me, the mental process seems more like a cottontail rabbit darting from clover patch to clover patch within a field. When I am in the midst of planning an article or a book, I draft in my head long before I sit at my computer and write. Ideas dance and dash in my head while I teach, chat with friends, or fall to sleep. I want my students to experience this mulling, too. I want them to be as fascinated as I am at the way writers discover new ideas as they draft, ideas that were not a part of their plan. As Ralph Waldo Emerson expressed, "Good writing is a kind of skating which carries off the performer where he would not go."

FIRST DRAFTS: LET THE IDEAS POUR OUT

While drafting, some students keep their notes and plans on their desks, perhaps for security, while others store them in writing folders. I encourage students to write their drafts quickly, which does not leave time to continually refer to notes. I do invite them to reread their notes and plans several times before drafting starts. "When you start drafting, let the ideas pour out," I say. "You'll be able to organize them and rewrite later." Donald Murray's advice mirrors my experience: "Put your notes away before you begin a draft. What you remember is probably what should be remembered; what you forget is probably what should be forgotten" (*Expecting the Unexpected*, page 151). Tell students that they can return to their notes and plans when they revise drafts to make sure they have not omitted points or details.

> ### TERRIBLE FIRST DRAFTS ARE OKAY
>
> Almost all good writing begins with terrible first drafts. You need to start somewhere. Start by getting something—anything—down on paper. A friend of mine says that the first draft is the down draft—you just get it down. The second draft is the up draft—you fix it up. You try to say what you have to say more accurately. And the third draft is the dental draft, where you check every tooth, to see if it's loose or cramped or decayed, or even, God help us, healthy. (Anne Lamott, *Bird By Bird*, pages 25–26).

I encourage students to write as if they were pilots on a nonstop flight—keep those jet engines humming without worrying about grammar, organization, spelling, and so on. Getting their ideas onto paper means that students will have a piece to read and revise. Judging and changing each sentence while drafting can be frustrating and can derail the drafting effort. I always think of Anne Lamott's words and share them with students:

> Just get it all down on paper, because there may be something great in those six crazy pages that you would never have gotten to by more rational, grown-up means (*Bird by Bird*, page 23).

While drafting, new and related details invade writers' minds. Fourth-grader Georgi expressed her frustration over what she called "idea attacks" during a brief conference: "New ideas come up when I'm drafting. If I start thinking about them, I stop writing. If I keep writing, I forget ideas that were good." To help student writers maintain the momentum of drafting as well as hold onto new ideas, provide strategies for completing quick jots while drafting.

STRATEGIES FOR RECORDING NEW IDEAS

My students jot down connections or new ideas that pop into their mind in the margins. A few use sticky notes. After completing the first draft, students can reread their jottings and decide whether to add these idea "invasions" when they revise.

Whether students add ideas on a handwritten or computer draft makes no difference. The point is that they immediately note details as they bombard their mind. Waiting until they finish the draft means a worthy idea may be lost forever.

Graves and Lasky on Keeping Track of New Ideas

Donald Graves: I write on the computer. I shift to italics to put new ideas in the text. I don't like to interrupt the flow, so I jot notes in the text so I don't forget. I keep the momentum going. The next day I reread what I wrote, cleaning up notes. This also gets me ready for the new day because now yesterday is in my head. Don't push kids on this. If they think it's a good idea, they'll steal it.

Kathryn Lasky: I use sticky notes. I also use sticky notes on the computer. When I'm working on a book, if something comes to me, I put it on a note on the screen. When I'm finished with the book, I go back and look at all the sticky notes. Did I put that in? Some things I don't use.

"Tell the Truth But Also Tell The Story": Transforming First Drafts Into Creative Nonfiction

Okay, so we've got our terrible first drafts. Now the fun part. I didn't say the easy part, but fun just the same, for now we begin to help students infuse their texts with narrative. As Homer Hickman, Jr., advises, "Tell the truth but also tell a story."

Remember, though, that storytelling is just one way to bring life to nonfiction topics, and not all your students will gravitate to it. So here and throughout, we'll look at other techniques that add color, such as word choice, dialogue, and quotes.

In Chapter 1, I discussed the phrase *creative nonfiction*; it's a pair of words I want students to understand deeply; a pair of words I want students to consider before they start drafting, a pair of words we continually discuss as we refine our writing.

Joyce Hansen's advice to student writers shapes my instruction of nonfiction writing:

"The research will probably be ongoing until the piece or book is completed. Once students begin the actual writing, think like a storyteller. This is a true story you are telling; provide interesting details, establish a sense of place, use words that appeal to the sense, and where possible, include people in your nonfiction, too. My Civil

An eighth grader rereads his draft.

War book, Between Two Fires, did not come to life until I found a way to include information about the soldiers in a dramatic way through letters, memoirs, biographies, personal reminiscences, and actual images of the soldier. — Interview 2003

PUTTING STORY BEHIND THE FACTS: STRATEGIES FOR STUDENTS

Here are some techniques for helping students bring narrative flair to their writing. Remember, though, that not every student turns in pieces that incorporate stories, and that's fine.

- **Look for a story in your research materials to include.** By story I mean a true event that has narrative elements—a conversation, an experience, or an unusual relationship. You'll find examples to share with students in such books as *Forging Freedom: A True Story of Heroism During the Holocaust* by Hudson Talbott, *When Plague Strikes: The Black Death, Smallpox, AIDS* by James Cross Giblin, and *Lives of Extraordinary Women* by Kathleen Krull.

- **Find a letter, quote, or part of a newspaper article to include.** Two books that show these techniques in action are *Through My Eyes* by Ruby Bridges and *Days of Jubilee* by Patricia and Frederick McKissack.

- **Include firsthand experiences.** Excellent examples of weaving personal experiences into nonfiction are in Stephen R. Swinburne's *Bobcat, Coyote,* and *Black Bear,* where Swinburne weaves his field observations into his text.

- **Create a scenario to function as a backdrop for the information you've researched.** Show students how to create a backdrop or setting—either real or imagined—in which they can embed their research.
- **Read aloud parts of nonfiction texts.** Encourage your students to discuss the backdrops that professional writers use to breathe life and humanity into their work (see page 100).

TWO STUDENT SAMPLES

Reading aloud excerpts is highly influential. Inspired by Jean Craighead George's "moon" books, sixth-grader Laura invented a situation in her lead paragraph for her article on Tasmanian devils. She wove a fact about these creatures' behavior into an opening she said "could have happened."

> "Excuse me, I was wondering, do you have any Tasmanian devils here at the zoo?" I asked one of the zoo employees.
>
> The woman cringed and said, "What could you possibly want with those creatures?"
>
> "What do you mean?" I inquired. She did not reply, but escorted me to the zookeeper. He told me that they used to have two Tasmanian devils, but as of yesterday, they don't have any. According to him, Bob ate Zuzu, which completely mortified the tourists, so they sent Bob straight back to Tasmania.

Jaime, a sixth grader, inspired by the work of Stephen R. Swinburne, weaves her personal experiences about snowboarding into the lead of her piece:

> With both feet in my fiberglass snowboard, I waited at the top of the hill behind three boys. As I watched each boy shove off the edge and descend down the powdery snow, I imagined my first run on my new snowboard. In minutes, my dream of a great first run turned to fear as I watched two of the boys glide over a large bump and roll downhill as easily as a barrel. Could I avoid the bump and make it, I wondered, as I clenched my fists and started.

Voice: What Is It? Can It Be Taught?

Along about now, as students write first and second drafts, you'll want to explore more explicitly qualities of writing such as leads, endings, and word choice. In the next chapter you'll find craft lessons on these elements. Voice, though, I explore here, as students ought to be aware of it early in the drafting process—indeed, early in their research.

What is a writer's voice? Voice has everything to do with how a writer presents himself on paper—how we hear the writer's unique diction and way of using syntax and words as we read because the writer is present, leading us through and enticing us into the text. It's the one thing that makes the reader decide "to stop or read on, to distrust or believe the writer, to reject or accept the writer's view of the world," says Donald Murray (*Shoptalk: Learning to Write with Writers*, p.127).

When I asked Lois Lowry how she would define voice, she offered some clues. During our conversation, Lowry first explained her view of voice, then offered suggestions for developing it:

> *Writer's voice has to do with a combination of language usage, cadence, flow, rhythm, and a particular combination of these that a writer uses in a unique way. There are writers who have a more powerful and identifiable voice, like Faulkner. The degree and power varies. Voice comes from being exposed to lots of language. Young children need to gain language experiences.*
>
> — Interview, August 1994

Sixth-grader Ethan points to a section of text with strong voice.

What I take from these insights from professional writers is that voice is an essential ingredient of writing, but because it emanates uniquely from each and every writer, it's a tough thing to teach. Indeed, I do not teach formal mini-lessons on voice. The lessons don't work for me, because I find it difficult to break the concept of voice down into discrete steps. However, in the next section I'll share strategies that I've used successfully and that uphold Lowry's implicit message: expose young children to lots of language.

Nonfiction Writing From the Inside Out

SIX WAYS TO DEVELOP NONFICTION WRITING VOICES

In my experience, the best way for me to develop students' writing voices is by helping them find topics they're passionate about and by providing learning experiences that raise their awareness of voice. Here are six ways to cultivate students' writing voices.

1. **Read aloud every day at school.** Read informational picture and chapter books, magazine and newspaper articles so students can hear the powerful voices of writers. Here are two excerpts I share with students:

From *From Slave Ship to Freedom Road* by Julius Lester:

> I think often of those ancestors of mine whose names I do not know, whose names I will never know, those ancestors who saw people thrown into the sea like promises casually made and easily broken. It was primarily the youngest and strongest who survived the Middle Passage, that three-month-long ocean voyage from the western shores of Africa to the so-called New World. My ancestors might have been young when the slave ship left, but when it docked, they were haunted by memories of kinsmen tossed into the sea like promises never meant to be kept, and of gulls crying like mourners. They could still hear the wind wailing at the sight of black bodies bobbing the blue water like bottles carrying notes nobody would ever read.

From *The Alamo* by Shelley Tanaka:

> It was time for Santa Ana's officers to wake the troops. The men had been sleeping since dusk. They would need that rest. In just a few hours, they would attack the fort . . . .
>
> It was crucial that the Texans did not hear, see, or smell them. Everyone was to move in absolute silence. Not a single shot was to be fired until the trenches of the Alamo had been reached and the Mexican soldiers were right under the nose of the enemy. When the bugle sounded to launch the attack, nothing must stop them from moving as quickly as possible.
>
> The Mexican soldados gathered in their formations and moved to the narrow wooden bridges that crossed the river. The houses of San Antonio were dark and empty. Many of the townspeople had already loaded up their oxcarts with their belongings, buried their money, and hustled their families out of town. Everyone knew the battle, when it came, would be bloody and merciless.

2. **Have students read a wide range of nonfiction texts at home and at school to experience the voices of others.**

3. **Invite students to share excerpts from books they are reading.** Set aside five minutes each day for several weeks and ask students to read aloud a short passage where they hear the writer's unique voice.

4. **Encourage students to write about what matters to them and their voices will carry the content.** Then, with students' permission, share samples with the class on an overhead projector or by printing them on chart paper. Here are two student examples: From his writer's journal by Spencer, Grade 8:

> It's Spencer again. What a bad day! I've a cell phone that I use fairly often. After seeing the bill, though, I realized that I had used my phone a bit too often. $150 over! My heart sank when my mom handed me the bill. I spent lots of time making that kind of money, and it goes down the drain to the bill. AAAAH! I have never been so royally pissed off. I ran around the house 50 times because of the fury inside of me.

From an article on the great fire of London by Jill, Grade 7:

> The fire grew four times its size in just twenty-four hours. A great wind helped the fire expand. The flames were so bright from Saint Paul's Cathedral, that a school boy could read from one mile away with a candle! The sparks looked like tossed grenades.

A fourth grader discovers what he knows about parrots.

Land fire streamed down the roads as if a volcano was erupting. "Nothing but the almighty power of God could save the city." (Quote from Struggle for Power by J. R. Unstead, London: MacDonald and Company Limited.)

5. **Use fast writes once students have enough information about a topic.** Pouring out ideas quickly often helps students write with their authentic voice, because they don't have the time to adopt the more stilted language they might think we want as teachers! When students have difficulty with a fast-write, ask them to dictate their ideas to you (see Scaffolding Ideas on page 81).

> **Do Now - Fast Write**
> Joanna
>
> My best friend is the most important person in my life. Ian is like my family; I feel so comfortable around him and can tell him anything that is on my mind. He listens, gives me advice, and always assures me that everything will work out in the end. We can talk for hours and many believe its more than a friendship since some people think a girl and a guy can't be best friends unless we have a crush on each other. However, its not like that at all. Hopefully, we will be best friends for life even when we go our seperate ways to different highschools. I couldn't live w/o him!

An eighth grader's fast-write provides her with insights into friendship.

6. **Ask students to read their writing aloud to themselves and to a partner.** Training students' ears to hear their voice enables them to figure out whether the voice is flat or strong. Eighth-grader Erin observed during a conference, "When I don't let the ideas pour out and I keep stopping to think of correct English, then I lose my voice." How right Erin is. Usage can be fine-tuned during revision; bringing back voice to a stilted piece is difficult.

Scaffolding Ideas: Letting the Writing Flow

Students who struggle with writing often have difficulty letting their thoughts flow freely. Instead, the harsh censor is at work, judging every word and sentence. I find that talking about a topic can be enough to build the confidence to write. However, talking might not be enough for some students. My goal is to show them that the exuberance of their talk can be captured on paper. So, first I listen to them talk about their topic, then I invite them to tell me what they want to write, and I record their talk on paper. I'll never forget Joshua's response when he silently read his dictated piece: "Man, that's not bad. Maybe I can do this."

FIVE WAYS TO DESTROY A YOUNG WRITER'S VOICE

With the focus in classrooms today on having students write to teacher-selected prompts, young writers' voices are becoming an endangered species. The list at right, then, is meant to remind teachers that it's all too easy to undermine students' confidence with writing, and destroy their voices. Sharing a part of yourself on paper for others to observe is an act of courage for students and professionals alike. Ripping a piece apart is an act of cowardice that can damage students' confidence and self-esteem. Janette expressed this feeling when she told me: "I dread getting back papers filled with red marks and rewrites by my teacher. I feel like I never want to write another word."

1. **Mark up papers correcting writing convention errors.** When teachers place commas, repair run-ons, mark paragraphs, and so on, they take the learning away from students. Eighth-grader Jason told me this literacy story in a conference at the start of the year. "I received a paper last year that felt like it had more red marks than my writing. I hated looking at my paper. I didn't care. I copied it over and turned it in. It wasn't my work anymore."

2. **Rewrite large sections of the piece.** Sometimes when I sit side by side with a student and show her how to use an introductory phrase to vary sentence openings, I jot down a sample rewrite on a sticky note. This way the student has a concrete model to refer to while revising. Rewriting entire paragraphs, on the other hand, and turning back your rewrites to students can deeply wound their fragile self-esteem. A solution is for students to return to "safe writing," as one sixth grader called it, leading them to focus on correct sentence structure more than the ideas they want to convey. In this situation, many students avoid experimenting with complex sentences, fearing they'll be marked down for incorrect punctuation. Instead, they play it safe and write short, simple, choppy sentences that destroy their voices and the fluency of their texts.

3. **Demand the first draft be a perfect piece.** I'm stunned when I hear of teachers asking students to complete a final draft of a short story or a personal essay over a weekend. Just thinking about such an assignment makes students so tense that the writing becomes an odious school task to be done as fast as possible. These assignments ignore the joys and benefits of revising.

    In my classroom, I note on the chalkboard, "Writing is Revision." Students understand that they will always have time to improve their first drafts. Robert Cormier expressed it this way: "The beautiful part of writing is that you don't have to get it right the first time, unlike, say, a brain surgeon. You can always do it better, find the exact word, the apt phrase, the leaping simile."

4. **Take large amounts of points off for incorrect use of writing conventions.** I recall my daughter complaining about a high-school teacher who took ten points off for each missing or incorrectly placed comma. Everyone earned D's and F's. The purpose? According to the teacher, to prepare students for the real world.

5. **Always choose the writing genre and topics.** "Writing is for school," a fifth grader wrote when I invited students to tell me why they write. She explained her statement: "I know it's for school because all we ever write about is what teachers tell us." If we offer students choice, they become motivated to write for themselves.

CONTINUE TO THINK ABOUT

Besides helping students find topics they care about, it's also important to encourage them to do "octopus" research. The glue that binds lessons on finding topics, generating lists of ideas, researching, planning, and drafting is the modeling you offer students by thinking aloud and writing to explain your process. But all of these predrafting experiences require time.

So make time a writing ally, for, like professional writers, our students need the time to drench themselves in a topic before drafting. As much as possible, have students research, take notes, plan, and draft during class. With you and peers available for encouragement and support, students will come to understand that prewriting is like playing soccer. Just as soccer players move back and forth over the field hoping to score a goal, writers move back and forth trying to find topics, brainstorm ideas, research, select details, and plan. For the soccer player the goal is scoring points. For the writer, the goal is pouring out a first draft.

Remember, too, that first drafts are meant to be imperfect. At this point in the process, content and passion are more important than missing commas and run-on sentences. Scholastic Book Editor Dianne Hess reinforces this point. Mull over her words and integrate their message into your teaching practices:

> I would never reject a fine story that had mechanical errors. I feel that every writer (and child) should try to do his or her best proofreading, but no one is perfect. I'd rather get a manuscript that says something of substance than a perfect one that has nothing to say. Punishing children for mechanical errors can turn them off writing.

CHAPTER FOUR

WINNING OVER THE READER WITH WORDS

Lessons and Strategies for Crafting Leads and Endings, and for Writing With Simplicity

In Their Own Words

What does a lead do for a piece?

Russell Freedman

Nothing is more important than a powerful opening. It is the lead that determines whether a prospective reader will actually go ahead and read a piece. A good lead may raise a question that the reader wants answered. It may focus on some strange or intriguing aspect of the subject. It may emphasize the unexpected, challenge the reader's preconceived notions. There's no hard and fast rule. Often, you don't discover your lead until after you've completed a draft or two of the entire piece. In any case, it pays to lavish plenty of time and attention on those crucial opening words, sentences, or paragraphs.

Homer Hickam, Jr.

My years as a freelance writer for a variety of magazines taught me the importance of hooking the reader very early in the manuscript. Editors will toss a manuscript on the return pile if that first paragraph doesn't grab them, so I learned quickly to gain their attention.

Stephen R. Swinburne

In the first sentence you want to win over the reader. You have to keep the reader reading.

David Quammen

My advice to young authors is that good writing requires careful, careful attention and determined writing. One of the hardest parts is to craft a graceful, lucid, enticing lead paragraph that reads as though it has fallen fluidly from the writer's fingertips.

What do you think are the elements of a terrific lead?

Jean Craighead George

Drama is the essence of a powerful opener.

Joyce Hansen

I think of a terrific lead as details—who, what, why, when, where—that make you want to read on and not put the essay, book, or article down.

Hudson Talbott

Catch readers off guard with something unexpected, so they'll want to read further in order to find out what you meant.

James Cross Giblin

In my leads and chapter openings, I try to grab the reader's attention and make him or her want to keep on reading. I have a similar goal when I write a chapter ending: I usually raise a dramatic question that can only be answered by going on to the next chapter.

Patricia McKissack

Tell the reader what and who the story is about right away. Put in action—that brings the reader right in. If by the second or third paragraph the reader is not hooked, you're not likely to hook them. We adults sometimes read a book with a poor opening and discover it was really good; young readers are not like that.

Sometimes my endings turn out to be my beginnings. I might take the last chapter of a book and make it the first chapter. When the shoe fits, you know

it. That's the way your lead is. Play with it and play with it and don't be afraid of tearing it apart and starting it over.

Michael O. Tunnell

A terrific lead should make the reader sit up and take notice. Sometimes it may mean asking a question of your reader. Or presenting some mind-bending bit of information. Or using a humorous anecdote. It may be the beautiful, stylish use of language that evokes a pleasant or startling image. Look at how Russell Freedman begins his biography of Abraham Lincoln: "Abraham Lincoln wasn't the sort of man who could lose himself in a crowd. After all, he stood six feet four inches tall, and to top it off, he wore a high silk hat" (*Lincoln: A Photobiography*, page 1). Hundreds, even thousands, have written about Lincoln. But Freedman found a fresh, new way to introduce the Great Emancipator.

INCLUDING AUTHORS' INSIGHTS IN INSTRUCTION

HOOK THE READER. All the authors I spoke with know that truth cold, perhaps having learned it the hard way, with rejection slips or frank comments from editors. They know that all the hard work of researching, planning, and shaping their rough drafts will go out the window if they don't invest time crafting compelling openings. They are aware that their audience—children—may be the toughest critics of all. As sixth grader David says, "If I don't like the opening sentences, I put the book back—even if I liked another book by that author."

In this chapter we continue to examine drafting, the process of transforming what's in our heads and our notebooks into polished prose readers can't put down. We'll first look at leads—how they help students determine where to go from there and how developing a compelling lead sets the bar high, making every sentence that follows live up to the lead's power. I'll then take you through several craft lessons on techniques that help writers bring color and cadence to their ideas, including using the "show, don't tell" maxim and the use of sensory images, strong verbs, and specific nouns. We'll then end the chapter by looking at strategies for crafting endings that are every bit as powerful as the opening lines.

I'm not worried about whether I use the right word.
I worry about whether I use the best word.

—Patricia McKissack

I am going to tell you about snakes.

You will learn about Columbus in this paragraph.

In my report I will compare and contrast plant and animal cells.

These leads are typical of students in grades four and up, even though they sound like the work of primary-grade writers. Why does this stilted writing persist? Because in school they have learned that the lead's function is to establish the topic. Our job, then, is to have students understand that above all, the lead must compel the reader to continue reading. They also need to understand that the lead must do "real work," as William Zinsser states in his book *On Writing Well* (p. 56): "It must provide hard details that tell the reader why the piece was written and why he ought to read it. But don't dwell on the reason. Coax the reader a little more; keep him inquisitive."

The best way of guiding students to appreciate a lead's function is to have them analyze opening sentences and paragraphs in books, magazines, and even newspapers. Once they identify the elements of successful leads, they can then practice applying the techniques to their own nonfiction pieces.

READING LIKE A WRITER

Cindy Potter, my teaching partner, rolls into the classroom the two-tiered cart, once again brimming with nonfiction picture books and chapter books. Our sixth-graders look at us dubiously. "We're going to learn about leads," Cindy announces after we organize students into pairs and ask each duo to select a book from the cart.

"Read just the opening of the book. Leads can be as short as one or two sentences and as long as a paragraph. Then use the questions on the chart to discuss the lead," Cindy tells students (for questions, see page 116). They spend five to seven minutes reading and discussing. She then asks pairs of students to take turns explaining to the class why they thought the lead was terrific or boring. Students state the title of the book and read aloud the lead.

After each presentation, classmates evaluate the lead, explaining why it did or did not catch their attention. According to sixth graders, great leads make you read on because they:

- raise questions that make you wonder;
- contain an anecdote that fascinates;
- create a mood that appeals to you;
- open with information that's new to you;
- introduce an unusual setting;
- have action that intrigues.

If time is an issue because you have only a 45-minute period, then schedule two or three paired presentations each day and limit classmates' queries and comments to one or two. A 90-minute block offers greater flexibility; you can reserve 45 minutes to hear seven or eight paired presentations each day.

The paired analyses that follow come from notes I took during sixth and eighth graders' presentations. I've included the title, author, lead, and a summary of each presentation.

Book: *Lives of the Athletes: Thrills, Spills, (and What the Neighbors Thought)* by Kathleen Krull

Lead: James Frances Thorpe's tribal name was Wa-tho-huck, which means "Bright Path." "I cannot decide," he once said, "whether I was well named or not. Many a time the path has gleamed bright for me, but just as often it has been dark and bitter indeed" (page 11).

Summary of Eighth-Grade Partners' Comments:

- The quote from Thorpe made us want to know the bad and good in his life and how he felt about these.
- The quote set you up for learning about both parts of his [Thorpe's] life.

Book: *From Slave Ship to Freedom Road* by Julius Lester, paintings by Rod Brown.

Lead: They took the sick and the dead and dropped them into the sea like empty wine barrels. But wine barrels did not have beating hearts, crying eyes, and screaming mouths (page 1 of unpaged picture book).

Summary of Eighth Grade Partners' Comments:

- We got choked up.

- We wanted to read on right away. We learned what the slave traders did—they had no feelings.
- In two sentences Lester grabbed our hearts.

Book: *Women of Hope: African Americans Who Made a Difference* by Joyce Hansen
Lead: Alice Walker is the youngest of eight children in a Georgia sharecropper family. When she was eight years old, one of her brothers accidentally shot her in the eye with a BB gun. She lost sight in that eye and, with her confidence shaken, she withdrew into herself (page 25).
Summary of Sixth-Grade Partners' Comments:
- She [Hansen] picked a gross story that made us wonder if she ever got over this.
- We learned this was about Alice Walker. We wanted to know more about her and why a short bio was written about her.
- We wondered how her brother felt and what happened to him.

Throughout the year, students pore over leads in nonfiction and fiction. It's a lesson worthy of repetition because it heightens students' awareness of the lead's importance while exposing them to a range of techniques for opening a piece, such as:

- a question
- a fascinating fact
- a brief story or anecdote
- a quote
- an action
- a brief dialogue
- a memorable image

A DEMONSTRATION LESSON ON LEADS

After a week or so of having students study leads written by professional writers, weave in lessons in which you model writing leads yourself, and then have students try their hand at it. When I teach, my end goal is to have students routinely write two to four alternate leads after they have completed a first draft of an essay, article, book review, interview, or other genre.

Here's how I begin the modeling:

I put on an overhead transparency a draft of a piece I've written. Here's the lead I share: *A brown bear for a berry-picking companion was not what I expected.* I compose three alternate leads, thinking aloud so that students can hear my thought process: *(1) The brown bear loping towards me was not the company I had hoped for while picking blueberries. (2) The handful of ripe blueberries never made it to my mouth when I noticed the brown bear charging toward me. (3) I closed my eyes, then opened them to check whether the brown bear loping toward me was a mirage.*

Next I point to my chart paper, on which I've written questions based on the nuggets of advice authors shared on pages 110–111. I invite students to use them to evaluate my lead.

Questions That Help Students Analyze Leads

Did you learn what the piece is about?

What did the author do that grabbed you?

What made the lead boring?

What did the lead make you wonder?

What details does the lead include?

How could this lead be improved?

Which lead would you choose? Explain why.

Next, I tell students to refer to these questions as they compose and mull over their own leads, on their own and with peers. I keep the questions on display, and give each student a copy of them to put in their class writing folder. You will also use questions such as these with the following variations on the demonstration lesson:

- Share writing and alternate leads by former students and invite the class to discuss these.
- Ask students in your class if you can read some of their alternate leads to everyone. Students can also read aloud and discuss their leads with a partner or small group of three or four.

A fifth grader works on leads.

Mini-Lessons on Leads

As with features and structures and virtually every aspect of composition, professional writers craft their leads intuitively. In other words, it's not as though they glance at a menu of types of leads and give one a trial run. Instead, to paraphrase Patricia McKissack, they play with the lead and play with it until the shoe fits.

Elementary and middle-school students, however, need a certain amount of deliberate practice with various kinds of leads. Once you see that students understand them, and can use them in their writing, the need for practice sessions fades away.

Each of the seven mini-lessons that follow shows you how to give students this practice. The basic structure of the lessons is:

- teacher brainstorms possible leads;
- teacher thinks aloud her process;
- teacher invites students to collaborate on writing a
  lead; and
- students evaluate their collaborative leads using the questions on page 116.

If the class or a group of students requires additional practice, invite partners to collaborate writing leads. *As soon as possible, move students from practice to their own writing.*

MANAGEMENT NOTE

When the class collaborates on writing a lead, students often will offer many topics for the lead, and then endlessly debate over which topic to work with—unless you step in. I give them two minutes to decide; if the class cannot reach consensus in two minutes, then I select one. However, I always add all the topics they've pitched to the class chart, as students like to refer to them when they're searching for writing topics later.

MINI-LESSON

Pose a Question

Purpose

To pose an irresistible question in the lead that readers want to have answered

First Day

I jump right in to brainstorming.

Robb's Modeling

I write my topic on large chart paper. Then I brainstorm two to three ideas and use these to pose a question. Here's what I write while fifth graders observe:

Topic: Picking Blueberries

Brainstorm: metal pot half filled with ripe berries; bear walks toward me.

Lead: What would you do if a brown bear loped toward you as you picked blue-berries and dropped them into a metal pot?

Robb's Think-Aloud: *I thought the bear was the key to hooking readers because this is an unexpected event. I used loped because it showed what the bear's walking looked like to me. The question set me up for writing what I did and getting the reader to consider what he would have done in my shoes.*

Second Day: Students Collaborate

I invite students to suggest topics and then choose one.

Fifth-Graders' Topic: Harry's run-in with leeches

Brainstorm: Field trip to get pond plant samples; Harry collected leeches. He put them on his tongue and showed the teacher.

Lead: What happened to Harry when he plastered his tongue with leeches he caught at Blandy Pond, then showed his black tongue to Mrs. Robb?

Students' Observations: We liked this because it made you wonder what happened to Harry. It gave details of where we were and what Harry did. The only thing it didn't have was what everyone else did. We could add that soon after the question.

MINI-LESSON

Lead With a Fascinating Fact

Purpose

To model how to stimulate readers' interest with an unusual fact

First Day

Robb's Modeling

Topic: The Hunting Habits of Crocodiles

Brainstorm: Egyptian plover walks into croc's mouth and picks food between its teeth without being harmed; huge jaw muscles snap tight to clutch prey, muscles that open jaws are weaker; can stay submerged for more than an hour.

Lead: A crocodile's razor-sharp teeth and powerful jaws can clamp down on an unsuspecting duck in a few seconds. Yet, when that same crocodile wants its teeth cleaned, it lets a tiny bird, called an Egyptian plover, walk into its mouth, pick food morsels between its teeth, and never once clamps down with its huge jaws!

Robb's Think-Aloud: *I picked this fact because crocodiles are known for their powerful jaws, which they use to catch and eat small and large animals. I thought the image was strong and the fact so interesting that you'd want to learn more about them as hunters.*

Second Day: Students Collaborate

Seventh Graders' Topic: Anaconda's Eating Habits

Brainstorm: Anacondas kill prey by squeezing—can swallow a small deer or pig whole and not eat again for several months; don't chase prey—wait in the water for deer or sheep to come to drink.

Lead: The moment the fawn dipped her mouth into the pond to lap water, a fifteen-foot anaconda seized the fawn's neck, coiled itself around its small body, and began to squeeze.

Students' Observations: We liked starting with a gross fact—something different from the way people eat. There's a lot of information in the lead—the size of the anaconda and how it kills the deer. We wanted to make readers wonder what the snake would do next. That helps us because we know what to write next.

MINI-LESSON

Lead With an Enticing Anecdote

Purpose

To show how to use an anecdote—a brief story—to introduce the content and set the tone of a piece

First Day

Robb's Modeling

Topic: First Haircut

Brainstorm: 14 years old; cut one pigtail under my ear; lost nerve to cut the other; parents prized my long hair.

Lead: I could hear Dad's voice saying, "Be proud of your long hair." But my fourteen-year-old mind hated the pigtails that reached beyond my waist. I raised my mom's sewing sheers and cut one pigtail just beneath my ear.

Robb's Think-Aloud: *I tried to show the contrast between my dad's feelings about my hair and my own. I also tried to make the reader wonder how I resolved this situation—that's what my memoir will be about.*

Second Day: Students Collaborate

Fourth Graders' Topic: Sharks Near the Shore

Brainstorm: Sharks spotted near the shore; my dad in the water; can't hear lifeguards' warning shouts.

Lead: "Sharks!" shouted the lifeguard. "Everyone out of the water!" Men and women headed for the shore, but my dad continued to swim.

Students' Observations: We wanted to make you [the reader] scared. You think, why did everyone leave but not the dad. That's what the story will be about. The lead kind of makes you know what you will write about. There were details—the ocean, sharks, lifeguards, and the dad.

MINI-LESSON

Lead With a Quote

Purpose

To demonstrate how a quote can introduce a topic and arouse readers' curiosity

First Day

Robb's Modeling

Topic: Lies and Friends

Brainstorm: tried to get in with the popular group who couldn't stand Bella by saying that she was the one who told the teacher on Janie—Janie cheated on a big test and someone told on her

Nonfiction Writing From the Inside Out

Lead: You'll regret that telephone call," my brother said. "Telling a lie about Bella will turn against you."

Robb's Think-Aloud: *I like starting an essay with a quote because it quickly sets up the points that I am trying to make. But, the quote doesn't give my position away—you don't know if I get in trouble and learn a lesson or if I get Bella in trouble and get the group to like me.*

Second Day: Students Collaborate

Eighth Graders' Topic: School Dress Code

Brainstorm: too limiting; shorts too long for some, short for others; don't like colors; want to express our individuality.

Lead: Yesterday, while studying in the library, I heard Mrs. Rockwood tell the librarian, "I'm tired of monitoring whether students are abiding by the dress code."

Students' Observations: We thought that an essay on this subject would be more effective if we could use something a teacher said to support our ideas. We could use arguments about why teachers are tired of this to support where we stand. The quote also lets you know what the topic of the essay will be.

Mini-Lesson

Lead With an Action

Purpose

To show how action can add excitement to the lead and draw the reader into the piece

First Day

Robb's Modeling

Topic: To Fly

Brainstorm: blue flying cape; tricycle for a start; tries to fly by jumping over the handlebars of a moving bike

Lead: Blue cape flying behind her like a sail that caught the wind, my friend Elaine pedaled her tricycle furiously, built up speed, and leaped over the handlebars.

Robb's Think-Aloud: *My friend Elaine and I wanted to fly in the worst way. We agreed to wear our capes, ride our tricycles, then jump in the air and fly. I chickened out and watched Elaine try—and fall quickly to the ground. I wanted Elaine's actions to make you wonder what*

happened after she leaped. I purposely didn't bring myself into the lead because I wanted to present Elaine's daring to make her dream real.

Second Day: Students Collaborate

Eighth Graders' Topic: Handling a Black Snake

Brainstorm: Mr. Legge warns students about never picking up a snake unless he's there; Bobby and Jim sneak in the empty lab at lunch and pick up black snake; snake hisses and bites Bobby.

Lead: Jim lifts the tank's lid and Bobby grabs the black snake behind its head, pulls it out, and screams.

Students' Observations: We like the way you didn't really know what happened. The screams could be from getting caught by a teacher or getting hurt. We want to let the reader wonder about it. There are lots of details—teacher leaving, the two boys, what they did.

Mini-Lesson

Lead With a Brief Dialogue

Purpose

To show how a person's inner thoughts or a brief exchange between two people can hook a reader

First Day

Robb's Modeling

Topic: Letting a pet die

Brainstorm: cat Leonora is thin; won't eat or drink; won't open eyes; time to put her to sleep—19 great years

Lead: "Is she purring?" Dad asked as he bent down to look at the cat.

   "No," said Anina. "She won't open her eyes. She always opens her eyes and looks at me—but not this morning." Her voice choked with sobs.

Robb's Think-Aloud: *I wanted this dialogue to set a gloomy tone. Having a sense of hope at first, then having the hope disappear helps create that tone. It's also more real, because my young daughter would have hope. The question the dialogue sets up is what will happen to this cat and family? Dialogue is an effective way to introduce characters, give some background,* *and set the situation. Dialogue is a good way to start a personal essay or memoir or even a magazine article.*

Second Day: Students Collaborate

Sixth Graders' Topic: Team Player

Brainstorm: Wally wants to be a forward on the soccer line; he wants to make goals. He always leaves his position and leaves a space wide open.

Lead: "Play your position," Greg hissed.

Wally hated playing halfback.

"Pass the ball!" hollered Greg. "Get back into position!"

"This goal is mine!" said Wally, wanting to make a goal and get cheers.

Students' Observations: We think the dialogue uses Wally's thoughts to show where he is and why he's made his decision to leave his position. It will help this essay, which is on the importance of being a team player, because we can use what Wally does to explain our points. You don't know if Wally makes the goal or not—that makes it suspenseful.

Stephen R. Swinburne's Examples of Leads

Share these tips and examples of leads from Stephen R. Swinburne's books with students. They provide good models of leads that grab the reader and announce the content:

Begin With a Question: Do you know that emperor penguins lay eggs when it's 80 degrees below zero?

Begin With a Dialogue: "I feel like a large caterpillar this morning," said George as he tumbled out of bed.

Begin With an Interesting Fact: Sloths don't poop in a tree.

Begin With an Unusual Image: The wind blew so hard it lifted the butterfly high above the waves.

Begin With Action: The pack of wolves woke, stretched and set off at a trot to hunt.

Begin in the First Person: On a frosty winter afternoon in Vermont, I find a set of tracks at the base of a rugged wall of rock.

Lead With a Memorable Image

Purpose

To show how painting a colorful, memorable image for readers can captivate them

First Day

Robb's Modeling

Topic: Trout Fishing

Brainstorm: mountain stream, fly rod, fishing for trout, silvery scales, leaps looking like a silver rainbow.

Lead: Hooked to my fly rod, the trout leapt out of the stream, a silver rainbow arched above the water, then plunged into the deep pool.

Robb's Think-Aloud: *Strong verb—arched—gives the shape of the trout as it hung for a moment over the water. Plunged is a contrast to arched because of its speed and energy. The metaphor of the trout as a rainbow helps build the image I observed. Strong verbs and figurative language can create powerful images.*

Second Day: Students Collaborate

Eighth Graders' Topic: Balloon Landing

Brainstorm: the sun is setting; strong winds; mustard plants make field yellow; balloon tries to land.

Lead: As dusk crept over the meadow, the wind buffeted the red balloon trying to descend and land on the field carpeted with yellow mustard.

Students' Observations: We thought dusk—one word—was better than the sun setting. Crept—personification—made dusk feel slow and stealthy. It gave color and time. The verb buffeted showed how the wind controlled the balloon—not the balloonist. It also gives a good image. The verb carpet was a contrast to the wind—it creates a soft feeling. We tried to use strong verbs and one figure of speech—too many won't work.

A fifth grader concentrates on revising leads.

Writer's Craft Mini-Lessons

This next set of mini-lessons addresses techniques that help students enliven their prose, such as showing instead of telling and using sensory images, strong verbs, and specific nouns. I want to emphasize that there is no perfect sequence for these lessons or any of the lessons in this book. For example, you could introduce some or all of these craft lessons before any of the lessons on leads. Take your cues from your students.

I like to present each of these craft lessons several times throughout the year—sometimes to the entire class, other times only to a small group. I've found that presenting them just once doesn't give students enough exposure to the technique to enable them to transfer it to their own writing. I present the lesson over a few days, as each is multiphased. I devote about 10 minutes a day, never more than 15 minutes.

Here's how each lesson works:

1. Students observe how their teacher analyzes an excerpt from a book or article. In a think-aloud, the teacher points out specific words, phrases, and figurative language that will deepen students' understanding.

2. Using the think-pair-share technique, pairs of students analyze a new excerpt the teacher put on the overhead projector.

3. Pairs of students look for a specific writing technique from their independent reading and share it with classmates.

Think-Pair-Share

Here are the think-pair-share steps students can follow:

1. Ask partners to each think about a sample piece of writing.

2. Have pairs take turns sharing ideas by discussing specific nouns, unusual verbs, and figures of speech. Discussions should pinpoint how the writer's word choice and combination of words exemplify the technique addressed in the craft lesson.

3. Invite pairs to share with the class what they have learned. During sharing, encourage partners to bring to the entire class insights that have not been presented by other pairs.

Writer's Craft Mini-Lesson

Show, Don't Tell

Purpose

To change "telling" sentences that are general and tell the reader what to think and feel into "showing" sentences filled with details that make the reader draw conclusions.

Materials

Students' independent-reading books; practice sentences (see sidebar for examples); 3 x 5 index cards

Example 1: From *Days of the Dead* by Kathryn Lasky, page 15.

They [the butterflies] have flown thousands of miles, some from as far as Canada. The rivulets of butterflies streaming in from the northeast will become thicker and thicker until they are like sparkling streams in the skies. The monarchs embroider the air with their orange-and-black finery as they glide on gossamer-thin wings to their roosting places in the trees. There they cluster on branches in immense bunches looking like tissue-paper shingles.

Example 2 for Think-Pair-Share: From *Rachel's Journal: The Story of a Pioneer Girl* by Marissa Moss, unpaged journal.

A different kind of storm passed us today—a herd of buffalo. It was as if the river had leapt out of its banks and taken solid form to chase us down. A thick cloud of dust surged toward us, then there was a tremendous noise, an earthly thunder. We could see their shaggy backs rising and falling like a great wave.

Guidelines

First Day: Study Literary Examples

1. Read aloud example 1, or another passage you've chosen and analyze it by thinking aloud.
   Robb's Think-Aloud:
   Instead of just saying that there were millions of butterflies, Lasky uses striking language to show us the

large numbers. "Rivulets, streaming in, sparkling streams in the sky" show readers how dense the air was with these. Lasky moves from water images that show the numbers of butterflies to the verb embroider, *which features the monarchs' colors and a simile—"like tissue paper shingles"—which shows how thin their wings are. It takes more words to show, but it's more effective than just telling.*

2. Organize students into pairs.

3. Have pairs take a few minutes to analyze the second passage and share their think alouds with the entire class.

4. Ask students to discuss why showing is more effective than telling. Here are the highlights of what eighth graders noted about the excerpt from *Rachel's Journal:*

- Moss compares the dust storm to a herd of buffalo charging and a river flowing out of its banks.

- She uses comparisons to show the huge amount of dust and how it was everywhere like the river. We could hear the dust across the plains because we could imagine buffalo charging.

- Showing made us get involved with the diary entry. It also helped us picture the power, the large numbers, the fur, and the sounds of stampeding buffalo.

Second Day: Students Study Their Independent Reading

1. Organize students into pairs.

2. Have pairs find a showing passage in their independent-reading book and discuss these.

3. Invite each pair to join a second pair and share what they have learned.

Third Day: Collaborative and Partner Practice

1. Write a telling sentence on a large sheet of chart paper. For my eighth graders, I write, "The waves are scary."

2. Invite students to generate some showing ideas with their partner and collect three or four ideas on the chart. Here's what eighth graders offered:

- walls of water

MOVING BEYOND
PRACTICE

After students show you they understand a writing technique, have them rewrite parts of a piece from their writing folder. Continually remind them to use specific techniques as they draft.

You can add a writing technique in your content criteria (for more about content criteria, see pages 259–261). For example, content criteria for a memoir can include: develop one key event from the past; show, don't tell; use specific nouns and strong verbs.

- waves reflect the dark gray storm clouds
- pound onto shore scattering birds and children

3. Ask students to compose one or two sentences using the brainstormed ideas. Here's what eighth graders wrote:
   - Like ten foot walls of water, the waves turned the color of the dark gray storm clouds.
   - One after the other, the waves pounded the shore, scattering birds and children to high ground.

4. Write a different "telling" sentence on the chalkboard.

5. Give each pair an index card and ask both partners to write their names at the top.

6. Ask pairs to brainstorm a few "showing" ideas on the index card, then compose an example in one to three sentences.

7. Have students discuss why taking the time to brainstorm is helpful.

8. Invite pairs to share and discuss their writing. There will be a variety of ways to transform the same telling sentence into a showing sentence.

9. Continue partner practice until students understand the technique. This practice may spill onto another day.

WRITER'S CRAFT MINI-LESSON
Sensory Images Stir Memories

Purpose

To show students how details in writing that appeal to the five senses—hearing, sight, touch, taste, smell—deepen a reader's involvement because they trigger personal memories and associated or connotative meanings.

Materials

Students' independent-reading books; practice words and phrases (see sidebar, next page)

Example 1: From *Forging Freedom: A True Story of Heroism During the Holocaust* by Hudson Talbott, page 35.

The blue-gray dusk of the wintry afternoon had already settled over the medieval town when they stepped off the train. Nightfall in Maastricht, like all of Europe, was unbroken by a single light that could attract the Allied bombers . . . .

Shortly after midnight a whistle pierced the stillness. With the screech of brakes the stations suddenly filled with German clatter. Jaap and Kreen quickly adopted the frantic mood, and pushed their way up the steps of the train. The car they entered was packed with a full array of the German military.

Robb's Think-Aloud:

Words that appeal to my senses involve me with the ideas and put me in the train station. **Wintry** *causes me to shiver and feel and taste the cold;* **blue-gray** *lets me see that the sun has set and night is coming. With* **whistle** *and* **pierced** *I hear the shrill sound combined with the shriek of train brakes, and I feel and picture the motion of Jaap and Kreen as they act* **frantic** *to blend in with the movements and sounds of German soldiers. The associations I make through my senses deeply connect me to the passage, and I use my senses to create more detailed, rich pictures.*

Example 2 for Think-Pair-Share: From *Winter Moon* by Jean Craighead George, page 81.

Around noon warm winds from the South blew into Tennessee, and the thaw began. The warmth remained for three days. A boulder near the bear snapped as the ice in its cracks let go. The snow began to melt and gurgle into the soil.

Guidelines

First and Second Days: Repeat steps for the mini-lesson Show, Don't Tell on pages 126 and 127.

Third Day:

1. Organize students into pairs.
2. Have partners brainstorm a short list of sensory images relating to a simple word or phrase (you can use the examples in the sidebar or think up your own), and then write vivid sensory sentences.

TEN MOMENTS FOR STUDENTS TO EMBELLISH WITH SENSORY IMAGES

- falling asleep
- feeding ducks
- snowboarding down a steep hill
- constructing a model boat, car, or airplane
- swimming
- entering your bedroom
- bathing your pet
- hearing your parent's or a friend's voice
- feeling happy
- feeling angry

3. Call for volunteers to write their sentences on the chalkboard. Here's what a pair of sixth graders wrote for "ice storm":

   Frozen water pinged onto cars, roofs, and roads, and silently enclosed tree branches and electric wires in layers of ice.

4. Ask students to discuss their sensory reactions. Here are some comments from sixth-graders:

   - *"Ping made me hear the ice hitting hard things. Enclosed helped me see ice wrapped around trees' branches."*
   - *"I could feel the chill and the danger with the word layers."*
   - *"It made me know that falling ice can make noise and come silently."*

5. Explain to students that sensory images help writers show and not tell.

6. Continue practicing, then instruct students to use sensory images when they brainstorm before drafting a piece of writing.

Bruce Brooks on Sensory Memory

I have a great memory of smells and vision from when I was small. I have wholeness of memory, not just sounds, but smell, sight, place. Hanging onto wholeness is important, and I have tried to remember one aspect of a conflict or a tender moment—the room, time of day, the feeling. I try to remember the entirety. Where I was, a piece of clothing, or crispness of air—all can allow me to place and recall an experience.

— Interview August, 1994

WRITER'S CRAFT MINI-LESSON

Strong Verbs Paint Images

Purpose

To replace weak, cliched verbs and adverbs with verbs that paint images.

Materials

Chart paper; scrap paper for students; students' writing

Example 1: From *Days of Jubilee: The End of Slavery in the United States* by Patricia C & Frederick L. McKissack, page 54.

Seven bells tolled the hour. The winter storm that pummeled the city with several inches of snow had passed. The weather had not dampened the enthusiasm of the crowd that had gathered at Boston's Tremont Baptist Church. The packed snow crunched under the feet of people rushing toward the church.

Robb's Think-Aloud:

Strong verbs paint pictures, appeal to the senses, and have specific connotations or associations. For example, **tolled** *conjures a mournful sound and* **pummeled** *makes me see snow continually bombarding the ground—like punches a boxer gives his opponent.* **Crunched** *helps me hear feet connecting with deep, powdery snow, making a crackling sound. Strong verbs also call attention to the meanings of other words in the sentences. Strong verbs eliminate the need for adverbs to help do the job.*

Strong verbs also help me understand facts and major historical events. This passage shows how even a snowstorm couldn't stop people from gathering at the church to hear whether Lincoln had freed the slaves.

Example 2 for Think-Pair-Share: From *Coyote: North America's Dog* by Stephen R. Swinburne, pages 19–20.

The coyote freezes in its tracks, every sense focused on one spot. It springs three feet in the air, eyes still glued to the invisible target below. It pounces on the spot and lands forefeet first, pinning its prey. The coyote's head disappears and then lifts with a snout full of snow and a mouth full of mouse.

Guidelines

First Day

1. Read aloud from the transparency the first example, or another passage you've chosen, and analyze it by thinking aloud. Include the strong verbs in your think-aloud, explaining how each one creates a powerful image. Point out the lack of adverbs or the need for them when the verbs are strong.

2. Organize students in pairs. Have partners discuss the second example by pinpointing the strong verbs and explaining how these triggered images in their minds.

3. Have pairs share with the class. Make sure students express how the verbs enable them

to recall key facts such as that the coyote *freezes* in its tracks before attacking and that it lands forefeet first to pin its prey.

4. Invite students to find and share strong verbs from their independent-reading books.

Second Day

1. Divide a large sheet of chart paper into three columns. Write these three weak verbs at the top of each column: *go, cook, make.*

2. Ask pairs or groups of four or five students to take a few minutes to brainstorm a list of strong verbs that could refine these weak ones and to jot them down on paper.

3. Encourage students to add their strong verbs to the chart, under the corresponding weak one. You may wish to get the ball rolling by writing three strong verbs on the chart. For example, I would print *stomp* under *go; grill* under *cook;* and *force* under *make.*

   Here's part of the list fourth graders created:

go	cook	make
trudge	boil	insist
race	poach	compel
run	broil	register
zip	fry	strong-arm
pedal	stir	pressure

4. Move students to their own writing. I circle three to five weak verbs on a piece composed by students in grades four to six. I ask seventh and eighth graders to circle verbs on their own, offering support to those who have difficulty.

5. Have students brainstorm, in the margin near the circled verb or on a sticky note, three to four alternate verbs. Encourage students to help one another as you circulate and continue to offer support.

6. Ask students to read their sentences aloud several times, substituting a different verb with each rereading. Then have students circle the verb they feel is the strongest.

7. Invite students to test the need for adverbs that surround the verbs they have replaced and remove those that now seem unnecessary.

> ## DISCUSSION POINT
>
> Discuss with students how strong verbs and specific details form a realistic backdrop that helps them visualize and recall key facts. When you or students think aloud, always include what you are learning and how vivid writing supports recall and understanding.

Nonfiction Writing From the Inside Out

8. Continue inviting students to use this strategy, emphasizing that it's one they will want to permanently integrate into their revision process.

WRITER'S CRAFT MINI-LESSON

Specific Nouns Create Clear Details

Purpose

To improve writing by avoiding adjectives and changing general nouns to specific nouns, so as to sharpen the images you are creating

Materials

Chart paper; scrap paper; students' writing

Example 1: From *Duke Ellington* by Andrea Davis Pinkney, unpaged picture book.

But with practice, all Duke's fingers rode the piano keys. Duke started to play his own made-up melodies. Whole notes, chords, sharps, and flats. Left-handed hops and right-handed slides.

Believe it, man. Duke taught himself to press on the pearlies like nobody else could. His one-and-two-umpy-dump became a thing of the past. Now, playing the piano was Duke's all time love.

Robb's Think-Aloud:

When nouns are specific, I can better picture what the author is trying to show me. I can hear the Duke's original melodies with nouns such as chords, sharps, flats, hops *and* slides. *The words, "one-and-two-umpy-dump" help me hear how ordinary his music was until he began to make up his own melodies. Unusual nouns such as* pearlies *for the white piano keys help me feel the music's rhythms as well as Duke's love for the piano and all the things he did with it to be original.*

Example 2 for Think-Pair-Share: From *Lives of the Writers: Comedies, Tragedies (and What the Neighbors Thought)* by Kathleen Krull, page 73.

He [Jack London] had a personal valet, who every evening arranged London's pencils and papers on his desk. London worked at night, sleeping on and off for five hours. In the afternoons he joined guests at the ranch for sports, practical jokes, and challenges—a guest might have to swallow a live goldfish or push peanuts up his nose. After dinner (London liked to eat raw meat—a "cannibal sandwich" of raw beef, perhaps, and as many as two barely cooked wild ducks a day), he played cards or read aloud until it was time to go back to his room to work.

Guidelines

First Day

1. Read aloud from the transparency the first example you've chosen and analyze it by thinking aloud. Include specific nouns, explaining how each one creates a powerful image and also conveys information about nineteenth-century life.

2. Organize students in pairs. Have partners discuss the second example by pinpointing the specific nouns and explaining how these triggered clearer images in their minds.

3. Invite students to find and share specific nouns from their independent-reading books.

Second Day

1. Divide a large sheet of chart paper into three columns. Write these three general nouns at the top of each column: *stuff, time, vacation.*

2. Ask pairs or groups of four or five students to take a few minutes to brainstorm a list of specific nouns that could refine these general ones and to jot them down on paper.

3. Encourage students to add their specific nouns to the chart, under the corresponding general one. You may wish to get the ball rolling by writing three specific nouns on the chart. For example, I print *hockey skates* under *stuff; yesterday* under *time*; and *scuba diving* under *vacation.*

Here's part of the list seventh graders created:

stuff	time	vacation
snowboard	midnight	camping in the Adirondacks
dirt bike	afternoon	Yellowstone National Park
in-line skates	dawn	ranch in Montana
ballet shoes	sunrise	mountain climbing
book bag	early spring	

Nonfiction Writing From the Inside Out

4. Move students to their own writing. I circle three to five general nouns on a piece composed by students in grades four to six. I ask seventh and eighth graders to circle general nouns on their own, offering support to those who have trouble finding nouns.

5. Ask students to evaluate the necessity of every adjective they use. Finding more specific nouns often eliminates the need for adjectives.

6. Have students write the more specific noun above the general noun in their draft. If a sentence has to be rewritten, students can use a sticky note or place a number next to the sentence in their writing, then rewrite next to the same number on the back of the paper or on a new sheet of paper.

7. Continue inviting students to use this strategy.

rough draft

Self-editing

Katie

① Pointe and Ballet are really the same... except for the shoes they use the same technique—that is why I had to take ballet over and over every year even though I was in a Pointe class. It got annoying, but the teachers just kept saying "Katie, you need the technique. If you quit ballet, you'll have to quit Pointe too." So I was stuck with ballet for another three years.

Note on ①... after ①, there will be a new paragraph.

② In my ballet classes, we do basically the same thing as in my pointe class. We don't put on pointe shoes though. It lasts the same time.... one hour. We do the same kind of warm-ups... 20 minutes of about 6 different exercises. Then we stretch out. After about 10 minutes of stretch out time, we practice our *new* dance moves. We have the same assignment as in my Pointe class.

Katie rewrites, keeping in mind the importance of showing and sensory images.

"We would put on our ballet shoes first"

Katie G.

Pointe, Ballet, & MY LIFE.

Ballet picture / *Ballet shoes*

"I wanted Pointe shoes so bad it hurt"

Pointe picture / *Pointe shoes*

Pointe and Ballet are the first things that come to my mind when I wake up in the mornings. They become a passion more and more each day as I think about them constantly. Every week, I anticipate my classes

① *New ¶* In my *Pointe* classes, we put on our ballet shoes and do some simple exercises to warm up. That takes about 20-25 minutes usually. After about six of those 20 minute exercises, we stretch out. That usually takes us 5

second draft

minutes at the most. ¶ Next, we put on our Pointe shoes. Our classes last about an hour... sometimes a little more if we need extra work. We are given an assignment—practice our new dance and the new dance moves we learned that day.

② *New ¶* Pointe is the type of dance I'm really focused *(sp?)* on, because ever since I started ballet and saw the "big girls" up on Pointe, I wanted Pointe shoes so bad it hurt. Now, I finally have them, and love them even as they grow

FROM STUDYING CRAFT & TECHNIQUE TO APPLYING IT

For students to truly absorb a writing technique, they must apply it many times to their own writing. To help make this transfer happen, I have students use pieces they are working on to practice a technique. I also help them maintain a writing folder, in which they keep lists and resources that foster their use of techniques. In that folder students also store:

- blank composition paper,
- a list of possible writing topics,
- brainstormed ideas related to a topic,
- writing plans,
- drafts,
- revisions and edits,
- publishable drafts,
- editing symbols (see Appendix page 324),
- a list of transition words (see Appendix page 323).

Rarely do I mark students' writing, for it's their work to improve, not mine. However, my students need guidance in order to progress, so I might ask questions in the margins, do a sample rewrite on a sticky note, or use editing symbols in the margin to signal a missing comma or other punctuation. (More on editing in Chapter 7.)

Crafting Endings

Writers in primary grades often close their pieces abruptly with THE END. It's a good way out when they are unsure of how to end their piece. There's also a bit of a power play going on—those big, all-cap letters letting us know *I'm done, finis, don't make me write another word*. As a teacher of older students I'd like to be able to say I see more finessed endings, but I don't. In this section, we'll look at strategies for pushing students in grades 4 and up to achieve a higher standard.

The authors I spoke with made it clear that crafting an ending should be given as much thought as crafting a lead. In his book *On Writing Well*, William Zinsser notes, "The positive reason for ending well is that a good last sentence—or last paragraph—is a joy in itself. It gives the reader a lift, and it lingers when the article is over" (page 65).

Unfortunately, in school students often learn that to end an article, essay, or interview they should review the main points or emphasize a point they think is paramount. It's a style teachers themselves may have been taught, and one that trickled down from academic writing. Academics still use this style. I see it quite clearly when I happen to read an article in a medical journal—and in that context the highly structured, highly predictable form is appropriate. An article that presents findings from medical research and posits their implications needs an almost mechanical consistency so that possibility for misinterpretation is minimized. But let's face it—in school children are not writing articles about medical cures, so it's time to question the suitability of these formal endings and find new models.

Writers on Endings

Knowing when and how to end a nonfiction piece can puzzle student writers. Sharing with them the advice of professional nonfiction writers can open discussions that lead students to think more carefully about how to end a piece and what techniques professional writers use.

JAMES CROSS GIBLIN: At the end of the book or article, I try to sum up what has gone before and, if possible, send a chill of excitement or satisfaction down the reader's spine.

RUSSELL FREEDMAN: An ending, I think, should try to distill some key point or theme, or perhaps reach a conclusion, or maybe leave the reader with a provocative thought or an unanswered question.

PATRICIA MCKISSACK: With endings I don't want to tell readers what to think once the story is finished. Show them what the person did, then let the reader come away saying, "Boy, this was a great person." I don't want to tell because the reader might be thinking something else that is interesting. So I try to show the reader all the information that is available, tie it up at the end, and then let the reader come to a conclusion.

JULIUS LESTER: As for endings, I want to leave the reader feeling satisfied. By that I mean that the reader isn't left dangling at the end, or not understanding. The reader may not agree with me, but the reader understands how I got from the first sentence to the last.

HUDSON TALBOTT: The ending sums up the emotional journey, leading the reader to an awareness and understanding of how the person grew from experiences and how the reader grew by following it.

IDEAS FOR STUDYING ENDINGS

Models of excellent endings abound, of course. Together, students and I read and discuss outstanding examples from nonfiction books and magazines. Presenting a mini-lesson isn't necessary; instead, we take turns thinking aloud about what makes a particular ending effective (see pages 139–142).

In addition, I share with students the reflections of professional writers (on previous page). If students require more support from me, I confer with them.

Here are some other suggestions I give students:

- Surprise the reader with an unusual fact or idea.
- Use some of the techniques that make a lead work: an anecdote, a quote, a brief but memorable scene, or a question that lingers with the reader.
- Reread notes and journal entries; skim through books you've used and study illustrations and diagrams, or reread fascinating passages.

These activities will reclaim thoughts and ideas tucked in the corners of students' minds or enable them to process a fact they had not noticed while researching or writing their notes.

It's okay for student writers to allude to something important they have already said, but they need to do it in an inspired way.

ENERGETIC ENDINGS TO SHARE WITH STUDENTS

Analyze the endings shown on the next page with your students. Use these questions to guide your think-alouds and discussions:

- What technique did the writer use: Summary? Quote? Anecdote? Memorable scene? Unusual fact? Dialogue?
- What lingering ideas and feelings did the ending stir?
- Did the ending surprise you? Can you explain how?
- Did the author use a figure of speech that was effective? Explain how.
- Were there strong verbs and specific nouns that appealed to you?

Discuss how these added to the ending.

For each example, I've included some of the points I share with students in the think-aloud sections. I want to give students the language to evaluate endings in the nonfiction texts they read, and in their own endings.

From *Confucius: The Golden Rule* by Russell Freedman.

And so, after twenty-five centuries, the pros and cons of what Confucius said or didn't say are still being debated. He trusted people to think for themselves. He was always ready to offer suggestions, but he insisted that each of us must find answers for ourselves. And admitted that he himself did not know the truth, only a way to look for it.

"If a person doesn't constantly ask himself, 'What is the right thing to do?' I really don't know what is to be done about him."

So said Confucius. (page 40)

> The final three-word paragraph sends readers back to thinking about the other sayings of Confucius.

Robb's Think-Aloud:

Freedman brings us back to wondering if all the sayings attributed to Confucius are true. He also helps us see how Confucius's thinking matches contemporary ideas of democracy because Confucius believed each person must find his own way in life. Having a last paragraph of only three words makes us consider carefully the saying Freedman quotes; it also brings readers back to other sayings in the book.

From *Bad Boy: A Memoir* by Walter Dean Myers.

Writing has let me into a world in which I am respected, where the skills I have are respected for themselves. I am in a world of book lovers and people eager to rise to the music of language and ideas. All in all it has been a great journey and not at all shabby for a bad boy. (page 206)

> The words, ". . . not at all shabby for a bad boy," show Myers's pride in his journey, and return us to thinking about the title and themes.

Robb's Think-Aloud:

This ending really hits my emotional center. Walter Dean Myers expresses his pride in becoming a respected writer and being part of the world of books and language. When he says his life has been "a great journey" he celebrates all of his experiences and finds positives in each one. By writing "bad boy" Myers sends readers back to the title and theme of his book, taking readers full circle and leaving us with much to think about.

"In Case You Ever Want to Go Home Again" by Barbara Kingsolver, from *High Tide in Tucson: Essays From Now or Never.*

I learned something else that November day, that shook down all I thought I knew about my personal, insufferable, nobody's-blues-can-touch-mine isolation of high school. Before the book signing was over, more than one of my old schoolmates had sidled up and whispered: "That LouAnn character, the insecure one? I know you based her on me." (page 45)

Robb's Think-Aloud:

Barbara Kingsolver's opening phrase in her final paragraph helps us know that she continually learns from life experiences. By doing so she extends the invitation to readers. By ending with that quote, Kingsolver artfully reminds us of the universality of certain experiences. The ending lingers as all good endings do.

"George Gershwin" by Kathleen Krull, from *Lives of the Musicians: Good Times, Bad Times (and What the Neighbors Thought)*.

In 1936, during a concert tour that ended in Los Angeles, Gershwin began having memory lapses and dizzy spells, with the sensation that he was smelling burning rubber. Six months later he died of a brain tumor at age thirty-eight.

He had two funerals at the same time. At the start of services in Hollywood, all the movie studios shut down for a moment of silence in his honor. In New York, the funeral music was Bach, Beethoven, and *Rhapsody in Blue*. (page 89)

Robb's Think-Aloud:

Krull returns the reader to the subtitle of her book, "Good Times, Bad Times," when she ends with Gershwin's illness. But she lifts us up and ends on a "good time" by telling us Gershwin had two funerals at the same time. With this ending, Krull helps us understand that Gershwin will live on through his music, especially when she links Gershwin with Beethoven and Bach.

From *Rebels Against Slavery: American Slave Revolts* by Patricia and Frederick McKissack.

Freedom proved to be a bittersweet victory. Although African Americans accepted the challenges and the responsibilities of their hard-earned citizenship, they soon learned that racism and discrimination could be just as cruel as slavery had been. Without justice there can be no freedom, and without freedom there can be no peace, for wherever there is oppression, there is bound to be resistance to it. (page 165)

Robb's Think-Aloud:

I like the way the ending forces readers to reconsider the belief that freedom alone is enough: "Without justice there can be no freedom. . . ." The authors use the injustices African Americans experienced through racism and discrimination to extend readers' thinking beyond slavery in America to oppressed peoples everywhere. That's a spectacular ending because of the connections it helps readers make.

From *The Children of Topaz: The Story of a Japanese-American Internment Camp* by Michael O. Tunnell and George W. Chilcoat.

Finally, Congress passed the Civil Rights Act of 1988, which made the recommendations of the CWRIC (Commission on Wartime Relocation and Internment of Civilians) into law. Of course, not everyone agreed that there had been a wrong that needed to be righted. Some people who played important roles in the relocation defended their actions. But in October of 1990, the first letters of apology, signed by President George Bush, along with the redress payments were mailed. For many, the apology came too late. (page 69)

Robb's Think-Aloud:

This ending makes readers think about the disagreements surrounding the harsh and unjust decision to relocate Japanese Americans during World War II.

The ending returns readers to the feelings this book stirred—anger at the injustice and unfairness of placing American citizens in internment camps and disrupting their lives. By ending with the words, "For many, the apology came too late," the authors help readers feel the intense pain of Japanese Americans. Why? Many of those who needed to hear this apology had lost their homes, jobs, and friends, and never recovered from their harsh experiences; moreover, many were dead.

"The Face of a Spider" by David Quammen from *The Flight of the Iguana: A Sidelong View of Science and Nature.*

And the question continues to puzzle me: How should a human behave toward the members of other living species?

Last week I tried to make eye contact with a tarantula. This was a huge specimen, all hair and handsomely colored, with a body as big as a hamster and legs the size of Bic pens. I ogled it through a sheet of plate glass. I smiled and winked. But the animal hid its face in distrust. (page 9)

Robb's Think-Aloud:

Humor can help readers consider a serious point.

Quammen creates a funny situation—a human being winking and smiling at a tarantula—to remind readers of his essay's main idea: "How should a human behave toward the members of other living species?" The image of a scientist making eye contact with a tarantula is so absurd that I will always vividly recall it.

From *Be Seated: A Book About Chairs* by James Cross Giblin.

> Chairs also reflect, as they always have, the customs and habits of the societies in which they are used. Just as seat furniture tells us much about life in ancient Egypt or medieval Europe, so your favorite chair conveys a great deal about you, and the time in which you live. (page 122)

Robb's Think-Aloud:

> *In this ending, the author points out that the chairs we love and use tell others about us and our times. This is a masterful way to remind readers that all historical artifacts reveal stories of culture—and invite readers to reflect on the objects in our lives today and what they say about our values.*

> Making a personal connection between the history of chairs and readers' lives helps readers connect to the past.

CONTINUE TO THINK ABOUT

Samuel Johnson said: "What is written without effort is in general read without pleasure." In order for students to heed Johnson's warning, you and I need to set aside plenty of class time so students can write at school, where they can tap into the expertise of teachers and peers. Writing at school should provide students with time to:

- experience writing as a craft,
- apply the recursive writing process to an entire piece, and
- let their writing "cool" so students obtain some distance before working on leads, endings, and awakening their prose.

It's also important for teachers to reflect on the kind of classroom environment that best supports students. When I talked with Donald Graves, he offered this thoughtful and sound advice about creating a writing environment that includes a floor area for writing, a conference area for talking, a quiet reading area, and a silent area for those who need silence to compose.

Writers are like the artists and musicians who continually work hard in order to effectively communicate ideas and feelings. And this hard work, this effort, takes time.

Nonfiction Writing From the Inside Out

CHAPTER FIVE

PART 1: FROM PARAGRAPH TO ESSAY

*Strategies for Crafting Paragraphs as a
Building Block to Writing Essays*

In Their Own Words

How do you narrow the scope of a topic for an essay?

Susan Bartoletti

I make the topic as specific as possible. For instance, when I wrote the nonfiction photo essay, *Growing Up in Coal Country,* I narrowed the topic to child labor in the anthracite region of Pennsylvania. Through preliminary research, I realized that the anthracite region and its people could serve as a microcosm for the study of industrialization, immigration, and labor throughout the United States.

Katherine Paterson

I start trying to look at the question from as many different angles as possible, trying to think of stories that illustrate the various points that seem important.

Personal essay is a broad genre. How would you define it?

Donald Murray

All writing is autobiography. The personal essay is the form of writing in which the authority comes from the writer's experience, how he or she reacts to what he or she has seen or felt.

The personal essay is the most important form of nonfiction. It allows an individual writer to speak to individual readers. Each reading produces the text readers need.

Katherine Paterson

A personal essay is one that presents the reader with one person's view on some aspect of human experience. It demands no research beyond the life experience and views of the writer.

David Quammen

I don't like genre definitions. They're more likely to restrict or calcify a form of writing than to liberate it or do justice to its plasticity.

What advice do you have for students who are writing essays?

Katherine Paterson

The best advice I ever got for writing fiction comes from Charles Dickens: "Make them laugh, make them cry, and above all, make them wait." It's not bad advice for a speech or an essay. I don't set out to make people cry, but if they laugh with you, it breaks down their defenses, and when you get to the serious points you want to make, they often respond at a deep level. You also want to have a strong thread that carries the reader or the audience from the beginning all the way through to the end. This all makes the tone a bit mixed, then—which is what I'm like.

Anne Scott McLeod

Know your subject, support your statements, be precise. Overgeneralization is the mark of the amateur. I despair when I read student papers confidently talking about "the nineteenth century" as though it were all the same for everyone for the whole hundred years. Keep a fairly narrow focus, write clearly. Writing's hard work and no one gets it right in one go.

Including Authors' Insights in Instruction

As the authors' quotes illuminate, the essay can take many forms. An essay writer may rely heavily on research, or may not use hard and fast facts at all to reveal some truth about life. As Donald Murray points out, all writing is autobiography; David Quammen bristles at defining genres at all, reminding us not to tamper with the plasticity of writing.

I imagine these writers would be disheartened to know that a simplistic, old-fashioned attitude about essays versus fiction prevails in many schools. The thinking is, any student can learn to write decent, factual essays, but only the talented, creative students can write fiction.

Behind this myth is an entrenched presumption that the goal of expository writing is to organize and present facts and ideas, and that's all. Some teachers who take that stance may even view nonfiction in this light. They may not have read writers who bring to essays much more than a neatly folded package of facts. Nonfiction writers such as Bailey White, David Quammen, and Lewis Thomas are as creative as writers of fiction in the way they observe, offer up insights about our lives, and say something unique about deeply felt issues, beliefs, and experiences of modern life. Nonfiction can call on the same powers as fiction; indeed, a handful of my favorite authors have written fiction and nonfiction, including Barbara Kingsolver, Joan Didion, and James Thurber.

Barbara Kingsolver discusses her teenage daughter and her mother in essays she calls letters. Bailey White's narrative essays offer glimpses of everyday events in a small southern town—events such as her mother eating mullet in the local restaurant, and the author's annual visit to the county fair. Joan Didion examines the absurdities of marrying in Las Vegas as well as keeping a writer's notebook, morality, and self-respect. Some essayists, like David Quammen, John McPhee, and Jacques Cousteau, write about issues in the natural world in such a way that we could swear we were in the field with them.

These writers knit self and world together, intertwining memories, facts, opinions, insights, and storytelling into an astonishing weave. Their clear and disciplined thinking enables them to knit their strands in such a way that one isn't fully aware of the logic at work until an essay's end—and then the reader is knocked breathless by the power of it.

Essays can argue, mourn, describe, analyze, make fun, propose, persuade, record,
entertain, irritate, discourage, confide, share, explain, document, criticize, celebrate.
In the essay, the writer sits on a bench beside the reader and comments
on the life they share.

—Donald Murray

I am in a fifth-grade class, observing a lesson on writing an informative paragraph. On the chalkboard the teacher has written:

Topic Sentence: introduces the subject of your paragraph

Body: three details that relate to your subject

Wrap-up: One sentence that repeats the topic sentence in a different way

"Feeding Your Pet" is the assigned topic. "I don't have a pet," a fifth grader says. Three other classmates echo this concern.

"Make believe you have one," the teacher responds. Then she adds, "You might have to write about something you're unfamiliar with on the test next month."

The term "essay" is a tough one to define, but I know this: the essay is not what was being taught in that fifth-grade classroom.

Webster's New Universal Unabridged Dictionary, Deluxe Second Edition, defines the essay as, "a short, literary composition dealing with a single subject, usually from a personal point of view and without attempting completeness." This simple dictionary definition is not a bad way to begin to build our students' understanding of essays. I might extend it to say: "A single subject from a personal point of view, with one or more of the following purposes at work: to inform, persuade, offer an opinion, analyze, entertain, or reflect on a life experience."

I will continue to define the essay later in this chapter. Suffice it to say, it's a sophisticated form of writing, and for that reason, I want to do it justice by showing you how to help your students work up to writing essays gradually, paragraph by paragraph.

Lessons for Writing Descriptive Paragraphs

The series of lessons that follow are on writing paragraphs that depict something with carefully observed details. I've outlined the lessons to span two weeks, but adjust them to suit your needs. As you explore them, underscore for your students that descriptive paragraphs can also contain information, opinions, and narrative elements.

Management Tips

- Do a think-pair-share to find out what your students know about paragraphs—it will help you tailor your lessons.
- Adapt these lesson ideas to your schedule and to students' needs. Like everything in this book, these are guidelines, not rigid steps to follow.
- Introduce students to one paragraph type at a time.
- Set aside 10 to 20 minutes daily for the lessons.
- After the lesson, have students do free-choice writing or complete a teacher-directed writing project until they reach the eighth day. At that point, students are ready to find topics and draft the kind of paragraph you've been discussing with them.

Guidelines for the First Day

1. Place a paragraph from a published work on a transparency and read it aloud. (The paragraph I use is from "A Mother's Love" by David Giannelli, from *Chicken Soup for the Pet Lover's Soul*. After helping to get a garage fire under control, New York City firefighter David Giannelli finds three kittens on the sidewalk in front of the garage, one in the gutter, and a fifth across the street. He decides to look for the mother cat.)

   A cop told me he had seen a cat go into a vacant lot near where I'd found the last two kittens. She was there, lying down and crying. She was horribly burnt: her eyes were blistered shut, her paws were blackened, and her fur was singed all over her body. In some places you could see her reddened skin showing through the burned fur. She was too weak to move anymore. I went over to her slowly, talking gently as I approached. I figured that she was a wild cat and I didn't want to alarm her. When I picked her up, she cried out in pain, but she didn't struggle. The poor animal reeked of burnt fur and flesh. She gave me a look of utter exhaustion and then relaxed in my arms as much as her pain would allow. Sensing her trust in me, I felt my throat tighten and the tears start in my eyes. I was determined to save this brave little cat and her family. Their lives were, literally, in my hands (page 234).

Robb's Think-Aloud:

This paragraph has descriptive elements and the author uses sensory details to help us see, smell, and feel the burnt mother cat. It also contains opinion, when the firefighter speculates that the mother was a wild cat. I also see narrative elements, in Giannelli's reaction and determination to save the cat. The entire paragraph is told in the order in which the events occurred. Writers refer to this as chronological or time order. But even with these other elements, I consider this paragraph to be descriptive. A paragraph is rarely purely one element.

2. Invite students to comment on the paragraph and your think-aloud.

Guidelines for the Second Day

1. Introduce or review the three basic parts of a paragraph: topic or lead sentence, body that contains details that support the lead, and a wrap-up or concluding sentence.

2. Analyze a model written by a student no longer in your school and delete the student's name. (I prefer to teach using examples of successful paragraphs, so that students can envision where they can go, though at times you may wish to look at one and discuss why it's not working.) If you're comfortable writing, it's also helpful to share a paragraph you composed. Here is a descriptive paragraph I wrote for a lesson for eighth graders:

> *The beach looked like a sandy morgue as the waves discarded dozens of mackerel heads and half-eaten bodies onto the shore. The air smelled of fish and fear. Anxious to haul in tonight's dinner, my dad abandoned his fishing rod, grabbed his net, charged into the foamy water, and swam after a school of fish riding a distant wave. For me, the rod was the fisherman's tool, so I motioned to my dad to come back, hoping he would return to the rules of his sport. He ignored my pleading and continued diving. Twice he emerged from the surf, plastered with churned-up sand and grinning as he tossed a bluefish from his net onto the dry sand. Just as my dad's body disappeared into a crashing wave for the third time, the lifeguard shouted, "Sharks!" My dad surfaced and swam for shore. On that last dive he had spied a shark chasing the bluefish. Since that day, my dad always fishes with a rod and reel. And he's quick to remind friends that what really makes fishing a sport is waiting on the shore for the big bite.*

I ask eighth graders to think-pair-share and discuss their reactions to and observations of the lead, the body, and the conclusion. Because students have studied and discussed paragraphs since second grade in the school where I teach, this is a review lesson. Here are some of their comments:

- The lead. It puts us on the beach; the tone is set with words like <u>morgue</u>, <u>mackerel heads</u> and <u>half-eaten bodies</u>. It makes me want to go on and find out what's happening here.

- The body. It has description of what's going on, but also narrative stuff like the dad tossing aside his rod, and what happens when he dives for fish. It's in time order. It's like a little essay because it makes a point—use your rod to fish. The word <u>sharks</u> builds fear and makes you think back to the second sentence.

- The conclusion. It's kind of funny because now the dad reminds friends of the lesson about fishing that he learned. It leaves you thinking about fishing as a sport and what makes something a sport.

Guidelines for the Third Day

1. Focus on topic or lead sentences. Note, on chart paper, two to three top-notch topic sentences by professional writers and/or by former students.

2. Ask students to discuss the examples and explain what they learn about the subject as well as what makes the lead sentence compelling, or, conversely, why it fails to grab them. It's helpful to remind students that leads for paragraphs or essays follow the same variety as those for informational texts, discussed in Chapter 3.

Scaffolding Ideas: When to Slow Down the Lessons

For students in grades 4 and 5, as well as students in grades 6 and up who struggle with writing, break your instruction about the parts of the paragraph into three lessons. First, study leads or topic sentences and collaborate to write some openings for specific topics. Next, analyze the details in the body and point out how they relate to the lead or topic sentence. Finally, move to the wrap-up and discuss how the writer keeps you thinking about the piece.

Nonfiction Writing From the Inside Out

Sample leads of essays by professional writers:

From "Family Values" by Bailey White in *Sleeping at the Starlite Motel*:

> My Aunt Eleanor was taking a shower the other day when the whole bathroom fell right through the floor and landed in the dust under the house (p. 9).

From "Letter to a Daughter at Thirteen" by Barbara Kingsolver in *Small Wonder*:

> Here's a secret you should know about mothers: We spy. Yes, on our kids (p. 145).

From "No Name Woman" by Maxine Hong Kingston in *The Best American Essays of the Century*:

> "You must not tell anyone," my mother said, "what I am about to tell you. In China your father had a sister who killed herself" (page 382).

From "The Crack-Up" by F. Scott Fitzgerald in *The Best American Essays of the Century*:

> Of course all life is a process of breaking down, but the blows that do the dramatic side of the work—the big sudden blows that come or seem to come, from outside—the ones you remember and blame things on and, in moments of weakness, tell your friends about, don't show their effect all at once (page 139).

Guidelines for the Fourth Day

1. If your students keep writer's notebooks, invite them to read through their notebooks to look for topics that lend themselves to writing a descriptive paragraph.
2. Have students think-pair-share for about 10 minutes to discuss topics they might want to write about.
3. Ask students to jot down a list of their ideas in their writer's notebooks or on a piece of composition paper.

Guidelines for the Fifth and Sixth Days

1. Model how you brainstorm ideas about a topic. Help students to see how you free-associate about recent everyday events, such as a funny or striking exchange in the grocery store or at home with your family, or an experience that happened in the past. Then show how you extend ideas and elaborate the details following the guidelines on page 163–165.

2. Demonstrate how you form these notes into a plan so that students observe your decision-making process (see page 166).

Guidelines for the Seventh Day

1. Discuss the wrap-up or concluding sentence. Help students understand that the conclusion ties together a key point but also adds something more for readers to think about.
2. Share models written by former students or professional writers. Be sure to show the conclusions from the *end* of a piece of writing; in other words, not a sentence that ends one of the interior paragraphs.

Here is a paragraph, written by a fifth grader, that you can use to discuss the concluding sentence as well as other parts of a descriptive paragraph.

> I enjoy the chaotic hubbub of the Apple Blossom Midway, a street with uncountable game and food booths lining both sides. All around is the aroma of funnel cakes, hot dogs, corn dogs, Polish sausages, caramel apples, and popcorn. Balloons pop while the game hosts scream like auctioneers, advertising their booths. People are all around me dressed in rich colors, walking in front of brightly painted booths with flashing lights. I love the sensation of being bombarded by fun from every direction when I'm on the midway.

Guidelines for the Eighth to Eleventh Days

1. Invite students to choose a topic and brainstorm a list of ideas or complete a fast-write.
2. Have students elaborate their ideas.
3. Ask students to create a plan. Read plans and offer feedback. Meet with students who need support as they elaborate ideas.
4. Establish guidelines for drafting with students. For example, paragraphs must include:
   - title
   - a lead sentence that introduces the topic and hooks the reader

> ### HOLD OFF ON TEACHING TRANSITIONS
>
> I don't share or discuss the last sentence of a paragraph I excerpt from *within* an essay because it isn't a concluding sentence. Instead, it's a transition sentence; I teach my students about transitions later, when they are writing and revising full pieces (see Chapter 7).

- descriptive details
- complete sentences
- correct use of uppercase letters

5. Ask students to draft paragraphs and check them against their guidelines, notes, and plan.

6. Circulate as they write so that you can respond to questions and confer with students who require extra support (see Appendix pages 316–319).

7. Have students peer-edit, using their guidelines.

8. Read students' work for these purposes:
   - to understand what mini-lessons they need;
   - to decide whether students are ready to move on to learning about another type of paragraph or whether they should revise their descriptive pieces.

9. Grade students' work using the guidelines (see page 260).

EVALUATING STUDENT PARAGRAPHS

When you read your students' paragraphs, look to see that students have done the following:

- written a short and snappy title
- written a topic sentence that does double duty (introduces the subject and hooks the reader)
- used details in the body of their piece that relate to the topic sentence
- organized the details in the body in one of two ways—in chronological order, or by presenting the most important points first or last. (This is especially crucial in opinion paragraphs, where the writer hopes to persuade readers to agree with her position.) and
- written a thought-provoking concluding sentence or ending

DECIDING WHICH TYPES OF PARAGRAPHS TO TEACH

Teachers often ask me: How many types of paragraphs should I teach? Such a question is best answered when teachers confer with colleagues in their school. Certainly, practicing all five kinds of paragraphs can take half a school year, and I don't believe that is a productive use of students' writing time. Spending four to six weeks on paragraphs leaves enough time for free-choice writing and learning about other nonfiction genres.

It's beneficial for faculties to make instructional decisions based on the populations they teach and their district's requirements. Decide which paragraphs to teach in grades four and up. Dividing the instructional load ensures that students will learn and teachers won't rush through modeling and discussing. Here's a plan teachers and I developed for a K–5 and 6–8 school in the same Virginia district. Use it to help create a plan that works for you and your colleagues.

	Grade 4	Grade 5	Grade 6	Grade 7	Grade 8
descriptive	✓		✓	✓	✓
informative	✓	✓		✓	✓
opinion	✓	✓	✓		✓
how-to		✓	✓		
narrative				✓	✓

Lessons for Writing Narrative, How-To, Opinion, and Informative Paragraphs

With this next set of lessons, I put at center stage paragraphs of professional writers and student writers. Students analyze them in pairs or small groups, discovering for themselves that "in real life," paragraphs serve various functions, and bend to suit the writer's goal for the content. Students become aware that writers rarely write a purebred paragraph; instead, they craft hardy hybrids that can, for example, narrate primarily, but also inform and deliver an opinion.

To help you launch these lessons I offer management tips, guidelines for teaching with the examples by professional writers and student writers, and questions your students can discuss in a think-pair-share.

Management Tips
- These are not full-blown mini-lessons. I'm giving you the raw materials—excerpts, a set of discussion questions, sample student comments—so that you can build your own lessons.
- When you create your own lessons, remember to pair a paragraph from a professional writer's essay with a paragraph written by a student writer that has the same prevailing purpose. In other words, your examples should each be doing one thing primarily—

informing or narrating or explaining, and so on.

- On the first day, explore the paragraph from a professional writer's essay. On another day delve into a student's paragraph.

- I tend to study each paragraph type for three class periods, but take more time with analyzing examples if your students' comments and observations are minimal or show confusion. To help you to plan your teaching time to support struggling or less experienced writers, return to the scheduling suggestions on pages 155–156.

- You can use the following suggested schedule and guidelines with every lesson, and you can present the lessons in any order.

SUGGESTED SCHEDULE AND GUIDELINES

The First Day

1. Place the example by a professional writer on an overhead transparency or print the paragraph on chart paper.

2. Have students read the example and use the discussion questions on page 156 to analyze it.

The Second Day

Repeat steps one and two using an example by a student writer.

The Third Day

1. Invite students to bring examples of the same type of paragraph from their free-choice reading and share with a partner.

2. Ask partners to share their reading examples with another pair; this gives students four additional examples to discuss, allowing them greater opportunity to absorb the fact that the content and purpose determine the nature of the paragraph.

The Fourth Day

1. Review with students what they have learned about paragraphs and their varied purposes. Help them to understand that though the overarching purpose of any paragraph is to inform or persuade, the content will influence the extent to which a writer uses narrative, descriptive, or other elements.

2. Have pairs or small groups compose an explanation of a paragraph's purpose based on their recent experiences. Ask students to be as specific as possible. Note their points on chart paper so that students can return to these when they find a topic, generate ideas, and draft a paragraph.

Discussion Questions

Print the following questions on a large sheet of chart paper. As students discuss them in relation to a text, circulate among groups, and guide their conversations.

- What is the author's purpose for this paragraph? What details support this purpose?
- Do you find more than one purpose? For example, did the paragraph both inform and describe? Is one purpose primary?
- How does the author organize ideas—by using chronological order, or by presenting ideas in order of importance?
- Did you notice any techniques you'd like to use in your own writing?
- Did strong verbs and specific nouns enhance the piece? Explain how.
- Did the author use figurative language: simile, metaphor, personification, onomatopoeia, alliteration? (See Appendix page 325.)
- Can you explain the elements of this kind of paragraph in your own words?

LESSON ONE

Narrative Paragraph

Narrative paragraphs tell a story by including specific events and people. They can contain snippets of a conversation, describe a person or setting, share a person's inner thoughts, and so forth.

Example by a Professional Writer

From "Rattlesnake Belt" in *Mama Makes Up Her Mind* by Bailey White:

The snakes live under our house, and as long as they stay there, sedate and well behaved, Mama leaves them alone. But when they crawl out on warm spring mornings and spread themselves out in the sun on the back steps, it's a different story. "Hospitality can go just so far," says my mother, wielding her walking stick as she heads out to the back porch. Through the years she has perfected her technique. She sneaks the screen door open and carefully pins the snake's head against the bricks with a piece of firewood. Then she gives it one smart whack on the neck with the handle of her walking stick, and when the snake quits wiggling, she throws it in the back of her pick-up truck and drives it over to the taxidermist (page 131).

Summary of Sixth Graders' Observations

- White used a quote by her mother. It helped me know how her mother felt about the snakes.
- The paragraph told the events of how her mother destroyed snakes that came onto the steps.
- It was funny when White described how her mother smashed snakes.
- It had description, too.
- It was in time order.

Example by Sixth-Grader Ethan

My sister Erin and I were having a water gun fight, and my water gun was the most effective one in our collections. Upset that I took the best one, Erin grabbed that water gun out of my hands. I quickly regrabbed it. Frustrated, Erin swung at my face with her fists. I backed away, trying to dodge my sister. But I fell against the wall. Erin then moved in for the strike. I stood there, waiting for the inevitable. When the inevitable happened, I ran to my mom knowing she would punish Erin. Was I in for a big surprise. Mom scolded Erin and grounded me for the rest of that day. I plotted revenge as I watched her ride her bike from my window.

LESSON TWO
How-To Paragraph

The how-to paragraph describes how to do something. For example, it might give directions for playing a game, explain how to make an herb garden or prevent erosion, or tell how to get from one place to another. Explanations are precise and organized sequentially. But as illustrated by the Bradbury excerpt, how-to paragraphs can also explain processes that are not as defined as a car route, such as how to become a professional ballet dancer, or how to find happiness in life. The Bradbury excerpt helps students appreciate that writers take liberties with traditional notions of paragraphs—Bradbury could have combined his sentences into one paragraph, but chose to present his "how-to's" as separate paragraphs.

Example by a Professional Writer

From "How to Be Madder Than Captain Ahab," by Ray Bradbury, in *Chicken Soup for the Writer's Soul:*

To sum it all up, if you want to write, if you want to create, you must be the most sublime fool that God ever turned out and sent rambling.

You must write every single day of your life.

You must read dreadful, dumb books and glorious books, and let them wrestle in beautiful fights inside your head, vulgar one moment, brilliant the next.

You must lurk in libraries and climb the stacks like ladders to snuff books like perfumes and wear books like hats upon your crazy head (p. 385).

Summary of Sixth Graders' Observations

- He [Bradbury] had lots of paragraphs. I think he wanted us to think about each one separately.
- The verbs like <u>lurk</u>, <u>wrestle</u>, <u>wear</u>, and <u>snuff</u> added humor.
- He compares books to perfume. That made me think about how books smell. Old ones smell different from new books.
- This was how-to and advice or his opinion of what to do to be a writer.

Example by Sixth-Grader Michael

Putting on your pants is one of the most important things you do in the morning. First, grab the knobs on the dresser drawer and pull it open. Take a pair of pants out; close the drawer. Next, hold the pants so the big hole faces upwards. Put your right leg in the right side hole and insert the left leg in the adjacent hole. After that, pull up the pants until the top is at your waist. On the waist band there is a button. Beneath the button is a zipper. If you cannot see a button or zipper, then the pants are on backwards. Now, zip the zipper and slip the button into the buttonhole. It's time to walk outside and have a great day. You have also dodged the embarrassment of leaving home without wearing pants.

LESSON THREE

Opinion Paragraph

In opinion paragraphs, also called persuasive paragraphs, writers clearly state their opinions about a topic. Often, writers place their strongest point at the start or near the end of the paragraph. Opinions can be more convincing when writers include facts, observations, and data collected from newspapers, interviews, or other research. As the writer expresses her opinion, she often desires to persuade readers to adopt her reasoning on the topic. Newspaper editorials are opinion paragraphs, and they often express the point of view of a specific newspaper.

Example by a Professional Writer

From "Somebody's Baby," in *High Tide in Tucson: Essays from Now or Never* by Barbara Kingsolver:

Taking parental responsibility to extremes, some policy makers in the U. S. have seriously debated the possibility of requiring a license for parenting. I'm dismayed by the notion of licensing an individual adult to raise an individual child, because it implies parenting is a private enterprise, like selling liquor or driving a cab (though less lucrative). I'm also dismayed by what it suggests about innate fitness and non-fitness to rear children. Who would devise such a test? And how could it harbor anything but deep class biases? Like driving, parenting is a skill you learn by doing. You keep an eye out for oncoming disasters, and know when to stop and ask for directions. The skills you have going into it are hardly the point (pages 102–103).

Summary of Eighth Graders' Observations

- She [Kingsolver] opens with a fact that lets her move to her opinion.
- Her comparison of a liquor license to a license for children shocks us. It makes me start thinking about her opinion. It makes me wonder who could impartially decide how to license couples to become parents.
- She uses questions that are great. She makes us think how subjective licensing a parent would be. It could create deep prejudices.
- She ends with her strongest point: "parenting is a skill you learn by doing."
- Bringing driving in and showing that parents and drivers have to look out for

"disasters" or ask for directions reinforces her point that doing, and learning
how to solve problems, are what's important.

Example by Eighth-Grader Sara

When people think of the "perfect woman," ten out of twelve times they
will think of a supermodel or an actress. The glamorous, long-limbed women
have dominated public attention forever: from runways to magazines, newspapers to TV shows. Males, used to the airbrushed images from the media,
set their standards impossibly high, making any "average" girl feel inade-
quate and inferior. But have our opinions of beautiful been stretched too
far? John Galliano, a prestigious fashion designer, recently stated that models these days have "no real physical beauty" and that "up-and-coming girls
are just extremely tall anorexics trying to look exotic." This may be harsh,
but unfortunately it's true.

LESSON FOUR

Informative Paragraph

The main purpose of an informative paragraph is to share information with readers about a
particular topic. Similes, metaphors, and descriptions can breathe vitality into informative
paragraphs. They may even have a narrative element—but the information predominates.

Example by a Professional Writer

From "The Beautiful and Damned," in *The Flight of the Iguana* by David Quammen:

Its [the cheetah's] favored prey species are modest-sized grazers like the
impala and the Thomson's gazelle, generally taken at weights less than the cheetah's own. But let an impala stand its ground (either from stupid daring or
because it's paralyzed by fear) and the cheetah will pass it right by, focusing
instead on one of the other herd members that has taken flight. For two or three
hundred yards the cheetah will pursue at top speed, until (on a successful chase)
it has pulled up beside the chosen impala's rear flank. Then it will do what is, to

my mind, a charmingly roguish thing: It will swing out a paw (in mid-stride now, remember, at seventy miles per hour) and trip the impala (p. 150).

Summary of Fifth Graders' Observations

- There's facts of the cheetah's prey and how it catches prey.
- He [Quammen] comments on things like the impala freezing and gives ideas why the impala would do this. It makes it more interesting.
- I like it when he makes us remember that the cheetah puts out its paw while it's running at seventy miles an hour.
- He made the information exciting.
- It's easier to remember this stuff because it's not just a list of facts.

Example by Fifth-Grader Zach

Robots will make our life easy because they are really good workers. Robots never feel tired or hungry. They always do their job and don't get lazy. Some robots have human-like hands that can use tools. In space, robots can do jobs that are too dangerous for astronauts. Robots can repair parts of a spacecraft. Robots can drive cars and fly spy planes. Scientists make the robots think. They give robots commands. Robots are great, but we do their thinking.

Students Write Their Own Paragraphs

Once your students understand how a specific paragraph works, it's time for them to apply what they've learned by writing a paragraph themselves. And with this, we're at the point in the writing process of finding a topic. As I emphasized in Chapter 2, your role is to help students find a topic that interests them; otherwise, their paragraphs will be perfunctory rather than inspired.

You'll find that students' choices run the gamut from lighthearted pieces about pet hamsters, to fact-filled paragraphs about World War II, to deeply personal accounts of losing a friend or relative. The important point here is, it's *their* choice. Keep in mind the following line from F. Scott Fitzgerald and you won't go wrong: "You don't write because you want to say something; you write because you've got something to say" (Winokur, 1999).

FOUR MINI-LESSONS THAT HELP STUDENTS GENERATE DETAILS

My students take from on to three class periods to mull over their chosen topics, while they gather ideas through brainstorming or fast-writes (see pages 80–81). I then guide them to expand on their ideas, a process which can be tough going. Elaboration is a key writing skill, but it eludes many students—or some students resist learning it.

Without sufficient detail, my students tend to write paragraphs that may have an impressively relaxed tone, but that lack force, or memorability, because there's nothing to sink one's teeth into as a reader. Donald Murray notes, "The tone may be conversational, but the reader will not read it unless there is an adequate delivery of information to satisfy the reader's hunger for specifics."

I've developed four mini-lessons that coax students to deliver detail to their writing: Wake Up and Smell the World; Rummage Your Memory; Note Your Notes; and Purpose, Please. Present and review these lessons whenever you sense your students need them.

Suggested Guidelines

1. The mini-lessons each feature a different writing technique; I recommend that you cover two techniques a week.

2. To present the mini-lesson, use a brainstormed list you composed beforehand—or, better yet, do your brainstorming in front of your students.

3. Encourage students to ask questions about your process.

4. After you've modeled and discussed the process, provide class time for students to apply these techniques to their own brainstorming or fast-writes.

5. Have students add notes to their lists, brainstorming beside each item. Have them use sticky notes to add extra details to fast-writes.

6. Ask students to have a partner read their expanded list and ask questions that help the writer collect even more details. Partners can write questions on sticky notes.

7. Display these expanded topic ideas on a bulletin board so that students can refer to them.

8. Set aside time for students to enlarge their initial lists in this way each time you ask them to generate ideas for expository writing.

> ### MODELING ADVICE
>
> Use the same brainstormed list or fast-write to model all four elaboration techniques. Students can see how the techniques help writers generate details in different ways.

Nonfiction Writing From the Inside Out

9. Ask students to consider their audience and purpose for writing the paragraph or essay. This will help them frame their ideas into a plan of their own. Or you can have students use their identified purpose and audience to complete the more formal plan on page 168.

MINI-LESSON 1

Wake Up and Smell the World

Encourage students to activate their senses—writing about what they hear, see, smell, taste, and touch can breathe life and energy into details. You can brainstorm a list in front of your students or prepare a list on chart paper. My original list is in plain type; additions are in bold (see pages 164 and 165).

Robb's Brainstorming for "Hiking Mountain Trails"
Equipment—light backpack so don't feel weighted down
food—peanut butter & jelly tastes like ambrosia when you're hiking and starved
drink—Gatorade, sweet
kind of day—clear and ideal for spotting birds
go with someone
where
look for things—animal tracks and droppings
rest—on velvety, pillow-soft moss or pine leaves

MINI-LESSON 2

Rummage Your Memory

Priceless details accrue in our memories, waiting for us to rediscover them and put them to good use. The only catch is, writers need to carve out time to recall. Set aside eight to ten minutes for students to chat about their ideas with a partner and reclaim experiences. Then set aside five to seven minutes for students to jot down their memories.

Robb's Brainstorming for "Hiking Mountain Trails"

equipment—light backpack so don't feel weighted down; **tell about first time when didn't take snakebite kit and copperhead bit friend; always have a snakebite kit or a knife; take field guide for what you're watching; I take guides for birds and mushrooms**

food—**take stuff that won't need freezer packs—these add weight to your backpack;** take 4 or 5 peanut butter & jelly sandwiches, **dried fruit, several protein bars**

drink—Gatorade, sweet, **keeps electrolytes—tell about feeling faint and another hiker gave you Gatorade; take water—sweat lots**

kind of day—clear to spot birds

where—**trails in state park about 20 minutes from home—can get help here from other hikers if someone is hurt**

look for things—animal tracks and droppings

rest—on velvety, pillow-soft moss or pine leaves

what to wear—long pants and long-sleeved shirt to avoid bug bites and thistle scratches; broken-in walking shoes or boots; light jacket if hiking into evening

go with someone—tell when you went alone and sprained your ankle

---

Mini-Lesson 3

Note Your Notes

Reflecting on one's notes and drafts is time well spent. I'm always amazed by how a fact or detail I may have glossed over before will suddenly seem neon-orange on the page and trigger an idea. Model this "aha!" moment for your students by rereading your notes aloud, and connecting one or two details to a newly emerging detail you want to include.

Robb's Brainstorming for "Hiking Mountain Trails"

equipment—light backpack so don't feel weighted down; tell about first time when didn't take snakebite kit and copperhead bit friend; **always have a snakebite kit or a knife & scarf for a tourniquet;** take field guide for what you're watching; I take guides for birds and mushrooms; bug repellent

food—take stuff that won't need freezer packs—these add weight to your backpack;

take 4 or 5 peanut butter & jelly **or peanut butter and banana sandwiches,** dried fruit, several protein bars

drink—Gatorade, sweet, keeps electrolytes—tell about feeling faint and another hiker gave you Gatorade; take water—sweat lots

kind of day—clear to spot birds; **cool so don't feel exhausted**

where—trails in state park about 20 minutes from home—can get help here from other hikers if someone is hurt; **stick to trail if you're a novice**

look for things—animal tracks and droppings; **wild flowers, ferns, trees**

rest—on velvety, pillow-soft moss or pine leaves; **tell about the barred owl you saw while sitting quietly**

what to wear—long pants and long-sleeved shirt to avoid bug bites and thistle scratches; broken in walking shoes or boots; light jacket if hiking into evening; **tell when you wore shorts and gotten bitten by chiggers and mosquitoes**

go with someone—tell when you went alone and sprained your ankle; **tell about finding mushrooms on a hike with friends**

MINI-LESSON 4

Purpose, Please

Defining the purpose of a paragraph or essay helps writers decide what details to include or exclude. For example, if I were writing an opinion paragraph about hiking without a companion, I'd select and massage only those details that help me lay out the benefits or drawbacks of hiking alone. If my purpose is to tell a story (write a narrative paragraph), then I'd organize my notes in a way that recounts a hiking adventure.

Closely related to the task of defining a purpose is the matter of defining an audience. For example, if my intended audience knows little or nothing about my topic, I'd select basic facts and ideas that will give them a strong foundation. If, on the other hand, my readers know a lot about my topic, then I wouldn't bore them with information they already have, but instead offer something new or a new twist or viewpoint (Zinsser, 2001).

I share these points about purpose and audience with my students, and also model my thinking process as I plan a piece, as illustrated here.

First, I model for sixth- and eight- grade students how I sort my notes into the pro and con structure of an opinion piece about whether middle-school students should have a mid-morning snack:

Robb's Plan for an Opinion Paragraph

Title: *Mid-morning Energy Boost*

Pros	**Cons**
work better	*takes too much time*
don't always eat breakfast	*leave a messy room*
pediatrician says it's good	*tend to eat lunch then*
"Teens burn calories as	*will eat high sugar and get hyper*
much as younger students."	
will keep snacks healthy	

Lead: *"Teens burn as many calories as younger children," Dr. Smithson told me during a telephone conversation about whether middle school students should have a mid-morning snack.*

Ideas in concluding sentence: *show benefits to students and teachers*

Next, I demonstrate for students how I write several sentences that weave opposing views into the paragraph. Then I write a first draft in front of students. When I'm done, I read it aloud.

Robb's Draft

Snacks for Students Support Learning

If possible, quote an authority to support your point.

"Teens burn as many calories as younger children," Dr. Smithson told me during a telephone conversation about whether middle-school students should have a mid-morning snack. Dr. Smithson also explained that school starts too early for teenagers—their brains are developing at such a rate that they need twelve hours of sleep—and most don't take the time to eat breakfast. Though many teachers feel that having a snack takes away from class time, I believe that teach-ers will benefit because students won't be daydreaming about food during class or dozing due to lack of energy. Sending a letter to parents can inform them of the problem of unhealthy, high-sugar snacks and encourage them to pack healthy, hunger-satisfying snacks so that students are less likely to down their entire lunch in the morning. I believe that stu-dents will toss wrappings and banana peels into the garbage can if teachers remind them

Weave in and address the opposite view-point from your own.

Nonfiction Writing From the Inside Out

to do so before snack. Reserving time for a morning snack will improve students' ability to learn and allow teachers to be more creative because students will be attentive during lessons.

After I read my draft aloud, I have students do a think-pair-share, during which they compare and contrast the plan and the paragraph. My students note the following:

- You changed the title.
- You put in the cons like the letter to parents
- It's more convincing because you addressed the cons and offered solutions.

I display my plan and draft on a bulletin board so that students can refer to it.

Helping Students Plan a Paragraph

In Chapter 3, I discussed and showed ways students plan their writing (see pages 91–96). Some teachers I coach prefer students to plan paragraphs or essays with a series of strategies that help them define their topic and target audience (see pages 87–88). That's fine. With paragraph writing I prefer having students complete a plan that encourages them to note details, anecdotes, and quotes, to compose a tentative title, lead or topic sentence, and to jot down ideas for their concluding sentence. I've developed a planning sheet that greatly assists my students with all of this. I encourage you to adapt it to your needs.

A couple of things to note about the sheet: I have not specified the number of details students should include, as this will depend on the topic and the type of paragraph they're writing. You may want to add a request that students list three or four points that support their topic sentence. And, although I have asked students to write a title, topic sentence, and ideas to include in their final sentence, I do not require them to adhere to these first attempts. As I noted in Chapter 3, plans naturally change during the drafting and revision processes. As Kurt Vonnegut said, "It's like a movie: All sorts of accidental things will happen after you've set up the cameras" (Winokur, 1999).

VARIOUS WAYS TO USE THE PLANNING SHEET

I use the planning sheet in four ways.

1. Students reread their notes and complete their plans.

2. Students evaluate their work by checking their draft against their plan and negotiated writing criteria. At this point students can add, delete, or refine ideas.

3. Peers can use the plan and criteria to offer feedback to a partner.

4. After self- or peer-evaluation, I can read the plans of any writers who are struggling and offer them feedback before they draft a piece. I always remark on the positives in students' plans so they know that their efforts are

Planning a Paragraph

Name _____ Date _____

Title:

Specific details to include:

Possible lead:

Ideas I want to leave the reader with in my concluding sentence:

noticed and appreciated. To foster reflection on areas of plans that require additional thought, I pose questions (see page 171).

Planning a Paragraph

Name Avery _____

Title: Bathroom Time.

Details to include in introduction.
- 1 hair per day (she does not have to have pony tails)
- Use a towel no need for my hair dryer
- get your own toothpaste

Details to include in the body. When she dose'nt listen, I help her with her hair.
- hair straitener
- Sara's burnt hair - she put her head in the sink
- spraying perfume all over the bathroom
- my mom telling me to "lighten up on the perfume

Our brief conference was truly productive. Here are some points you offered that will help you draft:
• Changing title to "Bathroom Law" sets the tone of you as the boss.
• Your point that the verbs should show the relationship is a good one.
• Can you return to your being "the law" in the closing #?

Details to include in the conclusion.
She'll never take my hair tie again, per day.

Questions are a kind way to stimulate thinking and encourage students to gather more details before writing.

Nonfiction Writing From the Inside Out

One hair tie per day, Sara does not have to ware her hair in ponytails one will do.

She can use a towel to dry her hair she doesn't need to use my hair dryer.

She can also get her own toothpaste and stop leaving the top off mine! These are just a

few of the bathroom rules that I took the liberty of laying down. When Sara doesn't

comply with these rules, I help her do her hair.

She shouldn't have used my toothpaste and left the cap off. I told her there would

be consequences the last time she violated that rule. So I helped her do her hair. I was

straitening my hair at the time when I realized her doo needed some styling. I took my

straightener and grabbed a piece of her hair with it. Unfortunately for her I held it there a

little to long. She started screaming at me because when I let go the bathroom filled with

the stench of burning hair. She looked at me with a look of horror. I assured her hair had

just been lightly singed.

The bathroom stunk, so Sara took out an old bottle of perfume and started

spraying it everywhere. The perfume only added to the stench in the bathroom.

My mom walked by our bathroom, then promptly turned around and stood in the

doorway. My sister and I hid the perfume and the straightener behind our backs and

struggled a guilty/innocent smile. My mom rolled her eyes and walked off. All I know is

the law is the law. Sara will never leave the cap off my toothpaste ever again.

Self and Peer Revision For Content

Name _Avery_____ Date_____

Directions: Next to each item, celebrate what worked well. Pose one or two questions to point to an area you feel needs revision. Use the content criteria to focus on specific items such as including a quote or short dialogue or making transitions from one paragraph to the next.

Title: none (Bathroom Love)

Lead: Good, makes me want to know how you do her hair

Can You Summarize the Purpose of this Piece?
to show sisterly love
she wants to tell about how her sister
doesn't follow her rules and the consequences

Content:
Good maybe use some dialogue
and make Sara sound
horrified

Ending:
Good
dialogue from your mom too (maybe)

~~Bathroom Love~~ Bathroom War

Avery

One hair tie per day, Sara does not have to wear her hair in pigtails, she can use a towel to dry her hair, she doesn't need to use my hair dryer. She can also get her own toothpaste and stop leaving the top off mine! These are just a few of the bathroom rules that I took the liberty of laying down. When Sara does not comply with these rules, I "help" her do her hair.

She should not have used my toothpaste and left the cap off! I told her there would be consequences last time she violated that rule. I was straightening my hair at the time I realized her doo needed some styling. I took my straightener and grabbed a piece of her hair. Unfortunately for her I held it there a little too long. She started screaming at me because when I let go of her hair the bathroom filled with the stench of burning hair. She gave me a look of horror. I assured her that her hair had just been lightly singed.

The bathroom stunk so Sara took out an old bottle of perfume and started spraying it everywhere. The perfume only added to the stench in the bathroom. My mom walked by our bathroom, but promptly turned around and stood in the doorway. My sister and I hid the perfume and the straightener behind our backs and struggled ~~a guilty/innocent smile~~ to hide our guilt with an innocent smile. My mom rolled her eyes and walked off. ~~All I know is the~~ My law is the law. Sara will never leave the cap off my toothpaste ever again!

Avery's first draft includes some revisions.

Bathroom Law

One hair tie per day! Sara does not have to wear her hair in pigtails. She can use a towel to dry her hair! She doesn't need to use my hair dryer. She can also get her own toothpaste and stop leaving the top off mine! These are just a few of the bathroom rules that I took the liberty of laying down. When Sara does not comply with these rules, I "help" her do her hair.

~~She~~ Sara should not have used my toothpaste and left the cap off! I told her there would be consequences last time she violated that rule. I was straightening my hair at the time I realized her doo needed some styling. I took my straightener and grabbed a piece of her hair. Unfortunately for her I held it there a little too long. She started screaming at me because when I let go of her hair the room filled with the stench of burning hair. She gave me a look of horror. I assured her that her hair had just been lightly singed.

The bathroom stunk so Sara took out an old bottle of perfume and started spraying it everywhere. The perfume only added to the stench in the bathroom. My mom walked by our bathroom, but promptly turned around and stood in the doorway. My sister and I hid the perfume and the straightener behind our backs and struggled to hide our guilt with an innocent smile. My mom rolled her eyes and walked off. My law is the law. Sara will never leave the cap off my toothpaste ever again!

Nonfiction Writing From the Inside Out

GIVING CONSTRUCTIVE FEEDBACK: SOME QUESTIONS TO POSE

Share the following questions with students, so they can use them as guideposts when they give a classmate feedback on a plan. In addition to posing these questions, students might also ask questions that are specific to the topic of the piece. I've found it works best to write comments in pencil directly on a student plan—that way the student has them as a resource. I also model the process of giving feedback a few times before inviting students to peer-evaluate. The rule for teachers and peer evaluators alike is to be sensitive to writers' feelings.

- Does your title relate to your topic? Can you make it shorter and snappier, to catch a reader's attention more?

- Can you write one or two alternate leads, using a different lead technique for each one?

- Can you narrow your topic so that it focuses on one or two aspects of your subject?

- Do you need more details to support your topic sentence? Can you ask questions that help the reader think in terms of specific details?

- Can you find another supporting detail? The criteria called for four details, and I find three here.

- What other ideas can you leave the reader with in your conclusion?

- What would you want to think and feel at the end? What can you include to help readers have these same feelings?

TEACH YOUR STUDENTS THAT CONTENT DRIVES FORM

There are two points that I want to reiterate before examining essay writing in the second part of the chapter. The first is that while I'm teaching various kinds of paragraphs, I assure my students that as writers, they don't need to get hung up on paragraph "types." What they learn during our study will give them the structures to mix together as they build a piece, not unlike how architects may fuse a few different styles into their creations. You'll see this blending of elements with more clarity as you explore Part 2 of this chapter.

The second point is that woven into the paragraph work is a lot of essay reading— my students read essays with relish during independent reading and thus get a sense of how this genre works, which eases their journey from writing paragraphs to composing essays themselves.

CHAPTER FIVE

PART 2: THE HEART OF THE ESSAY

*Composing to Inform, Persuade,
Remember, and Analyze*

In Their Own Words

How do you get ideas for essays?

Anne Scott McLeod

For beginners, this is a first priority skill. They must decide what question about the topic interests them most, then choose details, observations, quotations, and research finds that apply to the question. Not everything that emerges in your research is necessarily usable. You might learn in your investigations that Queen Elizabeth I wore blue the day of the Armada, but you must leave it out of a discussion of her foreign policy.

David Quammen

I begin with a fact, an idea, a topic that seems important but is not necessarily interesting. Just as often, I begin with an odd kernel of information that might seem interesting, but isn't important. I keep researching—finding interconnected lines of fact— until I discover a crossing point where the "interesting" vector converges with the "important" vector. That becomes my essay's center point. I narrow the scope by leaving out every-thing, *everything*, except what is neces-sary to do justice to those two considera-tions: the interesting and the important.

Katherine Paterson

Most of what I write has required some research. Ideas for writing essays or speeches often come in the form of ques-tions I am asked or that I have asked myself. I start looking at the question from as many different angles as possible, trying to think of stories that illustrate the various points that seem important.

What advice do you have for students writing a memoir?

Homer Hickam, Jr.

Tell the truth but also tell a story. This admonishment seems often lost on memoir writers. It's your job as a writer always to tell a story even within the restriction of truth. A memoir should have a plot with a beginning, middle, and end. To make a story with a plot out of real life requires very careful judg-ment, choosing only those episodes in your life that keep the story on track.

INCLUDING AUTHORS' INSIGHTS IN INSTRUCTION

The essays I read in high school and college were formal, serious essays by Thoreau, Emerson, Montaigne, and William James, and occasionally a humorous essay by Mark Twain. My memory of these essays is that, with the exception of Twain, they were boring. I certainly never read an essay on my own. I was a fiction and poetry addict during those years.

I've changed over time—I now readily read essays and other nonfiction—and I'd say the essay has changed too. The essay has evolved into an informal genre (Oates, 2000). Written communication in general has become less formal than a generation ago.

Essays are as varied in their purposes as human conversation. They can inform, persuade, analyze; they can address global concerns or deeply private ones, or merge the two in the form of a personal essay, which often comments on public events or universally felt themes through the lens of ordinary life. Donald Murray noted in his conversation with me that the personal essay is a form of writing "in which the authority comes from the writer's experience, how he or she has reacted to what he or she has seen or felt." Murray's is a helpful definition, because it differentiates the personal essay from an essay that may have a personal point of view, but whose authority does not solely spring from within the writer. Katherine Paterson helps us further define the personal essay when she asserts that it addresses "some aspect of human experience" and requires no research.

The line between personal essay and a memoir has become fuzzy, in that both use an intimate, first-person voice. In his foreword to *The Best American Essays of the Century* (2000) Robert Atwan states: "As writers began amplifying the personal essay into what is now known singularly as 'the memoir' the processes of confession would know no limits." And so, Atwan and coeditor Joyce Carol Oates included in this collection of essays, memoirs by Maya Angelou, Vladimir Nabokov, and James Agee.

In the book's introduction, Joyce Carol Oates asserts that the essay is a genre that "has evolved into a form closely akin to prose fiction and prose poetry, employing dialogue, dramatic scenes, withheld information, suspense" (p. xxii). The lines between fiction and non-fiction elements blur with essays just as they do with many informational books.

What does this mean for you as a teacher? It's good news, because your students' natural inclination to include narrative elements in essays has been sanctioned by two contemporary literary authorities on the genre. In this section you'll also see how I use complete essays and parts of essays to deepen students' knowledge of this genre and hopefully interest them in reading and writing essays on their own.

You will also notice that I emphasize that it's what students want to say that determines the length of their essay. Yet students never tire of asking, "How long should it be?" This question highlights students' insecurities as they embark on an essay-writing journey. By the time students generate ideas and create a plan, the question usually does not surface again.

The essay looks at narrative experience critically—emphatically but evaluatively—putting experience in a larger context, trying on the patterns of meaning hidden within the experience.

— Donald Murray

It's independent reading time in my eighth-grade reading-writing workshop. Today the boys get first dibs on the pillows and bean bags. In less than five minutes everyone has found a comfortable space. Before I settle down to read *Slouching Towards Bethlehem* by Joan Didion, I walk the room to note what students are reading. Amylee is reading *Chicken Soup for the Pet Lover's Soul*. In her last reflective piece on reading, Amylee wrote: "I started the year reading girlie books. Books about dating and romance and that whole scene. If anyone told me then I'd be reading and loving this book, I would have said, You're crazy."

Near the door, crunched together on a huge pillow are Nick, Michael, and William sharing Bailey White's *Mama Makes Up Her Mind*. Laughter and chuckles emanate from the pillow. Avery looks up and warns the trio, "Remember, I get it next. You promised."

It's scenes like this that deepen my belief in the power of reading nonfiction genres such as essays aloud each day as well as having students study and analyze them. By showing students that essays are fascinating, funny, sad, and true, I piqued their curiosity to the point that several began reading essays on their own.

Essays, like informational texts, tell the truth. And I want students to know that writing about the truth is often just as—or even more—exciting than creating fiction. In his book *On Writing Well*, William Zinsser stresses this point:

> The longer I work on the craft of writing, the more I realize that there's nothing more interesting than the truth. What people do—and what people say—continues to take me by surprise with its wonderfulness, or its quirkiness, or its drama, or its humor, or its pain. Who could invent all the astonishing things that really happen? (page 89)

Writing Personal Essays and Short Memoirs

"In the essay, the writer sits on a bench beside the reader and comments on the life they share," says Donald Murray. Murray's bench image is a useful one for us to have in our heads as we turn now to teaching students to write personal essays.

Our first step is to look at the work of published writers. There is no better way to introduce a form of writing than to look at the work of those who have mastered it. The models you provide enable students to build their own mental model of an essay.

Here I'll take you through a lesson I present using an essay by Jean Brody. Before introducing this kind of lesson, consider what you want students to understand and discuss. I've included "call-outs" to show you some points I emphasize. You might focus on the kind of essay it is, such as persuasive, its purpose, its narrative elements, transition sentences, the lead, the ending, and the body or heart of the essay. You might spend two to three days on one essay or look at two to three essays in a week. How you proceed will depend on the background knowledge and essay-writing experience your students bring to class.

Use my sample lesson as a model to devise your own lessons. In addition to analyzing entire essays, students and I also look at parts in isolation—leads, endings, and the body. More and more, I transfer the analytical process from my shoulders to students'.

I continue these lessons until I notice that students can discuss structure and purpose with ease and confidence. Usually, someone pipes up with, "When are we gonna start writing our own?" When lots of "yeahs" echo through the room, that is often a signal that it's time to get them writing.

A MODEL LESSON

From "A French Cat" by Jean Brody in *Chicken Soup for the Pet Lover's Soul*:

> *The lead announces the topic and piques our interest so reader wants to continue.*
>
> Recently my husband Gene and I traveled throughout Europe. We rented a car as we always do and drove along the back roads, staying in quaint, out-of-the-way inns. The only thing that distracted me from the wonder of the trip was the terrible longing I felt for our cat, Perry. I always miss him when we travel, but this time, because we were gone for more than three weeks, my need to touch his soft fur and to hold him close became more and more

intense. With every cat we saw, the feeling deepened.

We were high in the mountains of France one morning, packing the car before resuming our trip, when an elderly couple walked up to the car parked next to ours. The woman was holding a large Siamese cat and speaking to him in French.

> The last sentence about the French woman holding the cat transitions to the author watching in the next paragraph.

I stood watching them, unable to turn away. My yearning for Perry must have been written all over my face. The woman glanced at me, turned to speak to her husband and then spoke to her cat. Suddenly she walked right to me and, without one word, held out her cat.

> In the last sentence the French woman holds out her cat. This is a smooth transition to the author taking the cat at the start of the paragraph that follows.

I immediately opened my arms to him. Cautious about the stranger holding him, he extended his claws, but only for a few seconds. Then he retracted them, settled into my embrace and began to purr. I buried my face in his soft fur while rocking him gently. Then, still wordless, I returned him to the woman.

> The author returns the cat in the last sentence. This transitions to her reaction in the first sentence of the next paragraph.

I smiled at them in thanks, and tears filled my eyes. The woman had sensed my need to hold her cat, the cat had sensed that he could trust me, and both, in one of the greatest gifts of kindness I have ever received, had acted upon their feelings.

> The phrase "had acted upon their feelings" prepares readers for the conclusion

It's comforting to know the language of cat lovers—and cats—is the same the world over (pages 270–271).

> In one sentence Brody invites us to think about the universal language of pet lovers everywhere.

Robb's Think-Aloud:

<u>Title</u>: It's short and makes the reader curious about French felines. I picture a cat with a beret.

<u>Introduction</u>: The first sentence is not a grabber. But the rest of the introduction works because I can connect to Brody's feelings about her cat. She appeals to readers' senses with "touch his soft fur."

<u>Body</u>: Includes information—mountains of France, woman holding a Siamese cat, extending and retracting claws. There are also narrative elements—the author's inner yearnings for her cat, events such as the woman walking up to Brody, Brody taking the cat, and so on. Brody expresses her opinion when she states that this was "one of the greatest gifts of kindness." The essay focuses on one event or memory—finding a cat to cuddle in France—which is one of the goals of a personal essay.

Notice that essayists are careful to craft sentences that transition readers from one paragraph to the next. Let's look at the last and first sentences of each paragraph [see call-outs at the end of paragraphs].

By pointing out that no words passed between the author and the French woman, Brody
encourages readers to accept the language of feelings.
<u>*Conclusion*</u>: *Now, Brody states her point—that love for animals can become a universal lan-*
guage—in one sentence. The abrupt conclusion is effective because Brody leaves us with the
thought she wants readers to ponder.

After you've modeled how you study and analyze an essay, turn the process over to your students. You can divide students into small groups and ask each group to become experts on either the lead, ending, purpose, narrative elements, transitions between paragraphs, or any other aspect, and present their findings to the class.

Actively involving groups creates a student energy for thinking and learning. Groups' success is another barometer for deciding whether students are ready to write their own personal essays.

PLANNING A PERSONAL ESSAY

Students in my classes plan their essays using the reproducible on the next page. Under each heading on the reproducible, students jot down specific details they plan to include. While drafting, students can organize these details into paragraphs. If students need more room to extend their brainstorming, they can use the back of the plan or a piece of composition paper.

The processes of brainstorming, elaborating ideas, and getting feedback on an essay plan are much the same as they are for writing a paragraph. You may then wish to reread pages 162–165. The more detailed the list of ideas the richer the writing plan, and in turn, the essay.

Emily's plans are so detailed that, as she puts it, "The writing was fun because I could focus on expressing ideas."

> Planning an Essay
>
> Name Emily   Date_____
>
> Title:
> Uh..... there's something coming out of the microwave
>
> Details to include in introduction.
> "Um, there's something coming out of the microwave. I think its smoking," said the lady to the younger cashier. "Oh my gosh! Its smoking!"
>
> Details to include in the body.
> - We (Hannah, Rebecca M. & me) go to Daily Grind every thursday before Dance.
> - R.M ordered a Raspberry scone & wanted it heated up & to go.
> - D.G. normally heats scones for 15 seconds.
> - the cashier put the scone in microwave for 15 minutes instead of 15 seconds.
> - Some lady saw smoke coming out of the microwave & told the cashier.
> - Cashier opened microwave & all this smoke bellowed out
> - It was hilarious
> - the Cashier pushed the scone out w/ her hand & scooted the scone out the back door w/ her foot.
> - There was a smell of burnt rubber lingering through the building so they opened the back & front doors.
>
> Details to include in the conclusion.
> All this happened just b/c R.M wanted a warmed up scone to go. To bad Hannah missed it.

Nonfiction Writing From the Inside Out

Planning an Essay

Name _____ Date _____

Title:

Introduction:

Body:

Conclusion:

Writing a Personal Essay or Memoir: More Teaching Points

After students have filled out a plan, I emphasize that for the personal essay or short memoir to be effective, all details should relate to a single purpose or idea. I often ask students to reread their plans with these questions in mind: What point do you want to make? What is the one idea you are exploring? Do all your details further this idea? I also highlight that the lead paragraph of a personal essay or memoir contains the point—or purpose. A writer can embed the point at the start, middle, or end of the opening paragraph. Here are two lead paragraphs:

From "Life Is Precious or It's Not" by Barbara Kingsolver in *Small Wonder:*

> "Columbine used to be one of my favorite flowers," my friend told me, and we both fell silent. We'd been talking about what she might plant on the steep bank at the foot of the woods above her house, but a single word cut us suddenly adrift from our focus on the uncomplicated life in which flowers could matter. I understood why she no longer had the heart to plant columbines. I feel that way, too, and at the same time I feel we ought to plant them everywhere, to make sure we remember. In our backyards, on the graves of the children lost, even on the graves of the children who murdered, whose parents must surely live with the deepest emotional pain it is possible to bear (pp. 180–181).

From "Blood, Tears, and Joy" by Sally, Grade 6:

> When I brought my first pair of pointe shoes home, I had no idea that the shiny, pink satin would cause bloody toes, twisted ankles, and long hours of painful work. Ever since I started my dancing career at age three, I have envied the older and more experienced girls who danced on their toes. My envy became anger that my dream had been crushed with tears and soiled point shoes. Yet from that anger and pain emerged intense joy.

A writer usually doesn't just baldly state the idea. In other words, Kingsolver didn't begin, "The tragic killing of students in Columbine has colored all our lives forever." Instead, she deftly touched upon three "shades" of this idea:

- the topic

- how she feels about the topic
- the aspect of the topic she wants to emphasize

Teaching students the art of announcing the topic interestingly but subtly and clearly is a gradual process. Let's face it, it's a talent one hones over a lifetime. The best advice I can give you is to continually expose students to memoirs and personal essays by reading them aloud, studying them, and adding to your classroom library short and long memoirs.

PERSONAL ESSAYS AND MEMOIR IN ACTION: GRADES SIX AND EIGHT

Near the end of the school year I invite sixth graders to write a personal essay or short memoir with narrative elements. During the planning stage, Katie asks if she could just jot a few notes, then write. "It's all here," she says pointing to her heart and head. Some students, like professional writers, are able to plan in their heads. This essay, about the death of her uncle, pours out of Katie. Sometimes that occurs when the topic has great significance to the writer.

> Uncle George By: Katie G.
> Intro.
> He was sick & staying at our house.
> His appearance was horrible. Raggy clothes that almost fell off his body, socks too big for his feet, a shirt practically drooping off of him—like a drop of rain about to fall from a leaf. He was my Uncle George. My Uncle George with Cancer. He had a deadly cancer that was ruining his life. 3 children, 2 parrots, 1 dog, & his wife, he was leaving them all. He was letting himself die. And I didn't understand it. I didn't understand it at all.
> My Aunt Kim had asked us if we would please take care of him because her kids couldn't stand to see him in the position he was in. So we promised to take good care of him, and do everything in our power that we could. What I didn't understand was why he was letting himself look like this? He can take care of himself. He was a grown man! Why couldn't he take care of himself?" He's being rude to us. But, I still loved him very much. Little did I know it wasn't in his power to change the position he was in." I was only about 8." I had my friend, Melissa over, and I remember walking past our family room and seeing him very skinny, shorts basically falling off, droopy shirt, & very big, dark circles under his eyes. I remember, after Melissa left, crying. I didn't want my friends seeing him. Then, I overheard my parents..."He's dying. He says lately he's felt very cold."My mother's voice was quivering"We should put a heater

Katie's first draft about her uncle. Note the powerful details, strong voice.

Uncle George

By: Katie G

He was sick and staying at our house. His appearance was horrible. Ragged clothes that almost fell off his body, socks too big for his feet, a shirt practically drooping off him – like a drop of rain about to fall from a leaf. He was my Uncle George. My Uncle George with cancer. He had a deadly cancer that was ruining his life. Three children, two parrots, one dog, and his wife: he was leaving them all. He was letting himself die. And I didn't understand it. I didn't understand it at all.

My Aunt Kim had asked us if we would please take care of him because her kids couldn't stand to see him in the position he was in. So, we promised to take good care of him, and do everything in our power that we could. What I didn't understand was why he was letting himself look like this. He can take care of _himself._ He was a grown man! Why couldn't he take care of himself?! He's being rude to us. But, I still loved him very much.

Little did I know, it wasn't in his power to change the position that he was in. I was only about six. I had my friend, Melissa, over and I remember walking past our family room and seeing him very skinny, shorts basically falling off, droopy skin, and very big, dark, circles under his eyes. I remember, after Melissa left, crying. I didn't want my friends seeing him.

Then, I overheard my parents talking… "He's dying. He says lately that he's felt very cold." My mother's voice was quivering. "We should put a heater in his room." My dad's voice was very steady and calm. I couldn't believe it! DYING?! This certainly changed my point of view. I loved my uncle. I didn't want him to die. I look back now and see how selfish I was being…not wanting my friends to see him.

Some nights I cry over my loss of him. My dad feels it even more. It was his **_brother._** I feel SOOOOO sorry for my dad!! That's why I try not to bring it up in front of him. I know that my dad has strong feelings because whenever he talks about Uncle George, his voice gets a little shaky. But, I have never seen my father cry.

Katie's final draft.

In contrast to Katie, eighth-grader Joanna always plans on paper. Though many students complete skimpy plans after required practice, Joanna continued to plan on paper. "It [the planning] keeps me from rambling and going off on other ideas," Joanna tells me in a conference. "It helps when I write and see the ideas. I might change the plan, but having ideas on paper makes the writing easier." For writers like Joanna, reading a plan is the catalyst that stirs thinking about the ideas, whether the purpose of her essay is to inform or persuade.

> The Affects of Snow
>
> Joanna-Marie
>
> Intro: - waking up listening to cancellations
> - extremely thankful in having no school -escaped doing my chapel talk
>
> Body: - always loved snow
> - whenever it snows I take full advantage of it   - shoveling
> - snowball fights   - no school
> - snowmen   - additional h.w.
> - sleding
> - big snow - forts
> - fun getting snowed in, get things accomplished
> - ski down driveway
> - snow angels
> - messages in snow
> Conclusion: -you should always take the oppurtunity

Joanna's plan for her essay on snow.

Nonfiction Writing From the Inside Out

"Powhatan School...CLOSED"

Joanna

Last Monday, as soon as I woke up, I rushed to turn on the radio. I anxiously listened to the school cancellations. As they were going though the endless list of public schools, I was hoping and praying that there would be no school today. As they were gearing towards the end of the list, I felt disappointed. Catching me by surprise, at the end of the list was, "Powhatan School, CLOSED." A wave of relief and joy came over me for I knew a day filled with winter activities and adventures awaited me.

I have loved snow ever since I was little. Therefore, I always take full advantage of it. As soon as I heard there was no school, my sister and I headed outside dressed in several layers of clothing. We had snowball fights, built snowmen, skied down the driveway, sled down all the hills, and built snow forts until we were numb from head to toe. My dog, Mario, loves the snow too. We brought him sledding with us. I created snow angels and wrote messages in the snow for my mom to see from her window, which is one of my favorite things to do. Getting snowed in to the point where you can not even get out of your driveway means I have an excuse to have a stay-at-home-day and curl up by the fireplace in my pajamas. There are a few downsides though, which I have experienced, like shoveling, swerving off the road, receiving additional homework, and not being able to get where you need to be. Over all though, snow goes down as a positive thing in my book.

This much snow only comes once a year, so I always take advantage of the opportunity to go outside and enjoy it. So bundle up and let your winter land adventures begin!

Joanna's final draft.

EMPHASIZE THE WEAVE OF WRITING

When students allow content to drive their writing, then, like professional writers, their essays weave information, opinion, narration, and description. While fourth-grader Meg and I discussed her essay on Morgan and Abby, her grandparents' dogs, she was able to show me where she used description and narration and included information. "I didn't think about the kind of paragraph I was doing," said Meg. "After I planned, I wrote. It worked out that it had different stuff." Meg's astute comment reflects the fact that the content, not a formula, drives writing.

Note that Meg started this piece on January 13, worked on alternate leads and revisions, and completed her final draft a month later. For students to write with voice and organized thoughts, teachers need to reserve enough class time so that students can receive feedback from a peer or teacher. Her planning included detailed brainstorming.

Morgan and Abby

Meg #10

Morgan and Abby are my ~~very~~ ~~loving~~ grandparents dogs. ~~They are the~~ ~~most~~ ~~beautiful~~ Golden Retrievers ~~I've ever~~ ~~seen~~. Their golden-brownish fur is like a ball of spun gold. Morgan is a ~~boy with~~ boy ~~and with~~ ~~a furry nice body~~. Abby is a girl, a bad girl. Well, they are both bad but when there outside and you yell "Morgan, Abby, Treats!" Morgan comes ~~with~~ but Abby dosen't. She goes waddiling over to an empty flower pot. She hides in it. It is so funny. If you try to get her out she'll just bite you!

On the day we went to get Morgan ~~and~~ Abby basicly the whole family went to get them. ~~Well~~ my grandparents, Uncle, Emily, Tess, Grace, Maggie, My ~~owns~~ mom and I all went to~~,~~ West Virginia. Romney. Once we got to the guys house here they came around the corner. In his backyard we played with all ~~seven~~ puppies for an hour. Since ~~their~~ ~~was~~ was such a bunch of us we had to take two cars. In our car we ~~took~~ Morgan. When we got back I was just completly in love with puppies. ~~them.~~ I wonder what Morgan and Abby will do next?

An early (above) and final (right) draft of Meg's piece.

Morgan and Abby

Meg #10

Whenever I walk up my grandparents flight of steps all thats going through my mind is what will Morgan and Abby do this time? Morgan and Abby are Golden Retrivers. Their golden-brownish fur is like a ball of spun gold. Morgan is a boy and Abby is a girl, a bad girl. Well, they are both bad. When they're outside and you yell "Morgan, Abby. Treats!" Morgan the pig comes but Abby dosen't. She goes waddling over to an empty flower pot and hides in it. It is so funny. If you try and pull her out she'll just bite you!

On the day we went to get Morgan and Abby my grandparents, Uncle, Emily, Tess, Grace, Maggie, my mom and I all went to Romney West Virginia. Once we got to the house here they came around the corner. In his backyard we played with all seven puppies for a whole hour. Since there was so a bunch of us going to get them we had to take two cars. In our car we took Morgan. When we got back I was just completley in love with the puppies. I wonder what Morgan and Abby will do next?

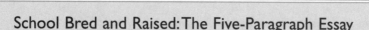

> ## School Bred and Raised: The Five-Paragraph Essay
>
> The five-paragraph essay is an example of a form that developed in schools and not among professional writers (Macrorie, 1985; Moffett, 1992; Murray, 1996). The essayists I interviewed agreed that the topic, content, and purpose of an essay determine its length (Murray, 2003; S. McLeod, 2003; Paterson, 2003; Quammen, 2003).
>
> Assigning a five-paragraph essay can limit the thinking on paper that students do and reduces the essay to a genre that lacks authenticity. If the number of paragraphs for an essay depends on the topic, then the number of paragraphs will vary when students choose their own topics.

The Persuasive Essay

To craft a convincing persuasive essay requires that the writer forms an opinion about a topic and then analyzes and evaluates her ideas. Analyzing ideas invites writers to consider the validity of each point. Evaluating means ranking ideas from least to most convincing, in order to determine one's line of argument.

In addition to collecting all the points and details that can support an opinion or position, it's important for the writer to understand all of the viewpoints the opposition might offer. Some essayists state a key argument of the opposition and explain its pitfalls, making their opinion more persuasive.

You can find examples for students to study in editorials and the op-ed (opposite the editorial) page of newspapers. I mine *Scope*, a Scholastic magazine for the middle grades, for persuasive pieces because these are on topics relevant to students. The essays reveal both sides of an argument but don't overtly take a position; that's for students to debate and decide. In fact, it's the invitation to join the debate that my students enjoy most about *Scope* opinion essays.

Most of these pieces comment on national and/or local issues. But for the purpose of giving you a model lesson on teaching persuasive essay writing, I've chosen one by Andy Rooney because of its humor and accessible topic for elementary students and teens. Though it doesn't exemplify how writers pick apart the arguments of the opposition, I use it with the idea I can show those examples later. In the beginning, it's easier for students to learn from a piece that, for the most part, presents arguments that support the author's opinion. Once students have developed their persuasive tactics, they can tackle topics by weaving in pro and con arguments.

From *Common Nonsense: Addressed to the Reading Public*, pages 200–201.

"To Each His Own—Bathroom" by Andy Rooney

If I had to choose between living with my family in a house with one bathroom and four bedrooms or a house with four bathrooms and one bedroom, I'd choose the one with four bathrooms.

Rooney prepares readers for his arguments for having his own bathroom.

It's not that I use a bathroom more than anyone else and need a lot of them, it's simply that a bathroom of your own is one of life's most civilized luxuries.

He brings in reasons that the opposition might make such as preparation for army life and traveling in other countries.

Four years in the Army gives anyone a lifelong appreciation of privacy and a bathroom of your own. The plumbing facilities in many foreign countries gives a traveling American reason enough to hurry home.

We had four children and one of the great things about having them grown now is that six of us no longer have to share the one upstairs bathroom in our house.

There are two bathrooms in our house and the one downstairs had a bathtub but no one wants to go downstairs to take a bath so the only person who ever bathed in that tub was Gifford, our white English bulldog.

Rooney adds humor to his opinion. The humor links readers' experiences to his.

We all like our own things in our bathroom. We don't want it all mixed in with everyone else's in the closet or medicine cabinet. It should be perfectly clear which toothbrush is mine. I even like my own tube of toothpaste. No one else squeezes it the same way.

Rooney offers additional reasons for having his own bathroom. He brings in the opposing points his children might make—that a towel on the rack is for anyone who uses the bathroom.

When the kids were home, I'd often wash my hands or take a shower and reach for my towel. At least half the time it was damp, good evidence that one of them had used it. I like my own towel, my own comb, my own glass, and I like to know where the aspirin and the Alka-Seltzer are so I can put my hand on either in the middle of the night without turning on the bathroom light.

When I'm feeling rich, I like to go into a good store and buy a couple of cakes of hard, milled soap or a cake of translucent glycerine soap like Pears. I like good soap. I'm generous with my worldly goods but I don't like sharing my expensive soap with someone who doesn't have the same respect for it that I do. Too many people leave soap in a pool of water.

The first thing I do when I go into the bathroom in the morning is turn on the radio. It's set to a station that carries nothing but news, weather and traffic. I want to know what to wear and I want to make my plans for getting to work. I have the dial set where I want it and I don't appreciate it when someone else has come in and put it on another station. Resetting the dial gets me off to a bad start.

> **Shows negative results of others fiddling with his radio.**

A man's bathroom ought to be his castle.

> **Closes with a familiar cliche that resonates with all of us.**

Robb's Think-Aloud:

Title: The title sets up the topic of having your own bathroom.

Lead: By juxtaposing two types of houses and creating the image of a family with four bathrooms all sleeping in one bedroom, Rooney states his position with humor.

Body: By focusing on his own experiences, Rooney makes this persuasive essay personal and captures the reader's understanding and sympathy. We've all experienced the frustration of searching for a misplaced toothbrush and toothpaste or stepping out of the shower only to discover that there isn't a dry towel on the rack.

He saves his most convincing argument for the last paragraph and points out that anyone who tampers with his radio is the cause of his bad start for that day. The reader can infer that Rooney's bad start affects everyone he interacts with that morning. Rooney explores multiple examples with humor—these connect us to the essay and the reader continually nods in agreement and chuckles throughout.

PERSUASIVE TECHNIQUES TO HIGHLIGHT

An important lesson for students to absorb before writing persuasive essays is that including statistics and quotes from respected people or organizations can greatly advance their argument. Also, make students aware that, in a persuasive essay, you raise the opposition's arguments and dismantle them or refute them, or concede them with a shrug. Point out how writers address main opposition points—even going so far as to include research data used by the other side, and getting a quote from an expert. Your study of persuasive essays by professional and student writers should encourage students to see the benefits of fleshing out both sides of an argument.

As you read on, you'll explore writing techniques to share with students—techniques that enhance persuasive-essay writing. Remember, these techniques emerge quite naturally once students have gathered the evidence for both sides of a position.

Below I've listed several techniques that students can use to craft a persuasive essay. Post them on chart paper and use them as the basis for mini-lessons. Use newspaper and magazine editorials, op-ed pieces, and editorials by former students as the models for these lessons. Have students work in small groups, reading various materials and searching for examples of the techniques.

- Start by stating your position. The position statement included in the lead of an essay can be expressed as a fact, a value, a consequence, a snippet of autobiography, or a policy.
  1. Factual statements point out that something is true or false.
     Example: "Though people fear bats and view them as evil creatures, bats are friends of the environment." —Matthew, Grade 5
  2. Value statements discuss whether something has worth or value.
     Example: "When teens choose their own school clothes instead of wearing a uniform, they can explore who they are and express their individuality." —Erica, Grade 8
  3. Consequence statements point out the results of decisions, actions, etc.
     Example: "Personal hardship, great expense, and troubled children are often the results of teen pregnancy." —Kayla, Grade 7
  4. Autobiographical statements derive from the writer's personal experiences.
     Example: "Taking an irritable, crying infant to a quiet restaurant can ruin the dinner for those seeking a peaceful and restful meal." —Sara, Grade 8
  5. Policy statements claim that something should or should not happen.
     Example: "It is time that every United States citizen had health care." —Douglas, Grade 6
- Include statistics to provide accurate data that support your position.
  Example: "Too many Americans die because they never seek health care. Why? More than 15 percent of Americans, or 44.6 million people, have no health insurance." —Ashley, Grade 8
- Make comparisons between how things are now and how things were in the past as they relate to your topic, clearly showing how the comparison supports your opinion.

Nonfiction Writing From the Inside Out

Example: "In the past, when men and women were driving their cars, they were unable to call for help. Today, with cell phones, the push of a button enables drivers to call for help if they are ill or in an accident." —Bobby, Grade 6

- Quote an expert and share what he or she has to say about your topic—as long as it supports your position. You can do this by quoting exact words or by paraphrasing. In either case, name the expert and the source.

  Example: "A recent news show came out with this statistic: 'By the time the average young adult reaches the age of twenty, they will have seen 4,000 virtual or real killings on television or video games.'"
  —Laura, Grade 8

- Add a prediction to convince readers. Forecast your arguments into the future and predict what might happen.

  Example: "When corporations have day care centers for their employees, moms and dads will be able to read to and play with their children during the workday." —Clint, Grade 7

- Bring in the opposition's points because when you include an opposing position, you have the opportunity to show how the main argument on the other side sounds good, but is really baloney. You strengthen your position when you know—and show you know—all the opposing arguments, and can show, point by point, why your side is better. Here are some words and phrases that can help you state opposing ideas:

even though	I will admit	I recognize that
I accept the fact	granted	

  Example: "Why do we have homework? Teachers say that it helps prepare you for the next class. But, most of us try to get it done as fast as we can so that we can chat on the phone or attend ballet class."
  —Dianna, Grade 8

WRITERS ON OPPOSING VIEWS

In order to be persuasive, it is generally necessary, yes, to have not just a knowledge but an almost visceral understanding of contrary viewpoints and attitudes. Righteous and blatantly tendentious writing is seldom either engaging or persuasive.
—David Quammen

I think writers need to know opposing views and take them into account. To much of this obviously becomes tedious, but not to recognize other views makes the writer look ignorant of the subject under discussion.
— Anne Scott McLeod

MORE TEACHING POINTS

Remind students to avoid the all-or-nothing pitfall. Tell them that when you use words such as *always, never, every, all,* or *none,* you are placing your ideas in frameworks that are tough to support.

Instead, choose words and phrases that won't box you into a corner:

almost	usually	maybe	perhaps	seldom
often	some	most	probably	rarely
overwhelming majority		nine times out of ten		

In addition, share these suggestions with your students:

- Be able to state your position to yourself, then make sure you state this in the lead paragraph or introduction.
- Open and end the body with your most convincing points.
- Address one or two main opposing arguments and offer support that makes each point support your opinion.

PLANNING A PERSUASIVE ESSAY

For student writers, the success of a persuasive essay lies in the thinking and planning. It's at this stage of writing that students formulate arguments to support their position and discover points the opposition will make.

Because thinking and talking are aspects of writing, it's beneficial to carve out time for pairs to explore topics and muster a list of pros and cons. Set aside two or three 15-minute time blocks for these conversations. Doing so will enable students to complete a planning sheet with ease and enthusiasm.

Planning an Essay

Name__Spencer_____Date_____

topic: water coolers should be set up by the playing fields for hydrating the student athletes and efficient practice time.

Title:
      Quench my thirst for coolers

Specific details to include:

pros — hydrate athletes and coaches with convenient coolers on the sidelines of fields
- efficient practices so kids won't take a long time at the distant water fountains
- kids will get water without waiting in a long line b/c there will be six coolers with water

cons — money $$
- kids spending too much time drinking and slacking off.
- transportation and how/where you fill up the water coolers.

(dialog)
Possible lead: For all the years that I have been in Powhatan's upper school athletics much time has been wasted and so many kids have been dehydrated because only one small, and distant water fountain was available to the sports field.

Ideas I want to leave the reader with in my concluding sentence:
- we should purchase these cheap, efficient coolers.
- Why did we not think of this before?
- maybe learn for the first time that by the time you are thirsty, you already dehydrated too.

Detailed plans enable Spencer to persuade others.

Nonfiction Writing From the Inside Ou

Based on my teaching experiences, the most successful middle-school persuasive essays deal with school issues, because students live with them and care about promoting change. Moreover, students can affect change by sharing their essays with the faculty and administration and, by lobbying, recognize the persuasive power of words.

Eighth-grader Spencer plans and drafts a persuasive essay on providing drinks for students during their sports period. In his plan, Spencer thinks through both the pros and cons of this issue.

A few weeks later, when I ask students to choose two pieces of writing in their folders to bring to final draft, Spencer explains why he wants to expand his essay: "I want to present more points and alternate solutions, then bring the issue to the faculty at a meeting." So in addition to developing his ideas in a longer essay, Spencer is also learning to move beyond complaining and use the democratic

---

① **Quench My Thirst for Coolers**
Spencer Burkholder

"Hey, Mr. Burke, do you think I could go get a drink?"

"Yeah, sure, but make sure you run there and run back; you've got three minutes. We lose all sorts of practice time because of this kind of stuff. I'll start timing you right now so start running or we'll all be running sprints."

Kids and coaches can both agree that up to ten minutes of practice time is lost because of water breaks to the distant fountain. When there is only one drink fountain that is 200 yards away from the field, what else can you expect? At Powhatan School there is an old drinking fountain that barely spits out the water after waiting about five seconds for it to even come out! Lines can build up to ten people easily. How are kids-like us- supposed to get back in two minutes when it takes that amount of time just to get to the front of the line?

I suggest that Powhatan purchase six coolers so that there may be three coolers for the two fields- three for the girls' field and three for the guys. In my diagram here, you can see that the coolers are conveniently located on the goal lines and on one side line. Many people question how the coolers would be transported and where the money would come from to buy the coolers. The coolers can either be filled up at the gym and then wheeled down to the sports fields or they can be filled up right at the field if a hose was run down to the bridge from Lee Hall. The captains could assign daily who has the responsibility of the water just as they do with the pennies, first aid kit and other sports equipment. However, it would be the responsibility of each student-athlete to bring his/her own water bottle so that paper cups wouldn't be wasted and litter our campus. As

---

② for the little money that we would need to purchase the coolers, an eighth grade bake sale could be held. If the students would be using the water then why not let them pay for it.

For practice efficiency the coaches could set out a certain time for water breaks, this would prevent kids from hanging around the coolers for a lot of practice opposed to practicing.

That's option number one. A second option would be to do what Hill does at their sports fields. At Hill there is a trapezoid shaped wooden stand that has water running through a hose inside of it and sprays out of the stand through metal spouts at about eight different spots. If we were to purchase these "water stands" then I would think that we would need only four of them. We could put one on each sideline of each field. My picture demonstrates what I'm talking about. I'm not trying to find Powhatan's every fault but why stop at the sports fields?

Our gym could also use coolers for basket ball season as well as for lower school sports. In the case that the lower school kids use the coolers, it would obviously be up to them to refill the coolers. In the gym, I think that it would be necessary for paper cups because the cups wouldn't be blown away by wind and the athletes could keep track of their cup- it's not the end of the world if someone loses their cup and get a new one. I know that coolers near the team benches would be a lot more convenient than our one water fountain out in the hall where the water isn't even cold. I really appreciated it when- at Wakefield – we played a basketball game and there was a water cooler near our bench. We lost both games but at least we weren't thirsty.

The Powhatan sports program will, without a doubt, benefit from the convenient coolers. Time will be used more efficiently because there would be six times as many coolers that are only a couple of paces away. Not only will there be more time to actually practice but we- the athletes- would give more of ourselves because our energy level would be greater and our intensity would greatly increase. I feel that a longer practice is a better practice and a hydrated athlete is a stronger athlete.

process to call the faculty's attention to a need he believes is important.

School issues can be personal and deal with relationships among students. Ciara, an eighth grader, tackles an issue that she and her girlfriends wrestle with: Do boys value girls' appearance more than their personality? "I want to help my friends value who they are more than what they look like," she tells me during a brief conference.

When you encourage students to write about their interests and passions, they write with strong voices that pro-

---

Planning an Essay

Name __Ciara_____ Date __March 4, 04___

Title: Appearance Overated

Specific details to include:

Can be- perdy & mean
    perdy & nice
    ugly & mean
    ugly & nice

Survey/talk to guys and see if they like appearance or personality better

Possible lead: (Start with a ratio)
1. 6/6 of (Give statistics)
2. 100% of
           a (girl) (to)
               (better)
All boys like the personality of girls more
(prefer)
Ideas I want to leave the reader with in my concluding sentence: than their appearence.
Girls { • should they do all they do?
  • should they care so much
Boys { • should they think differently

Overrating Appearance

Ciara

  After I surveyed six boys in Powhatan's eighth grade class, I wondered why girls worry about how boys will view their looks and clothes. Almost every eighth grade girl wakes up in the morning, styles her hair, applies make-up, and carefully chooses her look for that day. Would they continue this daily pampering and concern with appearance if they knew it might not make a difference?

  When six eighth grade boys were asked separately whether they preferred the personality or the appearance of a girl, each one said "personality" without hesitating. The guys said that if they were dating a girl who was extremely beautiful but had a dreadful personality, the relationship would end quickly.

  I believe that the eight grade boys should be applauded for their responses. I also recognize that not every male in the world prefers personality to appearance. But the girls in my class should heed the boys responses and focus on developing their unique personalities instead of dwelling on their physical appearance.

  I prefer to show my true self. I also believe that when the right person comes along, he'll like me for myself, not the fake made-up me others might prefer. The choice is up to my classmates. I hope they will base their decisions on the fact that eighth grade boys like what they see inside a girl.

Ciara's plan includes a survey she conducted of eighth-grade boys to make her opinion more convincing.

voke thinking and can convince readers to agree with their position.

  As you read about analytical essays in the next section, keep in mind that when students can choose the position they want to defend, they invest in the planning and writing of an essay that asks them to think about texts on paper.

Nonfiction Writing From the Inside Out

The Analytical Essay

With the support of their teachers, students can move from analytical and inferential discussions about literature to organizing their views into an essay. I find that students in grades 6 and up can analyze short stories in an essay far better than a longer, nonfiction text such as a biography. Moreover, by using the short story, students can read a selection at their independent reading level, so that groups within a class will analyze different short stories.

The analytical essay is similar to a persuasive essay in that the writer desires to convince the reader that his position is worthy. The difference is that the analytical essay examines some kind of text—the text may be a book, a body of work, a painting, a state of the union speech, and so on; the persuasive essay doesn't necessarily respond to a text or medium.

An analytical essay opens with an introduction that states the writer's position at the beginning or near the end of the introduction. This position statement is called the thesis. A body or supporting paragraphs prove the position the writer has taken. The number of supporting paragraphs depends on the guidelines students and teacher negotiate and is often influenced by how much the student has to say. In the conclusion, the writer needs to take the reader beyond the essay's thesis and extend thinking by adding a related idea or a new take on the thesis. The point is to keep the reader thinking about the essay.

The suggestions that follow can support your modeling and collaboration with students.

LITERATURE-BASED LESSONS: GENERAL GUIDELINES

Collaborate and Model: With students, plan and take notes for an analytical essay on a text with which you and students are familiar. Since students in one class are reading at different reading levels, I suggest you read a short story aloud for a common text. Provide students with a copy of the story. "On the Bridge" by Todd Strasser (1987) is a story I often read.

Offer Strategies for Creating a Thesis: With a thesis statement, students take a position about a character's actions, decisions, or motivations; or a situation or event in the story; or a theme. An effective thesis can be supported with two to four pieces of evidence, depending on the standards you and students establish. I model in a think-aloud how I create a thesis statement for "On the Bridge."

Robb's Think-Aloud:

> *I want my thesis to say something about Seth wanting to be considered cool and that that's why he chooses to follow Adam. But I also want my thesis to show that life experiences can change the importance of being cool and accepted by peers and also teach the importance of learning to think for yourself instead of following.*
>
> *Here's a stab at the thesis: Seth's experiences with Adam cause Seth to revise his definition of cool and the meaning of friendship.*

I explain to eighth graders that the thesis statement can open or close the introduction. In addition to the thesis, students must also include the title and author of the story in the introduction. Here's what they collaboratively compose:

> Todd Strasser, in his short story "On the Bridge," shows the struggles young teens experience when they make poor choices in order to be part of the in-group. In an effort to be tough and cool like Adam, Seth makes decisions that cause him to revise his definition of cool and of friendship.

Make Support Book-Specific: The next day, I discuss composing the supporting paragraphs, which should include the elements listed below. Depending on whether you have a short period or a block of time, you might want to complete this part over the course of two days.

- **General Statement**: a statement that introduces the point the paragraph will make.
- **Support From the Text**: Students collect specific details that prove the general statement. It is effective to quote phrases of text that emphasize your points.
- **Transition Sentence**: sets the reader up for the ideas in the next paragraph.
- **Connection to Thesis**: Students clearly show the relationship between the details and their thesis. Connections can be woven directly into the supporting details.

I wrote the opening general statement, and students completed the paragraph:

> Adam's bragging dazzles Seth and increases Seth's desire to act like Adam. Though underage and nervous, Seth follows Adam's instructions and illegally obtains cigarettes from a machine. The author describes Seth as "awestruck" because Adam makes out with girls who take Adam out. When Seth can't make a trucker blow his horn like Adam, Adam brags that he has "the right touch" because he was born that way. Seth wants to have a torn and

General statement

Evidence that supports the opening sentence.

bloody jacket like Adam so others will think he's tough. Though Seth is uncomfortable when Adam pretends to throw a rock at a car and flicks cigarette ashes onto the traffic below the bridge, Seth remains silent in an effort to appear cool.

Transition sentence; connection to thesis

General statement

Seth continues to be silent when three big guys confront the pair for hitting their car's front window with cigarette ashes. Seth is willing to take part of the blame because he did not believe in "squealing on his friends." Though Adam is responsible for flicking the ashes, he quickly blames Seth and watches as the boys bang Seth's face against the window and force Seth to lick off the ashes. Seth confronts Adam asking, "Why'd you point at me?" When Adam, now safe, starts bragging that he'll get those guys, Seth sees that being like Adam isn't so cool. On the way home, Seth looks at his denim jacket.

Evidence and connection to thesis

Transition sentence

Composing Effective Conclusions: On another day, reread the essay to show students how you can use the conclusion to go beyond the thesis.

Robb's Think-Aloud:

In the conclusion I want to use the denim jacket as a symbol of the changes in Seth and what Seth learned about Adam and coolness. Here are the points I would like you [eighth graders] to include: the jacket is a symbol of cool and means nothing because Seth throws it in a garbage can; Seth realizes Adam isn't cool.

I start the conclusion for students and invite them to complete it:

Now that Seth owns a torn and bloody jacket, a cool jacket, he no longer wants it. When Seth tosses the jacket into a garbage can, he also tosses in his wish to be like Adam. The smirk on Seth's face shows he knows that Adam isn't cool and Adam isn't his friend.

PLANNING AN ANALYTICAL ESSAY

Once students can use discussion to critically analyze literature by taking a position and finding support in the text for their viewpoints, they are ready to observe you plan and compose a short essay on a common text. Next, collaborate to plan and write one or more essays together. Students in grades 4 and 5 will need to write as a class several times. Middle school students might need to experience two or three collaborations before they write independently.

Students I work with agree that what enables them to successfully write an analytical essay is thinking about the thesis statement, gathering support, and completing a plan prior to drafting. William's comment illustrates students' attitudes toward receiving feedback before writing a critical essay: "When I get feedback from you or a friend on my plan, I can fix things before I write."

| Journal Work |
| So Far from the Bamboo Groove |

Meg

So Far From the Bamboo Groove, Yoko Watkins

Charecter's Name: Ko

Triats :	Proof from Book :
1. Protecter of Group	• finds food in garbage
	•steals corn
	• hides the knife on her
2. Pushy	• yells at little one
	•tells little one "It would be easier if you were dead
	• Tells little one to go through garbage
3. Smart	• Lies to farmer to get corn
	• hides the knife in a "cast"
	• makes a fake hurtful face when the searcher is feeling her cast so he went find the sword

Exploring ideas about Ko's character can give eighth-grader Meg ideas for analytical essays.

MORE TEACHING POINTS

Point out to students two things to avoid when writing an essay based on literature:

1. Avoid retelling the story. Be selective and choose details to support your thesis.
2. Avoid adding details that seem interesting but that don't support your thesis.

Here are some additional suggestions to share. Ask your students to reread their drafts to:

- check that the lead paragraph contains the position they will prove.
- make sure they have connected their ideas to the essay's thesis. This way the writers make their position more convincing.
- test that support includes specific details from the text.

ANALYTICAL ESSAYS IN ACTION: SIXTH GRADE

A group of sixth graders who read *The Pinballs* by Betsy Byars decided to write an essay that showed two changes in a character from the beginning to the end of the book. Below is Priyanka's plan. At first Priyanka had difficulty finding the change in the personality trait she observed in the beginning at the end. However, discussing traits with me enabled Priyanka to understand that some traits change and some don't; her essay needed to explore traits that changed. After our discussion, Priyanka completed her plan with assurance. In addition to the whole-class mini-lesson I present, I often have one-on-one dialogues with students who require these conversations to build a clearer understanding of the kind of thinking they need to do. On Priyanka's first draft, Cindy Potter, my teaching partner, poses questions for Priyanka to consider as she begins to revise her essay.

Students who have written analytical essays in grades six and seven, like Jeannette, find that the planning is easier. Jeannette's essay on Doris Lessing's short story "Through the Tunnel" reveals her depth of planning and well thought-out support (page 201).

Conversations, journal notes, teacher modeling, and student collaborations work in concert to support students as they write about their reading.

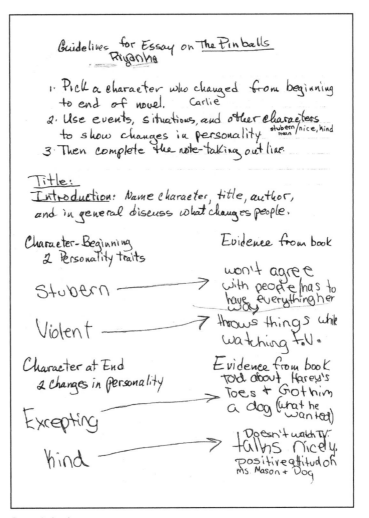

Priyanka's plan

People Can Change

"Bang!" Carlie missed. The lamp missed Harvey and hit the TV. In *be specific* the book, The Pinballs, by Betsy Byars, Carlie changes/a lot. The things that change people/vary in lots of different ways. In this case, some of the things that change Carlie are people and her surroundings. *friendship + surroundings*

How does this book show that people can change? what changes people? At the beginning of the book Carlie is very stubborn. She doesn't ② want to agree with anyone. She wants everything to go her way or no way at all. Carlie will not even think about accepting the suggestions or people that come her way. By the end of the book, she learns how to accept things and people. She gets along with Harvey and listens to what he has to say.

start it with proper name, not pronoun. ③ Another quality change she had was violent to kind and caring. In the book when Carlie watched TV, if anyone stepped in front of her she would throw what ever she could find like pillows or lamps. All she would do is ~~while watching TV.~~ watch TV. Its like she didn't even know that others where there. At the end of the book, Carlie is kind and caring. She stopped watching TV and started to help out. When Harvey's toes were swollen, she ~~stepped up to~~ tell Mrs. Mason. She did what ever was possible to make him feel better; she even *gives* got him a puppy.

Carlie changed from a rude and inconsiderate person to a nice and caring person. That just proves that people **CAN** change!

Priyanka's first draft with teacher feedback (above) and her final draft (right).

People Can Change

"Bang!" Carlie missed. The lamp missed Harvey and hit the TV. In the book, The Pinballs, by Betsy Byars, Carlie changes a lot. The things that change people vary in lots of different ways. Some of the things that make people change are usually their peers and their surroundings. In this book, that was the case.

At the beginning of the book Carlie is very stubborn. She doesn't want to agree with anyone. She wants everything to go her way or no way at all. Carlie will not even think about accepting the suggestions or people that come her way. By the end of the book, she learns how to accept things and people. She gets along with Harvey and listens to what he has to say.

Another quality change Carlie had was violent to kind and caring. In the book when she watched TV, if anyone stepped in front of her she would throw what ever she could find like pillows or lamps, ~~white watching TV.~~ Its like she didn't even know that others *were* where there. At the end of the book, Carlie is kind and caring. She stopped watching TV and started to help out. When Harvey's toes were swollen, she stepped up to tell Mrs. Mason. She did what ever was possible to make him feel better; she even gives him a puppy.

Carlie changed from a rude and inconsiderate person to a nice and caring person. Harvey helped her by listening to what she had to say and being her friend. Her reaction to that was to do just the same back to him. That just proves that people **CAN** change!

Notes for "Through the Tunnel"
TITLE: "Growing Up"
INTRODUCTION:
  TITLE: "Through the Tunnel"
  AUTHOR: Doris Lessing
  THESIS: Growing up involves proving your independence
    to your parents.
  TRANSITION:
    • relate (briefly) how Jerry grew up by proving himself
    • how he felt before and after
      ↳ Contrition → felt proud of himself for swimming through the tunnel.
      ↳ not so dependent on mother.

BODY:
  PROOF 1: Asked to go to the bay, proved he could be safe & happy alone.
    ↳ had to separate himself from contrition
        ↓
    Mother made him stay w/her → left w/out asking for permission.
      ↳ "wouldn't overdo it" she said
        ↳ he proved he could take care of himself.
      ↳ managed to swim through tunnel (she didn't know) → though stayed safe → proved to her.
  PROOF 2: Proved he could decide how to keep himself safe.
    ↳ "She was ready for a battle of the wills, but she gave in at once. It was no longer of the least importance to go to the bay"
    ↳ he realized he was tired – could make his own decision not to go.
    ↳ this shows independence.

CONCLUSION
  • thesis
    ↳ if one does not prove independence, may result in overprotection.
    ↳ in story, if Jerry had clung to mother w/out branching out on his own, his mother may have been tempted to become possessive & believe that she must rule his life.

Eighth-grader Jeanette uses detailed planning to compose her analytical essay on "Through the Tunnel" by Doris Lessing.

Growing Up

Growing up involves proving your independence to your parents. In the short story "Through the Tunnel" the protagonist, Jerry, must prove to his mother that he can function safely without her.

When Jerry first asked his mother to be able to swim in a deserted bay, she was apprehensive at first. Though she gave him her permission, she was not entirely satisfied with her decision and worried about her choice. Jerry proved he could be safe without her by swimming in the bay and returning safe and well. However, when Jerry's nose bled one night, his mother jumped to the decision that Jerry needed to be with her. She told him that he "shouldn't overdo it." The following day, Jerry left to go to the bay without permission. He returned fine again which helped his mother realize that Jerry could take care of himself.

Jerry also proved his independence by showing that he could make important decisions for himself. "After Jerry swam through the tunnel, he seemed tired. His mother advised him that he maybe should not swim any more. She had expected him to plead and try to convince her otherwise, but Jerry realized that he shouldn't swim. He agreed with her, which let his mother realize that he could make decisions on his own, and did not need to completely depend on her.

To grow up involves proving that you are ready to become independent of your parents. If this is not done, overprotection may result. If Jerry had not left to go to the bay, his mother may have continued to shield him from the world and Jerry would not have had a chance to naturally grow up and mature. Though it may often be difficult, one must always find a way to prove their independence.

Continue to Think About

Offer students many writing teachers by showing them the writing of professionals, peers, past students, and yourself. Help them view the essay as a highly personal and creative genre—a place where they can argue a point, celebrate an experience, explain how to do a task, persuade, record an event, or develop hypothesis and proceed to prove it. The essay is a satisfying form for students to experience writing as discovery of self, values, and ideas, for the essay explores students' experience, values, and beliefs. Donald Murray passionately makes this point in *Crafting a Life in Essay, Story, Poem*:

> As we place our life in significant contexts, as we create the legend or myth of our childhood, our schooling, our war, our profession, our marriage, we are changed. We become the product of our writing. As we find meaning in experience, we find ourselves (page 69).

Cindy Potter confers with an eighth grader.

Nonfiction Writing From the Inside Out

CHAPTER SIX

OTHER GENRES TO INVESTIGATE

Book Reviews, Interviews,
Biographies, and Diaries

In Their Own Words

ON WRITING BOOK REVIEWS
What do you see as the purposes of a book review?

Roger Sutton

Editor of *The Horn Book Magazine*

Reviewing isn't really about giving your opinion; opinions are easy. A book review is, first, news. The reviewer is telling his or her audience about a new book that might be—or should be—of interest. The reviewer has the responsibility to convey honestly what a book is about. Negative criticism can be strong, but it needs to be responsible as well—make your shots at the book, not the author, and not the genre or audience. The author is not the audience for the review, and woe betides the reviewer who forgets that.

Barbara Elleman

Author, Librarian, and
Former Editor of *Book Links*

The purpose of a book review is to give the reader information about the book under scrutiny and to analyze its strengths and weaknesses. Every point made should pertain in some way to the book itself. The review should not be a platform for the reviewer to expound on wayward theories and opinions. In the case of children's books, the review should take into consideration the wide variety of interests and abilities of child readers.

If you don't like a book, how do you go about reviewing it?

Barbara Elleman

First, I try to decide why I don't like a book: is it a personal or a literary objection? If it's a personal reason, I look for the book's strong points and concentrate on those to ensure my own prejudices aren't blemishing my criticism. When it is a literary objection, I try to redouble my objectivity, pinpointing specific concerns about plot, characters, writing style, illustrative matter, to be as clear as possible in my review. While my responsibility is to the reader of the review, I try hard to be fair, taking into consideration the author's hard work and the publisher's confidence in the book's worth.

Do you approach a book differently, depending on the genre?

Barbara Elleman

Yes, of course. In evaluating information books, the authenticity of material must be a consideration, whereas fluidity and turn of phrases are important in reviewing novels and poetry.

Roger Sutton

Whenever someone asks me about my "criteria" for a good book, I say that I don't have any. I don't think you can work from a checklist when reviewing. Each book generates its own criteria—as you read it, it tells you how to read it.

ON CONDUCTING AND WRITING INTERVIEWS
How would you define an interviewer's role in bringing out information for the audience?

Pat Cummings

Before interviewing a person, it's essential to understand the audience who will read the interview. That's why, before I interviewed the artists for my book, *Talking with Artists,* I chatted with sec-ond graders who suggested questions that I found surprising. Although I had developed my own questions, using elements of their questions enlivened the answers I received from the artists.

I knew from years of school visits that students who were interested in art wanted to read about the artists' techniques, sources of inspiration, and challenges. I framed questions that would reveal this information.

William Zinsser

Never go into an interview without doing whatever homework you can. If you are interviewing a town official, know his or her voting record. If it's an actress, know what plays or movies she has been in. You will be resented if you inquire about facts you could have learned in advance (*On Writing Well,* page 105).

What are the characteristics of a good interviewer?

Pat Cummings

You have to have a genuine interest in your subject and a clear objective for questioning a person. It's vital that you listen. Some of the most interesting information comes out when a thread is followed that was nowhere in your notes. I think you have to be sensitive to your subject's mood as well. It's important to put the people you interview at ease by treating their time as valuable, by being prepared, and by assuring them that they can review their interview before it is published. Be clear about how the interview will be used and make sure that you address any concerns the person has.

William Zinsser

When you get people talking, handle what they say as you would handle a valuable gift (*On Writing Well*, page 115).

ON WRITING DIARIES
Why keep a diary?

Hudson Talbott

Keeping a diary is a way of having a conversation with yourself. A diary is a way to understand our perceptions. By putting our perceptions and feeling into language we discipline ourselves to define and articulate them so we can interpret them for ourselves and others.

Marissa Moss

Diaries are a great outlet, allowing you to sort through experiences and understand them better. Whenever I'm upset, I've gotten the emotions outside of myself and onto paper where I can control them better. Writing in a diary also helps me clarify what I'm thinking. And then there's the pleasure of writing, of capturing memories so that they can be reread and relived later.

When writing historical diaries, how do you make the language sound authentic? Find that person's voice?

Marissa Moss

These are the tricky parts of writing historical journals. It can take a long time for me to find the right voice for a character. For example, I did three completely different versions of *Emma's Journal* searching for the right tone. While I'm writing a historical book, I only read material from that period, even for my own pleasure, so I can keep that language alive inside my head. In order to get all the details of daily life right, I research obsessively, taking notes on everything from foods of the time to the weather.

Nonfiction Writing From the Inside Out

Hudson Talbott

All of my characters, whether it's an Irish girl or a Masai shaman are ultimately reflections of some aspect of myself. The only authenticity I can count on is what I know to be true about myself. For example, I have no Irish ancestry nor had I ever been to Ireland when I was asked to do an Irish-themed story. But I knew the feeling that I had when I listened to the music of The Chieftains. I first seek the ground of authenticity within myself on which to stand and research and build my story.

ON THE CRAFT OF WRITING SHORT BIOGRAPHIES
How do you narrow the scope when writing about a person's life?

Kathleen Krull

Because my audience is young people, I ask myself what do they most need to know and remember about this famous person. I decide on one thing or maybe several things, and this gives me my focus on what to include (the information necessary to explain those crucial things) and what to leave out—everything else, even if it's really interesting.

Do you feel that narrative elements belong in biographies—conversations you recreate?

Kathleen Krull

I think that fiction and nonfiction are two different things and I would never try to make up or fictionalize something to go in a nonfiction piece. But I try to make biographies as dramatic as possible by using writing techniques such as putting facts into the most interesting order, asking rhetorical questions, shaping and sculpting information in unusual ways, varying the sentence structure and length, parenthetical asides, humor, irony, and other ways of twisting or spinning the facts without cheating and making things up.

What advice do you have for student biographers?

Kathleen Krull

After you've soaked up all your information, don't use it all. Being selective is the magic key. Use only the most savory, cream-of-the-crop stuff, plus facts that move your narrative along. Look for the arc, or shape of the person's life.

Including Authors' Insights in Instruction

Picture this scene: a group of students who are routinely saddled with writing traditional book reports, in a room with Roger Sutton, Barbara Elleman, and other book reviewers. A student asks, "What do you write for a living?" "Book reviews," they each answer. Jaws drop; stunned expressions cross every student's face. *Why would you ever want to do that?* they wonder to themselves, shuddering at the thought of a lifetime of churning out book reports.

In this chapter I explore strategies for enlivening our approach to book responses and three other genres—biography, interviews, and diaries—so that our students won't view them as merely school assignments, but as enjoyable avenues for connecting to people and ideas.

First, I'll show you how to move students from writing book reports to helping them know the ingredients of a fair-minded book review. I include mini-lessons that teach students to craft reviews in a manner that exercises their powers of comprehension and reflection.

Next, we'll look at conducting and writing interviews. Through interviewing, students gain skill in framing questions, listening, asking follow-up queries, and reading between the lines of what people say. Interviewing takes students outside themselves and invites them to learn from someone else. As one eighth grader commented, "After interviewing Mr. Seidner, I was able to understand how a young boy felt immigrating to the U.S.A. I always blew it off as nothing; immigrants were lucky to get into this country. But I learned that leaving your parents at fourteen, spending a week in the filthy hold of a ship, and working twelve-hour shifts in a shoe factory in New York stole his childhood."

Then I'll show you how students can use their interviews to write short biographies of classmates, friends, family members, or other adults. A short biography compels students to use the important skills of selecting and discerning, as they include only those details that advance their particular focus.

Finally, we'll look at diary writing, a genre that attunes students to their own thoughts and feelings. The lessons center on diary entries written by Marissa Moss, who researches an historical period, such as the Great Depression in America or ancient Rome, and then creates fact-based, fictionalized diaries of young people living during those times.

I've found that the more I'm able to define and articulate my personal point of view,
the broader and more universally understood my writing becomes.

— Hudson Talbott

I'm listening to a sixth grader read aloud her book report on Seymour Reit's *Behind Rebel Lines: The Incredible Story of Emma Edmonds, Civil War Spy.* The student is dressed up to look like a Union soldier—one of Edmonds's disguises—but despite the colorful costume, the student doesn't walk in the heroine's shoes, doesn't reveal any insights about the historical figure. After a few minutes of listening to a dry retelling of the book, her classmates grow restless and begin to shuffle their feet, look out the window, pass notes. This sixth grader has lost her audience.

Later that day, the sixth grader's teacher confessed to me that every student had handed in rehash-the-plot reports. "How can I change these lifeless retellings?" she asked.

"What do you want students to write about the books they've read?" I asked. She looked at me, a puzzled expression on her face. "I'm not quite sure," she said.

Book reports are a form of writing developed by teachers, but in the real world they don't exist. Perhaps when book reports first came into practice in schools they had an analytical thrust, but certainly that's gone now. In students' minds, report = retell. Yet, for all the book report's listlessness, teachers continue to assign it—like a habit that's tough to break.

In my early years of teaching I wondered how to move students away from retelling to evaluating books. I tried to do so by having them make mobiles, collages, and other creative projects, but these didn't show students how to analyze a book. Over time, as my own reading of nonfiction broadened, I figured out what to do: show students models of what I want. And so I began bringing in book reviews from the local paper as well as magazines such as *The Horn Book Magazine, School Library Journal, Instructor,* and *Booklist.* And just as we did with the other forms of nonfiction explored in this book, my students and I read the reviews with a writer's eye.

Directly and powerfully, the reviews do all of the following:

- demonstrate for students the genre's authenticity—presence in the world;
- show students what reviewers do—and generally do not—include in their reviews;
- introduce techniques for weaving informative details about the book with evaluative comments;

- provide examples of how to write honestly and critically while not attacking an author; and
- demonstrate that reviewers can have a speciality, such as children's books, or military history, but that collectively, book reviewers cover all kinds of writing—biography, memoir, autobiography, informational picture and chapter books, realistic and historical fiction, short story collections, fantasy, mystery, science fiction, poetry, and folk and fairy tales.

Writing Book Reviews: Introductory Lesson

Let's look closely, then, at a couple of published book reviews—one of a novel, the other of an informational chapter book. Why lead with a review of fiction? Because if your students are like mine, most of their book reviews will be of fiction rather than nonfiction. My students review biographies, informational chapter books and picture books, delve into topics that range from creeping spiders to exploring space, but fiction seems the most comfortable fit for them.

I will select teaching points appropriate for middle-grade and middle-school students from both reviews. I'll also share advice from Barbara Elleman on crafting reviews (see pages 215–216). You'll find these ideas in the guideline for writing book reviews for students in grades 4 and up (see pages 215–222).

MODEL BOOK REVIEW BY ROGER SUTTON

Roger Sutton's book review is from the May/June 2003 *Horn Book Magazine*. I give each student a copy of it, and also put it on an overhead transparency. I point out how Sutton threads in comments on the author's writing style, and evaluative comments on the use of plot and character development, with details about the story.

Together, students and I also notice that the review opens with a short summary of this utopian novel. It closes by helping readers infer that perhaps the author is considering a sequel, for she's left room open to do just that. I guide students to appreciate that Sutton's comments about the quality of writing are always well supported. In the call-outs, I highlight other teaching points.

Jeanne DuPrau *The City of Ember*

274 pp. Random 5/03 ISBN 0-375-82273-9 15.95

(Intermediate, Middle School)

Unlike the rundown dystopia of Lois Lowry's *Gathering Blue*, the darkness of Ember is essentially literal. Its people, by and large, are honorable and civilized; its governance is democratic if quasi-theocratic; its economy frugal but fair. But there is no natural light in Ember, and the blackouts of its antiquated electrical grid are coming more and more frequently: "running out of light bulbs, running out of power, running out of time—disaster was right around the corner." So thinks Doon, a curious twelve-year-old boy who, along with his spirited schoolmate Lina, determines to save the city. On a deliberately limited canvas, first-novelist DuPrau draws a picture of a closed society, all of its resources taken from vast but emptying storerooms, with no travel possible beyond the lights of the city. The writing and storytelling are agreeably spare and remarkably suspenseful, and rather than bogging down in explanations of how Ember came to be and how it functions, DuPrau allows the events of the story to convey the necessary information. There's a contrivance or two in keeping the narrative moving, but even the device of a hidden letter, complete with missing words, is used with such disarming forthrightness that readers will be eagerly deciphering it right alongside Doon and Lina. The two protagonists are good sorts, distinctively if not deeply etched, and fans (note: there will be many) will be pleased to know that while Doon and Lina's mission is triumphantly concluded, there's plenty of room for a sequel.

> The review states the book's problem, introduces the two who will try to solve it, and uses a quote.

> The reviewer points out that the author uses contrived devices, but gets away with it because it's done in convincingly.

> Connects the book to Lowry's utopian novel and provides general information.

> End of summary.

> Reviewer explains how the author uses plot to build suspense and explain details readers need.

> Sutton infers the fact that he enjoyed the book when he writes that there is room for a sequel.

MODEL BOOK REVIEW BY BETTY CARTER

I chose this review of an informational chapter book from the September/October, 2003 issue of *The Horn Book Magazine*. Freedman's book received a starred review, which indicates that all of the reviewers thought the book was outstanding. When I share it with students, I point out that the reviewer quotes from the book and discusses specific nonfiction features such as illustrations, statistics, Web sites, a list of Supreme Court cases, and an outline of some of the amendments to the Constitution. Carter's review reveals her delight in this book in the review's lead when she compares Freedman to a "gifted and practiced teacher."

Russell Freedman *In Defense of Liberty: The Story of America's Bill of Rights*
196 pp. Holiday 10/03 ISBN 0-8234-1585-6 24.95
(Intermediate, Middle School)

Like a gifted and practiced teacher, Freedman leads young readers through an explanation of the Bill of Rights. For each of the ten amendments, he outlines historical background that informed the original writing, provides an overview of controversial aspects, and discusses landmark cases. The tone of this literary lecture is friendly, as if Freedman were having real-time discussion with interested readers by sharing his thinking, answering anticipated questions ("can burning an American flag be a permissible exercise of free speech?"), citing quoted and statistical information, and appending several aids (a discussion of sources, pertinent Web sites, a chapter-by-chapter listing of Supreme Court cases and directions for accessing them, and an index) for readers to explore these ideas further. Numerous illustrations cover historical as well as contemporary issues, showing, for example, people of Japanese descent being transported to internment camps in 1942, Ernesto Miranda with his lawyer in 1966, and Charlton Heston brandishing a gun before the National Rifle Association in 2002. The book concludes with a brief outline of the Thirteenth, Fourteenth, and Fifteenth Amendments, added after the Civil War, to show that the national government would protect and guarantee individual liberties even when those rights were denied or restricted by the states. That the Constitution is a living document is evident in cited court reversals as well as the inclusion of contemporary cases, such as a 2002 ruling concerning mandatory drug testing in the schools.

> Carter explains that in addition to important information, Freedman also includes original writing and controversies.

> Here the reviewer lists additional information and nonfiction features found in the book.

> Carter addresses the tone and evaluates the style of the writing.

> Carter explains that Freedman connects the Constitution to issues middle-school readers struggle with today.

FOLLOW-UP LESSONS: CONTINUE TO LOOK AT REVIEWS

After you discuss one or two book reviews with the entire class, check out copies of *School Library Journal, The Horn Book Magazine,* and *Booklist* from your school or public library. Invite

The Last Burp of Mac McBerp
by Pam smallcomme
ISBN-1-58234-856-1

"The Surf and burp shop is right on schedule." These are the last words in The last burp of Mac McBerp. This ment that Mac is okay, and Liclo can still have The Surf and burp shop with Mac in the Bahamas.

Mac McBerp waunted to go to the burping contest in the Bahamas so he could look for a good spot for the Berp and Surf shop. But Mrs. Overbuddy the principal, wouldn't let him practice burping for the contest, so Mac travels to the Bahamas in an unusual way.

The author's imagination led to Mac being able to move objects with his burps. It was so funny, exciting, suspensful that I read it two time. A funny part was when Mac held in a burp so long that when he finaly got out into the teacher's parking lot and finaly let it rip it created a burp tornado.

I recomend this book to any one who likes a good funny book.

Artemis Fowl, The Eternity Code, Eoin Colfer
ISBN # 0-7868-1914 06

"Butler got that sinking feeling. The one you get when there are a dozen laser sights playing across your chest. Somehow Spiro had outmaneubered Artemis."
The Eternity Code is a well written fantasy book about a criminal mastermind named Artemis, who's only 13! He, along with his bodygaurd Butler, must steal back the elusive C-cube he built with fairy technology. If his magical comrades don't help him retrieve it, it will mean the end of both their worlds!
This was definitly a page turner because of all the wonderful characters, and the messes they get themselves into. There's a teenage criminal genius who wears Armani suits, and is the only person to ever outsmart "the people" (fairies). There's even a dwarf who unhinges his jaw and can eat through buildings! All the characters are lovable and quirky too. I love fantasy books because there aren't any rules to what the books should be about. When they're well written, fantasy stories make me want to believe what's in them. This book was full of surprises. I could never tell what was going to happen next because there was always a twist! One twist was the fact that, though fairies are usually thought of as tiny naked creatures that live under mushbooms, these fairies have neutrino guns, fireproof suits, and contacts that are actually hidden cameras! This book would probably be enjoyed most by anyone who likes things ranging from crime and computers, to creatures from the under world!

---

students to read reviews and discuss their basic elements. I also offer students book reviews by former students. By reading many reviews, students come to see the differences between a book report and a book review.

No More Dead Dogs
By: Gordon Korman

ISBN Number: 0-7868-1601-5

"Your pants didn't shrink, mommy…your butt got bigger." That came from the mouth of a four-year-old boy. Four-year-olds can usually get away with something like that…but what about a seventh grader?

Wallace Wallace is a seventh grade boy who wouldn't tell a lie if his life depended on it. He turns in a book report on a book called _Old Shep, My Pal._ He hated the book… so, naturally, he told the truth. His teacher gave him a detention and he had to watch the book that had gotten him a detention _PREFORMED ON STAGE._ He decides to change the lines…and soon, the play is turned into a roller-skating, rapping musical!! It's like he's a co-director. He gets off of detention, but quits football to continue 'work' on the play. But, unfortunately, someone keeps trying to destroy the play. Is it Wallace? Find out when you read this exciting fiction book by Gordon Korman!

This book was an ABSOLUTE page turner because you would want to find out who does what next. I would recommend this book to anyone who thinks if you see a book with a dog on the cover, "that dog is goin' down."

Book reviews by a fourth grader (upper left), by an eighth grader (left), and by a sixth grader (above).

Here are some observations my sixth- and eighth-grade students made after reading and discussing a dozen book reviews.

- It starts with a short summary.
- It tells the genre—fiction, biography, etc.
- It's like other writing—there are leads that grab and leads that are dull.
- There's opinion but it's backed up with stuff from the book.
- They discuss writing style and what about the writing makes the book successful or not. That would be tough for me to do.
- It's short, and some have the summary and evaluation in one paragraph.
- It doesn't tell the whole book and give the ending away.

These observations reveal that students can pinpoint what book reviewers do. However, when they write their own book reviews, most middle-grade and middle-school students have difficulty evaluating an author's writing style or commenting on the quality of literary elements. This is reasonable—many adults would struggle too. Students don't have the reading experience or life experience to review on par with Roger Sutton. Does this mean we shouldn't ask students to write book reviews? No, but we should guide them to review in an age-appropriate way, to draw their responses from what they do know. For example, in their reviews, students can comment on personal connections they made to characters, setting, and events. We can expect them to explain why they think a book bored or depressed them, and to use examples from the text to support their responses. When they have expertise with the book's topic, they can and should point out incorrect information. Students love writing reviews when you give them some boundaries. In fact, I tell my students directly that they do not have to evaluate writing style.

Five Building Blocks for Writing Book Reviews

I have broken the process of teaching students to write book reviews into five lesson clusters that I call "building blocks." Student reviewers in grades 4 and up benefit from a learning process that scaffolds the art of writing book reviews with a real immersion in the genre—sample reviews by professional writers, reading and thinking about the advice professionals have to share, and collaborating with a teacher.

I share published book reviews from magazines with students in grades 6 and up. For third, fourth, and fifth graders, I use reviews written by former students, as these are more accessible models for younger learners.

BUILDING BLOCK ONE:
COLLECT IDEAS FROM PROFESSIONAL REVIEWS

After you have read and analyzed professional writers' book reviews for three or four class periods, organize students into pairs or groups of four and give each group the same book review to read and discuss for 10 to 15 minutes. Ask students to discuss ideas for reviewing a book and jot these on notebook paper or in their journal. Then, collect students' input on a large sheet of chart paper. Here are some ideas I gathered from a sixth- and an eighth- grade class:

- Need a heading: These have title, author, ISBN, price, and age group.
- Tell the genre. That will help others find genres they enjoy reading.
- Have an interesting opening sentence.
- Quote from the book to make a point or show what you mean.
- Include a short summary so readers know what the book is about.
- Explain what makes the information interesting.
- Back up your points with examples from the book.
- Tell what you learned from reading it.

BUILDING BLOCK TWO:
CONSIDER BARBARA ELLEMAN'S ADVICE

During my interviews with authors, I asked noted author, librarian, and reviewer Barbara Elleman to e-mail me tips she would offer student book reviewers (see next page). Her ideas reinforce what students observed in the many book reviews they read and discussed. I have students discuss and comment on Elleman's points and compare her advice to their own experiences writing book reviews.

Most students have trouble with the third bullet Elleman shares, on the need for reviewers to assess the use of literary elements. Eighth-grader Erica commented to me: "Sure, I can say why I connected to the plot and characters, but I can't talk about literary elements the way they do in the reviews we read."

Barbara Elleman's Tips to Students for Writing Book Reviews

- Concentrate on summarizing the book in a few, short, meaningful sentences.
- Develop a good opening sentence and let your review flow from there.
- Focus your review on the major literary elements: plot, character, conflict, setting, theme, style, and so on.
- Center your comments on the main plot strand and major character to avoid a rambling review.
- Choose descriptive verbs to describe the book under review and use few adjectives.
- Review the book, not the author; avoid sarcasm and making remarks just to be funny; don't put anything in a review that you wouldn't say to the author's face.
- Write the review, edit the review, revise the review, and rewrite the review until you are satisfied that it is the very best you can do.

There's one additional issue I want students to wrestle with—an issue Elleman raises on page 204: taking care not to weave your personal objections to a book into the review. I tell students, "You are bound to read books you dislike." However, a review needs to go beyond emotions to providing specific reasons for those reactions, such as: there wasn't enough action, or the author didn't bring the topic to life. For example, Michael Renzi does this well in his review of Tolkien's *The Return of the King* (see right).

The Lord of the Rings: The Return of the King: Book 1
by: J.R.R. Tolkien
ISBN# = 0-618-26024-2

When I read The Lord of the Rings: The Return of the King: Book 1, a supposedly "famous" and "great" fantasy book, I was a bit disappointed, to tell you the truth. I did not really like it because it was not really my kind of book, and it was hard to understand. The whole plot of this story was about a place called middle earth where un-earthlike creatures live, such as orcs, hobbits and elves. In the story, a time of darkness has fallen and the story is about the battles among the different armies.

I did not think this book was a page turner because I thought it became pretty boring after the first couple pages. The whole book basically revolved around two of the main characters named Pippin and Merry going to different towns and talking to people. I thought this book was hard to understand. It was hard to understand because there were about four different scenarios that the book just kept switching back and forth through, and that would get really confusing when the story would be explaining a peak moment in a battle, and all of a sudden, they would be talking about people in towns conversing with their friends. I really did not like the style of writing in this story. The characters would always say words like "Lo", and "hither", and other midieval-like language that I could not understand, so it frustrated me. A good example of something the characters of the book would say in this kind of language is "And lo! The gate yonder opens ajar to reveal all that is hither." This was one of the main reasons I did not understand the book. Even though I did not enjoy reading this book very much, I think that anybody who likes midieval times or fantasy books would enjoy this story because this is considered to be one of the greatest fantasy books ever. Even though I did not like it, it was better then many other fantasy books I have read.

Michael's candid book review.

BUILDING BLOCK THREE
TEACH STUDENTS HOW TO SUMMARIZE

Summarizing a long text can be daunting for students because it requires them to select a few important details from a sea of thousands of details. Afraid of excluding a significant point, students will retell the whole narrative. Here's a strategy that scaffolds the summarizing process and reinforces students' understanding of narrative structure: SWBS or Somebody-Wanted-But-So (Macon, Bewell, & Vogt, 1991).

As these student samples show, this strategy provides a framework for taking notes and then drafting a summary. Let's look at how each section helps scaffold a student's ability to capture the essence of a story:

- Stating the "Somebody" compels students to identify the main character—the protagonist.

- Stating the "Wanted" helps students articulate the main problem(s) the main character faced—what that character wanted to solve.

- In stating the "But," students must consider the conflict—also thought of as the antagonistic forces that create conflict.

- In stating the "So," students must define how the

> Dancing in my Nuddy-pants
> cKat
>
> Title: Dancing in my Nuddy-Pants
> Author: Louise Rennison
>
> Somebody: Georgia Nicholson
> Wanted: She wanted to have a good boyfriend.
> But: There were two guys who wanted her, but she couldn't decide them
> So: Her rock-star boyfriend is going America and she can't go with him, So her and Dave (old boyfriend) are left alone.
>
> Summary:
>
> In the book Dancing in my Nuddy-Pants by Louise Rennison, Georgia Nicholson is faced with a hard decision. She really wanted a boyfriend, but she likes two guys, and they both liked her back. Her old boyfriend Dave the laugh never gave her up, but her new rock-star boyfriend is usually gone with his band. So when her boyfriend leaves for America, and Georgia and Dave are left alone, what will happen?

Eighth graders use SWBS to take notes.

> Lucy,   SWBS
>
> Somebody- Anna M. Pavlova
>
> Wanted- to dance; to dance for people to make them happy
>
> But - she got hurt, World War I, people were unhappy in general life, she was poor, she almost cared too much? - the people were her "children" she said
>
> So- she danced no matter what, she lied, NOTHING stopped her from dancing, she danced the day she died

problem was resolved— without giving away the ending of the story.

It's helpful to model how the SWBS strategy works using a common text you've read aloud or one students have read independently. You'll find that the points students select will differ, which is fine since a rich text will have many layers.

Summarizing Informational Texts, Biography, and Autobiography

To help students summarize nonfiction texts, my students and I have developed a strategy we call TFLC—*Topic*, Fascinating *Facts*, what you *Learned*, and how the information *Changed* your thinking. Under "Topic," students note the subject of the book. With Fascinating "Facts," students record one or two incredible things that relate to the topic. "Learned" invites students to jot down one to two new things they learned or understood better by reading the book. "Changed" asks students to consider any ways the book altered their thinking about the topic.

For biography and autobiography, some of my students found that SWBS was helpful. Eighth-grader Gordon observed, "But it won't get at why we read biographies. You want to learn what that person did and who helped them do it." So Gordon and some classmates developed SWSS which stands for Somebody-Wanted-Support-So. The two parts that change focus for this genre are "Wanted" which explains what the person wanted to do with her life. For "Support," students noted the people and events who greatly influenced and supported the person.

I encourage you to invite your students to develop an acronym that works for them. Doing so stretches their thinking, and gets them to apply their knowledge of a genre to the development of a scaffold for summarizing.

BUILDING BLOCK FOUR
MODEL AND COLLABORATE ON NOTE-TAKING

It's helpful to think aloud and model how you go about taking notes for a book review. Then have students help you compose one so that everyone understands the process. I often read aloud a one-page biography of Maya Angelou from *Women of Hope: African Americans Who Made a Difference* by Joyce Hansen (page 19). Here are the notes that I jot on chart paper using Somebody-Wanted-Support-So.

Nonfiction Writing From the Inside Out

Somebody	Wanted	Support	So
Maya Angelou	to make the world a better place	grandma believed in Maya	poet
		teacher introduced her to literature	journalist
			playwright
		son caused Maya to educate self	actress
			activist
		showed she could teach him	

Students use notes like the ones shown above to write a summary. Since the biography is one page, the students' summary, based on the details in Hansen's text, is short.

The next day I invite eighth graders to work in groups and jot down some notes for the second paragraph. Here's what I collect:

- Awful things happened to her—one so terrible she didn't talk for five years. She used adversity—being poor, abused, going to a segregated school—to change her life.
- Helped others—raised money for civil rights, studied dance, performed and wrote plays, won Pulitzer prize.
- Include quote at end: "All of my work is meant to say, you may encounter many defeats, but you must not be defeated."

Students Collaborate on a Review

On another day, I reread the one-page biography and invite students to compose the book review. Before we began composing, students read and discussed the "Book Review Guidelines" on page 221.

Collaborative Book Review, Grade 8

"She refused to be controlled by a society that defined her as inferior because she was black and female." These words, written by Joyce Hansen, show Maya Angelou's determination to make the world a better place for African Americans and all people. Angelou devoted her life to doing that. Her grandmother recognized Maya's talents as did a teacher who introduced Maya to literature. At sixteen she had

> Short summary based on information in the one-page biography.

her own child. Teaching her son to read and having to answer questions that stumped her drove Maya to libraries and reading. Reading changed her life.

Angelou's story is an inspiration to never give up. Even though terrible things happened such as poverty, abuse that stopped her from talking for five years, and attending a segregated school, Maya Angelou worked hard to "invent" a new self. Instead of becoming bitter because she was black and female, she dedicated her life to learning, dance, acting, reading, writing, and raising money for civil rights. We recommend this biography to everyone because it celebrates individuality and the fact that it's possible to turn life's negatives into positives. We think the author's use of quotes helped us know Angelou better. As Angelou said, "All of my work is meant to say, you may encounter many defeats, but you must not be defeated."

After I reread the notes and the collaborative book review, I invite students to discuss with their group how the guidelines supported their writing. Here are their observations:

- The summary was easy to write from the notes.
- Having possible ways to start the review helped.
- Knowing what we would include in the second paragraph before writing made it easy to write.
- Using quotes that make a point works well.

BUILDING BLOCK FIVE
DEVELOP GUIDELINES FOR STUDENTS

On page 221 are some guidelines to adapt to your needs. Give your students a copy of these guidelines to keep in their journals or writing folders. Review them with the class each time you invite students to write a book review.

Nonfiction Writing From the Inside Out

Book Review Guidelines

Length:
One handwritten page or three-fourths of a double-spaced typed page.

Heading:
- Write your name and the date at the top of the page.
- Skip a line and write the title, author, and ISBN number.
- Write a lead sentence that includes one or two of these elements:
  — a short quote from the book
  — a statement that gives the book a thumbs-up or a thumbs-down
  — a brief description of a character or an especially great part of the book.

Paragraph One:
Write a summary of your book and identify the genre: fantasy, science fiction, realistic or historical fiction, biography, autobiography, nonfiction chapter or picture book, poetry, photo essay, and so on.

Take notes before writing the summary, using the acronym that works best with the genre of your book.

Paragraph Two:
Here is where you inform readers about the strengths and weaknesses of your book. Support your points by providing specific examples from the book. From the list of prompts below, choose two to three review points to address in this paragraph.

Closing:
Explain why you would or would not recommend this book to others. Offer one or two reasons that made the book a great or boring read.

PROMPT IN MORE DETAIL

On the sample sheets for students on pages 223–224—for both nonfiction and fiction reviews—I've provided examples of further questions you might pose to students, especially those who need more prompting in order to elaborate. Adapt the sheet to your needs, and hand it out with the book review guidelines.

POST REVIEWS

Display students' book reviews on a bulletin board. Showcasing book reviews has a lot of teaching power—students see how peers express and support their opinions, gleaning ideas for their own writing and motivating them to read new books. Says Avery, "William's review made me check out *Labyrinth*. He said girls would like it even though it was about boys."

And Serge noted, "I would never have chosen *The Life and Death of Crazy Horse* on my own. But when Nathaniel wrote that he couldn't put it down and that the story made him angry and tearful, I checked it out."

Lessons on Writing Interviews

"Let's talk about interviewing," I tell my eighth graders. Nick pipes up with, "We do interviews in history and science all the time—why in English?" A chorus of "yeahs," from his classmates follows his lament.

"I'll let you know why tomorrow," I say, chuckling to myself as I use my time-honored tactic of delay—which always affords me time for reflection. I take my students' resistance to heart; I've learned that doing so improves my teaching. It's not that I always cave in to their pressure, but sometimes student resistance challenges me to present content in a new way. So the next morning I tell them that they are going to do interviews as a means of writing short biographies. They're receptive. They have just completed a study of biography and autobiography and enjoyed reading about people from Joan of Arc to the band Nirvana. Several students ask if they can write short biographies about friends. I tell them that's a great idea, but that before they choose their subject, we need to sharpen our interviewing skills as a class. In the sections that follow, I'll show you how I navigated them through this newly minted reading/writing unit, courtesy of ever-challenging Nick!

Prompts for Book Reviews About Nonfiction

Did you enjoy special nonfiction features?
Discuss information learned from sidebars and captions, unusual photographs, or excerpts from diaries, letters, and newspaper articles.

Was the writing interesting or boring? Was it tough for you to concentrate on the reading?
Did the author include stories that held your interest? Or was the book a list of facts? Can you select a story and explain how it kept your interest or helped you understand a concept?

What new understandings about history or the topic did you develop?
Discuss whether the book enlarged your knowledge of a topic, and be specific about what you did or did not learn. Did the author change the way you viewed the topic? Why or why not?

With biography or autobiography, how did you connect to and react to the life experiences of this person? What did you find fascinating about your subject's life and achievements?
Explain what this person did that changed the course of history or others' lives. Are there characteristics of this person you admire? Explain why. What decisions changed this person's life? How did other people affect his or her life?

Were the photos or illustrations effective?
Explain why these intrigued you. Did you learn information from them? Did you see things that you never saw before?

Prompts for Book Reviews About Fiction

Was the book a page-turner? Why or why not?
Describe how the events kept the pace of the book exciting and made you want to continue to read. Or describe why the character's problems and conflicts—and all that happened as he or she tried to solve them—held your interest.

Was it hard to concentrate on the story? Was it boring? Explain why.
Discuss that the story contained very little action—nothing much happened in each chapter. Perhaps the plot didn't make sense—events weren't connected or events were presented that did not have much to do with the character's problems. Did too many depressing things occur?

Did you connect to one character, event, or conflict? Explain why.

How was a character like you? Do you have the same feelings? Reactions? Worries? Problems? Hopes? Dreams? Have you lived through similar events? Did you react to the event the way the character in the book did? Explain.

What about this book or story made you enjoy or dislike the genre?

Think about what you expect from a specific genre. Did the book meet your expectations? Show how. For example, were the clues misleading enough so that the mystery held your interest until the end, when you finally discovered the murderer?

Were there surprises in the story that held your interest? Explain one.

Did the plot contain unexpected twists that you enjoyed? Did a character solve his problem in a different way from what you expected?

Did chapters end with cliff-hangers?

Did each chapter leave you wanting to find out immediately what would happen next? Give one example and explain why as a reader you like or dislike this structure.

Was the plot believable or unbelievable?

In all fictional genres, the plot has to be believable enough for readers to connect to what happens. Even science fiction must be, on some level, believable. Give two examples that show the plot was believable or two that show it was too far from reality.

What new understandings about life, people, or an historical period did you develop?

Think about what the author was trying to tell you about how people behave and react, or about parents, siblings, friends, teachers, or relatives. Did you learn what life for children, adults, rich, poor, or soldiers was like during a specific historical period?

Did you enjoy the fantasy and magic?

Can you describe an example of fantasy or magic that made the book exciting or a page-turner? Did the fantasy elements have some reality? Can you give an example of this?

BEFORE THE LESSONS: DISCOVER WHAT STUDENTS KNOW

The first step is to make sure your students grasp the fundamentals of interviewing, for whether engaging a best friend or the Queen of England, the interview won't go anywhere exciting unless students use certain techniques. To find out what they know about this art, ask your students: "What do you know about conducting interviews?" When I pose this question to my eighth graders, their responses shock me. "You just read off questions from index cards," was the general reply. So even if they've learned it before, you'll probably have to discuss with them some interviewing basics. Together explore such questions as: How do you decide on the focus of the interview? Is it important to know where you're headed? How do you help the person relax? How do you know what questions you will ask? What happens if you can't get all the words down as notes? What is an important job you have during the interview?

Once your students understand the process, they start developing the confidence and skills needed to conduct interviews. I find that setting aside 15 to 25 minutes of class time over three days helps students reflect on and absorb material. To stimulate thinking and conversation, I write the Interviewing Tips (see pages 226–227) on chart paper. While students work, I circulate around the room and listen to conversations, and discuss the three lessons (pages 225–226). You can shorten or lengthen the lessons that follow; your students' understanding of interviewing will determine the amount of time you need to invest.

Lesson 1: The First Day

Organize students into partners and ask them to discuss the questions on the chart. Have partners join another pair and share ideas. Reserve 4 to 5 minutes for students to fast-write in their journals everything they recall.

Lesson 2: The Second Day

Ask students to reread their fast-writes and clarify their ideas. Then ask partners or groups of four to create a list of important interviewing points.

SCOPE OUT INTERVIEWS

SCOPE, a Scholastic magazine for middle-school students, includes an interview with an author, musician, artist, or sports celebrity in every issue. Besides the interview, which is written in the traditional question/answer format, SCOPE also contains interviewing tips for teachers to share with students. To order, write to: Scholastic, 2931 East McCarty St., P.O. Box 3710, Jefferson City, MO 65102-3710

Lesson 3: The Third Day

Collect students' points on chart paper. Give each group one or two points to discuss. Groups choose a spokesperson to present the key points of their discussion to the class. Allow time for the listeners to clarify points and add ideas.

Here are the points that I gathered from groups of eighth graders and noted on chart paper. I've elaborated each point to help you build students' understandings. Display the charts on bulletin boards and classroom walls. These are terrific resources for students to consult.

Interviewing Tips

Know the topic and person. *Before you meet the person or call him or her on the phone, figure out the purpose of your interviewing. This will help you pose a series of questions that build on one another and don't jump all over the place. Detectives might call it "a line of questioning"—you're trying to uncover something in particular. For example, if a student decides she wants to interview a local politician, she might focus on studying the politician's record on civil rights issues and then ask questions pertaining to this. Or maybe the interviewer will focus on three issues—civil rights, capital punishment, and environmental protection. The point is, it's not reasonable to pose questions about a subject's entire career.*

Students need to know something about the person already, articulate what they hope to learn from the interview, and formulate questions that may provide insight into these things—all of which still leaves plenty of room for surprise discoveries. Tangents are a natural part of conversation, after all.

Put the person at ease. *Begin by asking the person warm-up questions about his or her interests and hobbies—sports, music, hiking, traveling. These "easy-to-answer" topics will get a relaxed conversation rolling, and can pave the way for asking—and answering—more difficult questions.*

Be a great listener. *Tune in to every word the person you're interviewing says. Listening carefully helps you cast fruitful follow-up questions.*

Ask follow-up questions. *Even expert interviewers will ask a question that doesn't elicit a sufficiently detailed response. An interviewer can rescue the question by promptly asking the question in a different way, or by asking the person to elaborate.*

Pause a moment before asking an unscripted question. *Impromptu follow-up questions can put wind in the sails of an interview that has suddenly stalled, but try to avoid posing questions that move the person far away from the topic; you might find it difficult to get your bearings again.*

Ask the person to repeat what she said. *If you're taking notes and fall behind, wait for the person to finish her thought, then ask her to repeat ideas. Explain why—that you want to get all the ideas down.*

Don't interrupt. *Interjecting a comment while the subject is talking can cause that person to forget key points. If a follow-up question pops into your mind while the person is speaking, jot it down on paper and pose it when she stops talking.*

Use a tape recorder. *Eliot Wigginton (1985) had his students use tape recorders for interviews. If this equipment is available to students, then offer the option of taping and transcribing.*

Be positive. *Take the time to respond to the person with enthusiasm. Show your appreciation for the person you're interviewing. It's also helpful to send the person a copy of the written interview.*

FURTHER LESSONS: THE ALL-CLASS INTERVIEW

When you provide students with one or more collaborative interview experiences at school, you can guide them through the planning phase, have the entire class experience and observe an interview in action, and debrief to learn from the process. Here is how I go about it with my eighth graders:

Select a Subject. First, I ask them to choose a person to interview. They decide to interview John Taylor, a new administrator at Powhatan. Partners in each section discuss possible topics, share these with peers, and then choose a focus, all of which takes about half an hour.

Morning Class's Topic: Intrigued by the fact that this tall, energetic man plays the bagpipes and coaches basketball, one class chose as its topic: To learn about Mr. Taylor's interests and why he enjoys them.

Afternoon Class's Topic: More interested in his background as a teacher and administrator, this eighth-grade class wants to know what events and people contributed to his decision to enter education.

Students in each class developed warm-up questions and prepared a set of questions related to their topic. All of them took notes.

Work in Two Groups: Before the interview, I divide the morning class and afternoon class into two groups:

- Group One asks warm-up and prepared questions.
- Group Two decides whether each question generates enough specific details from Mr. Taylor. If not, this group has to probe with follow-up questions.

This strategy permits all students to directly experience one aspect of the interview process and observe either asking prepared or follow-up questions. After Mr. Taylor departs, I ask students to reread their notes and write a summary of the high points. Completing this immediately

Rebecca B. - Interviewing

- ask questions about the topic under consideration
- Warm-up questions - get to know personally - creates comfort
- Avoid yes and no questions or if you do have one ask a good follow up question
- Be a good listener

Focus: Get to know Mr. Taylor's interests beyond education

- Did your childhood have any effect on your life today?
- Where and when were you born
- What are your hobbies
- Do you have any pets?
- When you were a kid, what did want to be when you grew up?
- What's your fav. vactioning spot?
- What do you like to do in your spare time? Why?
- Do you have a family? Tell us about them

Prepared questions for interviewing John Taylor.

after the interview guarantees that students remember what the shorthand notes meant. Rebecca's notes and summaries at right illustrate how much more in-depth summaries are compared to shorthand notes.

Next, I had groups of four debrief and consider two questions: What worked? How can we improve? Groups shared their ideas, which I noted on chart paper. Jeannette's notes celebrated the fact that students put John Taylor at ease. Though they had wanted to find out the story about his junior high school days he preferred not to tell, students respected Taylor's wishes and dropped that line of questioning.

In both sections, students agree that when Taylor spoke in generalities, such as "I enjoyed school for the most part" or "I did get in trouble and do pranks," the follow-up query encouraged him to be specific. For example, to illustrate the kinds of pranks, Taylor told the story of how he released a group of horses into a parade marching through town. "I regretted my action afterwards," he told students. "But it did seem like a great way to stir up more excitement. My punishment—apologizing to everyone—helped me see the results of my impulsivity."

> • What is your favorite childhood and adult memory? Explain why?
>
> Rebecca B. – Interview with Mr. Taylor
> 1) Where did you grow up? Eastern shores of Va. lived w/ grandparent, for 1 year, South hill Va., + Rocky river
> 2) What did you enjoy when you were growing up?
> • reading, Mrs. McBride instilled his love of reading in him
> • sports - football, basketball, track, b-ball in summer
> • outdoors -fishing, camping, w/ friends-still in contact w/some.
> 3) Did you ever get in trouble as a kid
> Yes. At Anually Harvest Festival Parade, he set horses free during parade, good idea till it happen. Had to apoligize to many, did get to go anywhere for a month, disappointed many w/ the stunt tough time, was shunned by some adults.

> 1) Where did you grow up? Mr. Taylor grew up on the Eastern shores of Virgina for a little while. Then he lived with his grandparents for about a year. He also lived in Rocky River, and South hill Virginia from age 12 thus his

> college graduation. Somethings he enjoyed when he was growing up were, reading, thanks to his neighbor Mrs. McBride who instilled his love for reading into him, playing sports such as football-he was the captain 1year, -basketball, track, and base ball in the summer. When we asked Mr. Taylor if he had ever gotten into any kind of trouble as a kid he said yes, and told us that at one of the Anual Harvest Festival Parade, he set free (2 tons worth of) horses during the parade. Mr. Taylor said he thought it was a good idea untill he let the horses go. His punishment was to apoligize to many people, he didn't go anywhere for a month, and he dissapointed many people so he was shunned by a couple of adults, which made him feel bad.

MAKING INFERENCES BASED ON THE INTERVIEW

Soon after the class interviews John Taylor, Cindy Potter asks students to reread their notes and summaries and draw some conclusions about John Taylor's personality. "I want them to interpret some of this material so they do that in their biographies," she tells me. Cindy and I also know that these inferences could help students decide the one or two points they want to convey about their person to readers.

Here are some of the inferences students made by reading between the lines of John Taylor's quotes:

- He's honest. He didn't withhold bad things he did.
- He got in trouble outside of school and in school. He wasn't Mr. Perfect and he let us see that.
- The few teachers that talked to him and helped him succeed in school influenced his choosing teaching, then administration.
- He has a great sense of humor. He can still laugh at his pranks even though he got in trouble.

- He loves playing bagpipes and plays in a group at parades and special dinners and celebrations. Music means a lot to him. He's not embarrassed to wear a kilt—he's proud of his Scottish heritage.
- He loves sports, but especially basketball. That's why he coaches it.

The class interview and daily Read Alouds pump students' enthusiasm for selecting a person to interview for writing a short biography. I ask students to choose a person they know well, so that it will be relatively easy for them to come up with an angle for the interview. I prompt them with questions such as: Are you intrigued by a hobby of theirs? Travels? Sports interest? Music? Job? A specific time in their life? Several students plan to take photographs of the person or ask for a photo for their piece. All agree that they want a time line at the end.

Writing Short Biographies: Craft Lessons and Think-Alouds

While students are thinking of a person to interview and then scheduling it, I give them a copy of Kathleen Krull's piece, "Advice for Young Writers." We discuss the first part, which addresses interviewing:

> Are you nosy? This is the key to writing a biography. Pick a person you'd love to know better—someone you really like. The more passion you have for your subject, the more energy you'll spend, and the better your biography will be. Make a list of nosy questions. If the person you pick is someone you know personally, conduct an interview. Take notes and listen carefully— you'll learn more than you could have imagined.

Next I use excerpts from Kathleen Krull's books (see page 238 for a list) to present lessons on writing short biographies; specifically, on writing lead paragraphs and closing paragraphs. We'll also discuss paragraphs from the middle of a biography that remind students to include, as Krull says, "only the most interesting stuff, plus the facts that get you from beginning to middle to end."

In this section, I share some of these lessons. You can print the excerpts you use on chart paper or create transparencies to use on an overhead projector. I like to present sample lead, ending, and middle from the same biography because I find students can better observe and understand the points I am making than if I were to pull from a few different books.

Although I provide you with one lesson for each writing technique, you will probably have to present several. When students can discuss what makes a lead or ending unique, and the kinds of details that move the biography forward, that's a sign they have absorbed the lessons.

The biography I use for the three lessons that follow is "Jackie Robinson" in *Lives of the Athletes* (pages 51–53). For modeling, I choose men and women my students know something about. When I think aloud, I start the analysis process, but leave room for students to notice points and share them.

LESSON ONE: The Lead Paragraph

It is difficult today to imagine the bombshell impact of August 28, 1945, the day John Roosevelt Robinson signed a contract with the Brooklyn Dodgers— the first black to play on a major-league team. As with much else in America at the time, organized baseball was reserved for whites—blacks were banned.

Robb's Think-Aloud

In this lead as in others I've read aloud, Krull sets the tone of this biography with words like bombshell *and* banned. *She also focuses us on the main issue of her short piece—how Robinson will deal with being the first black player in the majors where prejudice abounds.*

Summary of Eighth Grader's Observations

- She keeps it [the lead] short.
- It raises many questions, which we learned is a trait of an excellent lead.
- Here are some questions: Why did Robinson sign? How would he deal with the anger of whites? Why did the Dodgers decide to deal with prejudice?
- The questions drive us to continue reading.

LESSON TWO: Paragraphs With Terrific Details

To prepare Robinson for his new job in the major leagues, Rickey [the Dodgers' manager] and others acted out insulting scenes to demonstrate the hostility he would face and gave him a book about the life of Christ. They also asked him to take a three-year pledge of silence so he would keep his feelings about his treatment to himself . . . .

Once the three-year silent period was over, Robinson's fans admired him more than ever for saying what he thought, even talking back to players who taunted him. When he developed diabetes and lost the sight in one eye, people wrote to him, offering their own eyes for transplant.

Robb's Think-Aloud

Notice how these paragraphs contain only details that relate to the focus of the essay: that the sport, up to this point, had banned blacks from the game, and thus Robinson was breaking "the color barrier." Krull also offers tidbits that readers can enlarge by making inferences. For example, I infer that Ricky was a thoughtful man for preparing Robinson for the insults that would be hurled at him; the three years of silence suggests to me that Ricky was wise about human nature and race relations. He knew they would come to respect Robinson as a ballplayer, and then they would be more receptive of his opinions. Robinson's agreeing to the ban suggests that Robinson understood that candidly sharing his feelings could harm his position and chances for other African Americans to enter the majors. And I infer that the public loved Robinson and looked beyond the color of his skin with the detail that some fans offered him their very sight, their own eyes for transplant!

Summary of Eighth Graders' Observations

- The details move the story along. You start with the three-year ban, then she tells you what happened after the ban has been lifted.
- I think the part where we read that Rickey made Robinson role play shows us that Rickey wanted him [Robinson] to succeed. Rickey wanted him [Robinson] to know how bad it would be.
- Waiting three years was good. The fans loved Robinson. They even admired his answering back when he could. That wouldn't have happened if Robinson had answered back right away.

LESSON THREE: The Closing Paragraph

A year after his troubled oldest son died in a car crash, Robinson died at the age of fifty-three of a heart attack. At his funeral Reverend Jesse Jackson called Robinson more of a chess player than a ballplayer: "He was the black knight and he checkmated bigotry. . . . No grave can hold that body down because it belongs to the ages."

Robb's Think-Aloud

The biographies by Kathleen Krull that I've read to you, and the others you have shared, all use the closing paragraph to tell when the subject died and any interesting circumstances surrounding the person's death. In addition, here Krull also helps us see one of the main goals of Robinson's life when she quotes Jesse Jackson. She keeps us thinking about the legacy he left for all future generations because we will always have to fight bigotry.

Summary of Eighth Graders' Observations

- The first sentence makes you wonder if his son's death caused great anxiety and eventually a heart attack.
- The quote and metaphor to chess—to a knight—makes you know that he fought a tough battle to stop prejudice and hate but that he won. Like a chess player, he used his mind and his talents to checkmate people who don't like blacks.
- When Krull quotes Jackson—"he belongs to the ages" she causes us to think about what Robinson left people.
- I think belonging to the ages also means that we should remember Robinson because we will have to keep the fight going.

At the same time that I present these lessons, which deepen students' knowledge of Kathleen Krull as a writer, I share some of the tips she has prepared for students on biography writing (see reproducible, p. 235). I ask students to work in groups to discuss them, and to use them as they plan their own short biographies. (You'll find these and other tips on Krull's Web site, www.kathleenkrull.com.) I tell them that their biographies should be a maximum of three double-spaced typed pages, plus a time line of five or six key events in that person's life.

Here are some ideas that students generated, based on Krull's planning ideas:

Suggestions of What to Include in a Short Biography

- Note when and where the person was born.

Kathleen Krull's Tips for Writing Biographies

- Are you nosy? This is really the key. Start by picking a person you'd love to know better; the more passion you have for your subject, the more energy you'll spend and the better your biography will be.

- Make a list of nosy questions, and actually interview a favorite relative, neighbor, friend, or even teacher. Try not to be afraid or shy. Take notes and listen carefully—their answers will get your thoughts flowing, and they might tell more than you could have imagined.

- Look for juicy details to make your information come alive. What did they wear? What did they do in the middle of the night? How weird was their family life? What did they crave? While researching Beethoven, I found out one day that his favorite meal was macaroni and cheese, and this tidbit helped me focus on other concrete details.

- After you've soaked up all your information, don't use it all. Being selective is the magic key. Use only the most savory, cream-of-the-crop stuff, plus facts that move your narrative along. Look for the shape of the person's life. Aim for the most dramatic part and tell what led up to it. What traits enabled them to overcome what obstacles?

- Try tweaking your story by taking a point of view other then the standard third-person omniscient. You can use bystanders or the neighbors. You can divulge faults as well as redeeming qualities. Ask yourself, how would the person tell their story? How would one of their children? How would one of their teachers?

- I'm always trying to use combination of words and ways of telling the story that are unique to me. Some other clues to pithy writing include:
  - Think simple, clear, vivid and concise, and rethink cliches.
  - Stick to facts—interpret but do not make up facts or dialogue.
  - A sense of compassion helps—some lives are more tragic than comic.
  - Humor really helps—look for little ironies (unexpected twists and turns in a person's life).

- Collect something about the person's family and education.
- Look for juicy tidbits about that person.
- Find his or her quirks—what makes this person unique and interesting.
- Get more information than you need. Reread your notes and circle what you want to include.
- Find out who your subject admires and hangs out with in his or her spare time.
- Make a list of questions that will help you collect details.
- Discover things about your subject that others want to know. Collect lots of information about this stuff.
- Have a great lead.
- Decide which events your time line will present.

As a result of this pooling of ideas, several students think it would be neat to have two interview sessions. The first would be exploratory, discovering what's fascinating about that person. The second would occur after they have prepared questions based on their first interview. If you don't think it's feasible to have students conduct two interviews, have them choose some-

one they know fairly well so that it's more likely they will have sufficient information for their biographies.

Students work with a partner to fine-tune questions and to gather additional questions. The interviews occur outside of school and students have eight days to complete them. The planning and writing occur during class time where students can support one another as well as receive support from me or Cindy Potter. I reserve 40 minutes of a 90-minute block for planning, conferring, and writing three times a week. It takes students three weeks to a month to complete their interviews and a draft of their biographies. Though students

> David!
>
> I will interview Josh Mosser.
> Josh Mosser is a laid back school teacher that loves to teach.
>
> WARM UP Questions
>
> ① Where did you live as a child?
> ② Do you have a family? Tell me about them.
>
> Questions
> ① Did you get in trouble a lot? Give examples
> ② What is your favorite childhood memory?
> ③ How did you become a teacher/coach?
> ④ Do you have any hobbies? As a kid? What are they? How did you get started w/ them.
> ⑤ If you could describe yourself what would you say.
> ⑥ If you could go anywhere in the world, where would you go & why.
> ⑦ What other jobs do you see yourself doing? Why?
> ⑧ Why do you love teaching?
> ⑨ Where were you born?
> ⑩ What problems did you have growing up? Was that your biggest problem?
> ⑪ Is there anything that you've wished you'd never done? What?
> ⑫ Have you ever had a life changing event (if so, how'd your life change)
> ⑬ What was ur 1st impression of Jennifer? How'd you meet?

David's prepared interview questions

Nonfiction Writing From the Inside Out

Biography Plan

① Lead - grabs attention

② List some details for the middle juicy tidbits.

③ End

~~From failing heath class to becoming a college baseball coach,~~ ~~the~~ Josh Mosser is a

DOUBLE SPACE

[Lead] He failed heath class, met his wife in a bar, & crashed his dad's car. But that didn't keep Josh Mosser from becoming a great teacher & coach.

¶ Growing up in Allen Town, PA, Josh had a normal life with 2 ~~younger~~ brothers. Early on he got interested in video games & crossword puzzles because his grand parents played them. At age 10 he moved to Clouster, NJ. In his 5th grade year he decided to put a small assignment & then forgot about it. It turned out that the assignment was actually a big part of the grade & he failed the class. Josh's dad wasn't too pleased." After Clouster, the Mossers moved to Springfield VA at the end of 7th grade

---

Good, Bad, and Goofy Times

David   The Life of Josh Mosser

He failed health class, met his wife in a bar, and crashed his dad's car. But that didn't keep Josh Mosser from becoming a great teacher and coach. Growing up in Allentown, Pennsylvania, Josh had a normal life with two younger brothers. Early on, he became interested in video games and crossword puzzles because his grandparents played them. At age ten, he moved to Closter, New Jersey. In his fifth grade year, he decided to put off a small assignment in health class, and then forgot about it. It turned out that the assignment was actually a big part of the grade and he failed the class. Josh's dad wasn't too pleased.

After Closter, the Mossers moved to Springfield Virginia at the end of seventh grade until the end of high school. When Josh was 15, his parents decided to get a divorce. "This was one of the hardest things he had to deal with." He says. Another problem he had growing up was that he was a year younger that everyone else in his class.

When Josh went into high school, he won the Baseball state championship. He says, "That was the most memorable moment of my childhood."   Josh Mosser went to college at Mary Washington and after college he decided to be the baseball coach there. He planned to continue as a baseball coach until the night he met his future wife Jennifer. He was running a scouting camp at Episcopal High School when one of his friends called Josh. He was invited to a bar to celebrate another friend's birthday. He was a little late, and Jennifer had stayed late at the bar which is why they were both there. When they met,

they talked for one and a half hours. Josh says that his first impression of Jennifer was WOW!

Before meeting Jennifer, Josh had a job at a camp in Maine, but he decided to become a teacher to stay with her. The reason Mr. Mosser decided to become a teacher instead of a coach is because of the camp in Maine. He loved working with kids and decided, "That's what I wanted to do."

Powhatan School, in Boyce Virginia, hired Josh Mosser in 2000 as a fifth grade teacher. Now Josh Mosser is a eighth grade homeroom teacher, seventh grade science teacher, an advisor, and a fourth though eighth grade sports teacher. He lives with his wife Jennifer, and his dog Lucy in Winchester, Virginia, and plans to continue teaching.

---

think ahead about the focus of their interviews, I encourage them to gather more information than they need to ensure that they have collected many interesting stories and quotes.

I've included the interview questions, a plan, and the biography by David Strider. Notice the richness of detail in the interview. David creates a brief plan for his biography. "It helps me pick the details," he says. The plan reminds David to craft a lead that pulls the reader into his piece, to include juicy tidbits in the middle, and to end with two stories.

David opens his biography of his science teacher with great tidbits, but he also gives some background material to move the biography forward. He starts with several pages of interview notes, develops his focus, selects details, then composes a first draft.

Michael opens his biography of his best friend, Nick, with a quote that makes the reader wonder if there will be more about Nick's philosophy of life. His closing paragraph uses a unique metaphor that shows Nick's humanity and his capacity for change: "It is said that a person's life can be shown as a piece of glass. Well, if Nick's life was changed into a piece of glass, it would be a little jagged at the edges, but it would still make the strongest window around."

Krull-Inspired Titles

In each class I noted several students reflecting on Kathleen Krull's titles for her biographies. They decided to imitate Krull's use of a phrase above the person's name. These phrases were either a quote by that person or Krull's own words that captured an aspect of the person's character, behavior, life, or dreams. Once students shared their discovery with the class, every student started writing titles à la Krull. I included a few from eighth graders' biographies to demonstrate how effective these two-sided titles are.

"Blind Runner and Toilet Climber: Avery McIntosh"

"Life in a Picture Frame: The Biography of Rick Foster"

"Allyson Croce: Car Chaser and Candy Bar Thrower"

"Conquering the Odds: Jennifer Doerwaldt"

> **SHORT BIOGRAPHY COLLECTIONS BY KATHLEEN KRULL**
>
> Harcourt publishes all of these books.
>
> *Lives of Extraordinary Women* (2000)
>
> *Lives of the Artists* (1995)
>
> *Lives of the Athletes* (1997)
>
> *Lives of the Musicians* (1993)
>
> *Lives of the Presidents* (1998)
>
> *Lives of the Writers* (1994)

ILLUSTRATED AND ANNOTATED TIME LINES FOR BIOGRAPHIES

While students typed the final drafts of their biographies, they designed time lines that included five or six events in their subject's life.

First, students and I studied examples of illustrated and annotated time lines. Mikie Jones, our school librarian, helped me with this project by finding books with time lines for students to study. Besides dates and annotations, time lines contained photographs or illustrations. Students' own time lines reflected these discoveries.

Key Events In David Harrys Life.

Dylan used present-day photographs of his dad's face in a unique and humorous way.

Rosalynn designs a timeline for her friend Garland whose passion is dancing. On the timeline are illustrations of the different dance shoes Garland has owned.

As you read on, you'll explore other ways teachers use interviews to capture students' interest in issues as well as men and women of the past.

TALK SHOW INTERVIEWS

It's good to look beyond the notion of written biographies; some students can best show their understandings verbally and collaboratively. For exam-

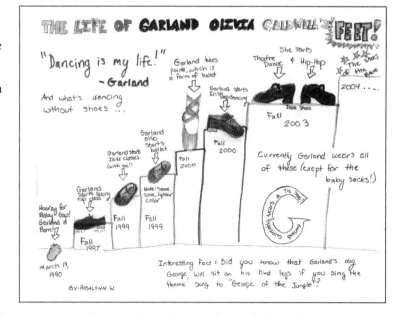

ple, Debbie Gustin, fourth-grade teacher at Powhatan, enlivens her teaching of the Civil War by having her students pair up to present researched-based talk-show simulations. Students read at least two biographies about a person who lived during the Civil War. They also collect additional information from the Internet. So instead of *writing* a biography, fourth graders pretend to be the person they researched and answer questions about their lives during an interview. Students work in pairs and alternate the roles of interviewer and the historical figure being interviewed. Partners plan their interviews together.

Ms. Gustin organizes pairs of students for their talk-show project by asking students to list their first three partner choices on scrap paper. Most students pair up with their first or second choice. Partners share their research through discussions, then work together to develop interview questions and responses. Students write questions and responses on 4 x 6 index cards.

① Interviewer

Hi! I'm Jim Simple interviewing Jubal Anderson Early. So, Jubal, how did it feel to surrender at the battle of Waynesboro?

② Jubal

First, I'm Genral Early to you! Second my defense of the Valley of Virginia in the Civil War postponed the Union Victory 6-9 months! Third and most importantly I NEVER SURRENDERED

③ Interviewer

O.K Mr., I mean Genral Early, did the end of the Civil War disappoint you most because your secession ideas failed?

④ Jubal

I was actually one who didn't wan't to seceed from the Union until the last moment, but I finally went with the Confederates.

⑤ Interviewer

Did the "Battle of Winchester, Virginia" have any significance to you?

⑥ Jubal

Yes they surley did. I didn't fight in the 1st or 2nd battles but the 3rd one I did. Richard Ewell and I fought the battle on September 19, 1864.

Ms. Gustin schedules four talk-show presentations each morning for a week at 8:30 A.M. so that parents who work can attend. Students write invitations and arrive dressed in costume. In the excerpt from the interview that follows, Nathan is Jim Simple, who interviews Jubal Anderson Early, researched and portrayed by Joseph.

Interviews Extend Learning in Social Studies: Grade 8

Interviews can support and enhance social studies curricula. At Powhatan, Dick Bell invites eighth graders to interview a person of color to enhance students' study of the civil rights movement. He shares the following guidelines with students, and discusses them with the class. "I also share notes and essays of students no longer at Powhatan, " Mr. Bell says, "so they [students] can clearly visualize and understand my expectations."

Recording information: In your journal, carefully record information received from the person you have interviewed. Make sure you have several direct quotes.

Synthesizing information: Discuss your notes with two third parties—a parent or caretaker, sibling, friend, or teacher. There will be time set aside for this during history. Have that person suggest what you may need to make your essay more thorough.

Focusing your paper: Concentrate on three aspects of your interviewee's story. Using that information, write a well-thought-out paragraph for each aspect.

Introducing and Ending: Develop an introduction and a conclusion that leave the reader thinking about the points you have made. Remember, an anecdote and direct quote create memorable beginnings and endings.

Length: No more than two-and-a-half double-spaced typed pages.

John Lathrop, head of Powhatan, also teaches history to eighth graders. An annual project students complete is to interview a person who experienced segregation. Mr. Lathrop works with area senior citizen groups to help students find someone. Like Dick Bell, Mr. Lathrop prefers eighth graders to compose an essay based on the interview.

Eighth-grader Erica interviewed Mr. James Tolbert to learn about segregation from a community leader who experienced it firsthand. Before reading her essay to the class, Erica noted: "Mr. Tolbert taught me how important it is to be socially responsible and use nonviolence to spread your message."

Each year I team with Dick Bell for a study of the Holocaust. Students in the eighth grade choose their interview topics, which range from questioning a Holocaust survivor to discovering adults' experiences with prejudice and stereotyping. Ali interviews her mother to discover if her mother ever experienced prejudice while growing up in the one Jewish household in a small West Virginia town.

As I trust these samples have shown, interviews are primary sources that can open a meaningful dialogue between students and adults—one that might never have occurred without the school assignment acting as the catalyst. Interviews hold the potential of bonding generations as students seek to learn about and gain insights into the past and

---

Ali   An Interview with Mary Recht

Ali: What is your name?

Mrs. Recht: Mary Ellen Recht

Ali: What is your profession?

Mrs. Recht: I am a wife, mother, and a teacher.

Ali: What are some of your intrests?

Mrs. Recht: I like reading, walking, historic and romantic comedy movies, gardening, and rose and formal gardens.

Ali: Did you ever experience prejudice? When? What happend?

Mrs. Recht: Yes, when I was in my first year of teaching in 1971, in a small cole mining town. The children and their parents had never seen or had a Jewish teacher befor. Several of the students parents felt that because I was Jewish I would not be able to do the Christmas play. The parents complained to the principal, but he convinced them otherwise, and I directed the play just fine.

Ali: How did this event make you feel? What did you do?

Mrs. Recht: I felt like I was truly diffrent from everyone, like a black person in an all white school. I felt like people were always watching me, and waiting for me to do somthing wrong. I felt very awkward, and alone.

Ali interviews her mother.

A Life Dedicated to Equality

Erica

"Fighting didn't help," was Mr. James Tolbert's initial reaction when asked about segregation. His struggle took place in Jefferson County, West Virginia where for about the last fifteen years he has been a leader of the NAACP. Mr. Tolbert's earliest childhood memories include segregation and discrimination.

As a young child, Mr. Tolbert remembers, "being pointed and laughed at by white kids." One time he was pushed too far and decided to fight back. It didn't get him anywhere though so he gave up fighting for nonviolence. Mr. Tolbert also remembers grocery stores where blacks were only let in one at a time.

In 1954, Mr. Tolbert joined the Air Force and traveled to Japan. While there he said, "he respected whites and whites respected him, but when he was disrespected he wouldn't back down." Mr. Tolbert stayed in Japan during the time schools were being desegregated and when he came home he expected schools to be desegregated. Much to his dismay, they weren't and Jefferson County was threatening to close public schools rather than integrate them. In 1966, Mr. Tolbert wrote to the governor of West Virginia and told him about Jefferson County's situation. After receiving the letter, the governor came to Jefferson County and told the school system that if

they didn't desegregate he would cut all funds from the state. Jefferson County integrated soon after that. More recently, Mr. Tolbert marched on Shepherdstown, West Virginia one Saturday morning against segregation.

Sadly, Mr. Tolbert notes that he still sees discrimination now in Jefferson County. " I could have been waiting in line with a white person behind me, and the white person would be waited on first," said Mr. Tolbert. Mr. Tolbert also mentioned that one of his black friends was threatened with a gun and called racial slurs for hunting where he was allowed to hunt. The white guy didn't believe his white friend would allow black people to hunt on his land.

Struggling to have racial equality has played a large role in James Tolbert's life. His first struggles included violence until he later used methods of Dr. Martin Luther King's nonviolence method to protest discrimination. Mr. Tolbert is still working today to change the country's racial discrimination and inequalities.

Erica transforms her interview into an essay.

Nonfiction Writing From the Inside Out

present experiences of family members and other adults. Diary writing moves students from understanding others to understanding themselves. It is a genre that allows students to relive and reflect upon past events in their lives.

Writing Diaries

The first time I asked sixth graders to complete several personal diary entries, the typical entry went like this:

> *Dear Diary,*
>
> *This weekend it rained. I went to the movies with Dawn. My dad picked us up and dropped Dawn off at her house. Then I went home and watched TV.*

This piece reminds me of Stephen R. Swinburne's first journal entry: "It was a very cold Monday and nothing really happened." No voice and only a few details.

Students' work expressed a need for mentors and models. One sixth grader confessed, "We thought it was an easy, not-much-to-write assignment." Now, before I invite students to write diary entries, we study a variety of texts written as diaries.

In the section that follows, I'll share a couple of model lessons so you can see how I help students write meaningful entries. Generally speaking, your aim is to share excerpts from diaries by professional writers—as Read Alouds and as passages you put on the overhead projector for discussion. You then invite groups to study other published diaries by former students.

Sharing a variety of models helps transform students' diary writing from general and ordinary to detailed and extraordinary, as these two examples show.

Diary Entry #2

Alexandra

Today I woke up, took a shower , got dressed and then I went to do chores around down with my mom. We went to the paint store to get some paint for my sisters bathroom. Then we went to Jo Ann Fabrics to get me some material for my curtains. Then my mom , my dad and me all meet at Cici's Pizza, it's my favorite place to eat. I just loved to be the only kid for the day! Then because tomorrow is my dad's birthday, he is turning 46, my dad's staff had a dessert party for him because he isn't going to work on his birthday or the rest of the week. (LUCKY!) Then we went to get Heather from school. After that we went home grabbed our purses and left. We then went to Party Supplies in the city. Then Calico Corners, while my mom was in there Heather and I jammed the music to Dave Mathews Band. Everyone was looking at us. Then we did the real shopping. We drove down the road to Dulles Town Center. We shopped around till 9:30pm. We went to a lot of stores! The for dinner ,at 9:30, we went to The Big Bowl. I had Veggie stir-fry and my mom had some kind of noodles and Heather had Rice and Chicken. Then we drove home and showed my dad our clothes.

Sixth and eighth graders wrote these diary entries over winter or spring break. I often invite them to compose three or four diary entries when school closes for vacation, as it keeps students in a writing state of mind.

DIARY-BASED LESSONS THAT WORK

Here is the framework for the two lessons that follow:

- Ahead of time, select several diary entries that appeal to you and that show various approaches at work.

For example, in the first model lesson I chose an excerpt from Anne Frank's diary because I wanted to show the reflective nature of diary writing.

For the second lesson, I chose a passage from *Rachel's Journal: The Story of a Pioneer Girl* by Marissa Moss.

This is a fictional journal based on extensive research. I've included Moss's work because her journals are superb models of this genre and include doodles, diagrams, and drawings that offer students a different take on diary writing.

- Put the excerpt on an overhead transparency and read it aloud to students.
- Display the questions on page 245 on chart paper.
- Think aloud your response.
- Using the questions to spark discussion, have students discuss with a partner what they observed from your think-aloud, and from their own reading of the passage.
- Share ideas as a class.

Nonfiction Writing From the Inside Out

Questions to Help Students Read Diaries With a Writer's Eye

- What was the topic?
- Was the topic developed with specific details?
- Did the author weave emotional reactions into the entry?
- What did the author do that connected you to the entry?
- Were there doodles, drawings, or photographs?
- Did the author use dialogue? Quotes?
- Did the entry contain an anecdote or brief story?
- Did the author pose questions? Were they all answered? Explain why.

LESSON ONE: Excerpt from *Anne Frank: The Diary of a Young Girl* (pages 124–125)

Saturday, 15 January, 1944

Dear Kitty,

There is no point in telling you every time the exact details of our rows and arguments. Let it suffice to tell you that we have divided up a great many things, such as butter and meat, and that we fry our own potatoes. For some time now, we've been eating whole-meal bread between meals as an extra, because by four o'clock in the afternoon we are longing for our supper so much that we hardly know how to control our rumbling tummies.

> Anne writes as if she is talking to her diary, which she's named Kitty.

Mummy's birthday is rapidly approaching. She got some extra sugar from Kraler, which made the Van Daans jealous as Mrs. Van Daan had not been favored in this way for her birthday. But what's the use of annoying each other with yet more unkind words, tears, and angry outbursts. You can be sure of one thing, Kitty, that we are even more fed up with them than ever! Mummy has expressed the wish—one which cannot come true just now—not to see the Van Daan's for a fortnight.

> Anne uses a brief anecdote to show emotions from jealousy to annoyance.

I keep asking myself whether one would have trouble in the long run, whoever one shared a house with. Or did we strike it extra unlucky? Are most people so selfish and stingy then? I think it's all to the good to have learned a bit about human beings, but now I think I've learned enough. The war goes on just the same, whether or not we choose to quarrel, or long for freedom and fresh air, and so we should try to make the best of

> Posing questions and answering them helps readers see Anne's struggle to understand the other family in their Secret Annex.

our stay here. Now I'm preaching, but I also believe that if I stay here for very long I shall grow into a dried-up old beanstalk. And I did so want to grow into a real young woman!

Yours, Anne

Robb's Think-Aloud

In the first two paragraphs, Anne uses minute details such as the Frank's frying their own potatoes and the short anecdote about Mrs. Van Daan's jealousy to show us how two families sharing close quarters struggle with day-to-day living. Anne deals with her emotions and the emotions of others in the annex. The questions Anne raises and her attempts to answer them in the third paragraph let us into her mind and her emotional state. She gives her concerns a positive spin by focusing what she has learned.

Summary of Eighth Grader's Observations

- It's like she's talking to me. I can hear her voice.
- She helped me see that being hungry all the time is tough.
- She tells us her fears of never growing up because she's in hiding.
- I feel her emotions from being hungry to worrying about the arguments.
- She doesn't just list stuff. She pours her heart out.

LESSON TWO: Excerpt from *Rachel's Journal: The Story of a Pioneer Girl* by Marissa Moss (unpaged journal)

July 5, 1850

Pa says we are not leaving the states, we are going to Opportunity. Besides, California will be a state someday, now that we have won the war with Mexico. Mother says not to count on that. But there is already a provisional American government in California, with a governor in charge, so I agree with Pa.

> Rachel retells what her Pa and Mother say. That helps us see the tension of different opinions and why Rachel sides with Pa.

July 7, 1850

I wanted to climb Chimney Rock when we came to it today, but passing between us and it was a large train of Sioux, moving their entire village. The chief and his daughter rode over to visit us. The girl looked like a princess, and we could see how proud the old chief was of her. Ben gave her biscuits and sugar (until Prudence glared icily at him). I wanted to give her something, too, something that would last, not be eaten and forgotten. I begged Mother to let me give her a small looking glass, and when I did, she gave me such a sunny smile, I see it still, hours later. She let me pet her pony and showed us the tricks she could do riding it. Even Frank fell in love with her. He offered her his treasured knife!! She took it, waved her hand, and was gone, like a rainbow vanishes after a shower. I did not climb Chimney Rock, but I will have wonderful dreams tonight, galloping on my own pony next to the princess.

> Simile helps readers imagine how quickly the princess was gone.

> Details of the Chief's and Ben's reactions to the princess let us know how special she is.

> Rachel makes the encounter personal and carries this personal connection to her dreams.

Robb's Think-Aloud

The details Rachel includes make readers feel as if they are with her. We also see Rachel as human when she begs her mother for permission to give the small mirror. We see Rachel's kindness and pleasure in meeting the princess. Rachel tells us her brother and sisters' reactions to the same event. In fact, with this one event we see Rachel's feelings, experience her excitement, and know the event's importance because Rachel will dream about it.

Summary of Fifth Grader's Observations

- One entry is short. But it says a lot about how they feel.
- She doesn't write every day.
- She tells what Pa and Mother say.
- She tells a story about what they did with the Indian princess.
- She tells her sister's reaction and that makes it real.
- I see her feelings for the princess. When she talks about dreaming, I know she doesn't want the meeting to end.
- The whole entry is about meeting the Indian princess. You can do that.

Invite Students to Study Diaries in Small Groups

After two or three think-aloud lessons, students work together to study excerpts from a variety of texts to deepen their understandings. You'll need several diaries for groups to browse through, read selections from, and discuss. I set aside about twenty minutes a day over two weeks. Some of my favorite titles are listed in the box on page 251.

Next, groups of students share with the class what they have observed from their reading. Based on their responses, I decide if they've learned enough to start diary writing, or whether I should continue to share models and think-alouds and guide group work.

MINI-LESSON

Examining Diaries and Journals

Purpose

To deepen students' understanding of what makes a terrific diary entry

Materials

Two to four diaries and journals by professional writers for each group of students (see the list of books I use on page 251).

Guidelines

1. Divide the books among the groups in your class. I like each group member to have a book, but you can also have pairs share a title.

2. Have each student browse through the book and read several entries.

3. Invite students to discuss what they noticed and collect their ideas on chart paper.

4. Display the chart; then before students write their own diary entries, reread their observations.

5. Repeat steps 2 and 3 until each group member has dipped into each one of their group's books. Here's what sixth graders noticed:

   - This one has lots of doodles and drawings. They make it real—that's what we do in our notebooks.

   - There's dialogue and quotes from others.

   - This one retells an adventure—it's like a story in a diary.

   - Mine has the person's feelings.

   - You can get angry and say why.

> **WHEN TEACHER READ-ALOUDS PARALLEL MINI-LESSONS**
>
> As students read and discuss diaries and journals by professional writers, read aloud a diary selection each day. As you read, think aloud, sharing your observations and reactions in order to model how you interact with the text.

Nonfiction Writing From the Inside Out

- The details make others see and feel like they were you.
- Sometimes they [the authors] develop one idea or one feeling and go on about it. That's what makes it more interesting.

6. Have groups exchange titles at least two times and share their observations. Students will notice different points, and your goal is to collect a treasure box loaded with ideas.

7. Ask students to share with classmates a short passage from a diary that touched them or made them want to read more. Hearing many examples read aloud will tune students' ears to this genre.

My students learned about the craft of writing diaries by reading like writers and sharing their understandings. The entries that follow have much to communicate. Students scrambled to share these with their groups. Reading them was not a chore for me; I never once thought about time or other tasks I had to complete because students completely connected me to their experiences.

On Another Day

1. Organize students into pairs or groups of four.

2. Make an overhead transparency of a student diary or journal entry. Use the work of a student no longer in your school.

3. Here is part of an entry I offer by Isabel, a sixth grader:

> April 24
>
> 4:30 in the morning. Everything is silent. The sun is not up yet, but I am. I change into my jodhpurs and turtleneck. Butterflies

The difference between a smart person and a wise person is that a smart person knows what to say and a wise person knows when to say it. —unknown

My bedroom, my Dad's house

Right now I am stressing out about my History interview. The person I was going to interview has been in the hospital and I haven't been able to interview them yet! We are supposed to write a twopage paper on what they said about the Great Depression and it's due Tuesday. Maybe I could call them on the phone and do it. It's going to be dissappointing to go back to school and everyday activities because the holidays have been so relaxed and worryfree. Oh well. I hope I don't forget my yearbook picture+quotes, but I don't see why we have to have them in so early. It seems as if they could at least wait until February or March. Maybe they have to check our quotes to be sure they're properly quoted. Or maybe, it's to make sure the pictures copy well. Anyway, I hope that nobody else has the same quotes I do. Later. % X

Found some!
98-99, 99-00, 96-97

This is the size of my last paper

History

This is my next paper

YEARBOOK!!!

This eighth grader's diary entry reflects Moss's influence.

form in my stomach, I am not hungry but I eat a banana for energy. Fox-hunting brings an adventure every time I go. The sun has risen and I go to get my pony, Izzy. She loves hunting and knows that is what we are going to do because I am up so early. The pony that usually runs away comes willingly to me.

This is when the day gets hectic. The sun is warming quickly and I have to get my hat, tie, and jacket into the truck and also get my boots on. Then I lead Izzy into the trailer. All this organizing has to be done quickly or else we will be late.

4. Invite partners or groups to use the prompts to help them analyze the diary entry.

5. Here are sixth graders' observations.

- She made us feel like we got up that early.
- She told us how she felt—butterflies in her stomach.
- She made it like a story, but it was true.
- It was neat to know all the things that had to be done.
- I wanted to read the rest.

When I asked why Isabel had made students want to hear more, Michael said, "She built up to the fox hunt, and you didn't include that part." Priyanka observed, "She got me with all the details, especially the opening in the dark and all." With sufficient modeling, students can write diary entries that enable readers to live through their experience and emotions with energy, capturing readers' interest. What a difference reading and discussing the diaries professional writers compose makes!

Nonfiction Writing From the Inside Out

Diaries and Journals to Share with Students

Anne Frank: The Diary of a Young Girl, Simon & Schuster, 1972.

The *Dear America* Series published by Scholastic

Galen: My Life in Imperial Rome by Marissa Moss, Harcourt, 2002.

Hannah's Journal : The Story of an Immigrant Girl by Marissa Moss, Harcourt, 2000.

I Thought My Soul Would Rise and Fly: The Diary of Patsy, a Freed Girl by Joyce Hansen, Scholastic, 1997.

Joshua's Westward Journal by Joan Anderson, Morrow, 1987.

The Journal of Ben Uchida: Citizen 13559 Mirror Lake Internment Camp by Barry Denenberg, Scholastic, 1999.

Max's Logbook by Marissa Moss, Scholastic Press, 2003.

My Year by Roald Dahl, illustrated by Quentin Blake, Viking, 1993.

Rachel's Journal: The Story of a Pioneer Girl by Marissa Moss, Harcourt, 1998.

Rose's Journal: The Story of a Girl in the Great Depression by Marissa Moss, Harcourt, 2001.

Safari Journal by Hudson Talbott, Harcourt, 2003.

Trapped by the Ice! Shackleton's Amazing Antarctic Adventure by Michael McCurdy, Walker, 1997.

The Winter of Red Snow: The Revolutionary War Diary of Abigail Jane Stewart by Kristina Gregory, Scholastic, 1996.

CONTINUE TO THINK ABOUT

The four nonfiction genres in this chapter are my students' favorites. They open possibilities for students to find topics they care about. Through diary writing, students can find their voices because they are writing about what they know and feel. If students review a book they adore or dislike, their voice and passions become bright writing beacons. Interviews and biographies encourage interactions with people students want to know better. Rebecca's words crystallize her peer's thoughts: "These genres come from things I love. So I want to work hard and make the writing sing."

That's why information gathered from direct experience or research can be transformed into a nonfiction literary genre, encouraging students to use their imaginations to make sense of history and their world. Taking facts and transforming them into creative nonfiction is an invitation for students to become alchemists, mixing in the same cauldron information, language, and imagination. Unlike the alchemist trying to create precious metals, our students can transform "just the facts" into writing that communicates meaning and emotion to others.

CHAPTER SEVEN

REVISING, EDITING, AND GRADING

Strategies for Improving and Evaluating Writing

In Their Own Words

What advice do you have for students on revising writing?

Donald Graves

Revision is happening just about every day. I keep changing and changing and the text gradually evolves into something. Sometimes it's an insertion of a brand new idea. Sometimes I want to look at my first five verbs. Are they active? Where is the beat of this piece? So I read from the standpoint of where is my voice the strongest. I try to find that and build on it. Sometimes I do a tight reading on adjectives and adverbs. Can I get rid of the adjective by changing the noun? Can I get rid of the adverb by changing the verb?

Kathryn Lasky

Each book sort of demands its own kind of revision. The shorter the book, the harder the revisions because every word has to count. Revision can be turning something inside out—taking on a new voice or point of view. Revision is tightening, kissing good-bye to something you think is great.

Stephen R. Swinburne

After I finish writing a book, I wait a week or so to let the writing cool. I then come back to the manuscript and reread for such things as spelling mistakes and awkward sentences. You can often see what you've written in a better light after being away from it for a while.

How do you test your essays/writing for clarity?

Anne Scott McLeod

I reread what I've written, and sometimes I corral someone else to read it. Mostly though I read it aloud. This won't always catch lack of clarity about ideas, since I am so familiar with my own thinking; this is where an outside reader is so helpful. But reading aloud does tell me how the sentences go, how the words sound aloud, whether I am repeating myself or being long-winded or, in my case a greater danger, too condensed.

Donald Murray

Doing three readings sounds like a triple assignment, but it actually is a time-saver. Trying to read for content, form, and language simultaneously causes the writer to do an unnecessary amount of scurrying back and forth. There is enormous waste of motion and a great deal of doing over. It is a time-saver to read three times, because the first two readings are relatively quick (for meaning and organization), and the time and care it takes for the third reading (reading for language) cannot be spent efficiently until the questions brought up in the first readings are answered (*Write to Learn*, page 169).

David Quammen

I reread them [essays] carefully with the reader in mind. With every sentence, every paragraph I write, I'm thinking about the reader, trying to imagine his or her responses, expectations, desires, possible confusions. What does the reader want? Is the reader bored at this point? Does the reader need a surprise, an informal remark, a joke, to refresh interest? Clarity is part of this. It's important for a writer to imagine, foresee, and then bypass any possible confusions that might come from what he has written. Misinterpretations are generally the writer's responsibility more than the reader's.

Including Authors' Insights in Instruction

Taped on the wall above Katherine Paterson's desk is an index card, on which she has written a Greek saying translated by Edith Hamilton.

BEFORE THE GATES OF EXCELLENCE

THE HIGH GODS HAVE PLACED SWEAT

(*Gates of Excellence*, page 3).

Paterson understands that excellence is earned. Like the professional writers quoted previously, she knows that revision is when real writing begins as writers prune and rearrange paragraphs, eliminate unnecessary phrases, clarify ideas, and make every word live up to their standards of excellence.

Student writers, however, find the exercise and sweat involved in revision and editing for conventions distasteful and unnecessary. Some of this resistance is kids-being-kids, resisting hard work, but some of it may be a reaction to a teacher's unrealistic expectations for revision. In this chapter, I show you an approach to this final phase of the writing process that I think is realistic for students and satisfying for them. In the course of describing it, I'll answer three questions that teachers often ask me as I coach them in schools:

1. How can I guide students' revision process?
2. How much editing for conventions should students do? How much should teachers do?
3. How do I grade students' work and give feedback that can help them become better writers?

As a first step in guiding revision, I encourage you to share the author quotes at the beginning of this chapter with your students, because they so clearly underscore that *everyone's* writing needs "a lot of tinkering" to be good.

> ## WILLIAM ZINSSER ON CLEAR WRITING
>
> The newly hatched sentence almost always has something wrong with it. It's not clear. It's not logical. It's verbose. It's clunky. It's pretentious. It's boring. It's full of clutter. It's full of cliches. It lacks rhythm. It can be read in several different ways. It doesn't lead out of the previous sentence . . . . The point is that clear writing is the result of a lot of tinkering (*On Writing Well*, pages 84–85).

Nonfiction Writing From the Inside Out

Writing's hard work and no one gets it right in one go.

— Anne Scott McLeod

L et's face it, students resist revision. As I said, some of this is because, developmentally, they're hardwired to move on, and some of it might be that they bristle at revision demands that are overzealous. Also there may be a fear factor: to them, a teacher asking for revision means their writing is awful, incorrect, in need of tons more work. Further, revising may stir up feelings that they are untalented or have nothing to say.

Revision and editing are delicate matters for even the most successful professional writers, and I think sometimes we teachers forget our students' fragility and the lasting effects of negative feedback. Shares writer Steven Kellogg: "Insensitive reactions to a student's efforts to express ideas, thoughts, and feelings on paper can undermine the self-confidence of young writers and cause them to withdraw from participating in a form of communication that they have learned to associate with harsh judgment and humiliation."

In the following letter to me from Rosalynn, an eighth grader, you can see just how easy it is to shake young writers' confidence, and how being given kind feedback is at the forefront of their minds:

> I suppose my advice to you would be to not critique my writing too harshly.
> Sometimes last year, I'd get discouraged when I'd get a story or poem back and
> there'd be a million red marks on it. (Robb, 2000)

Voicing positive comments to students is vital, for students can only build on what they are doing well. It's our responsibility to raise their awareness of what's working and what they can do (Calkins1986, 1994, Graves 1983, 2003). During our interview, Kathryn Lasky discussed memories of her student years and what she perceives an expert editor accomplishes:

> My memories of being edited as a young student were a lot of red pencil
> marks. Sometimes teachers wrote something in the margin like "silly," and
> that's not helpful.
>
> Editing should be a conversation between two people. If you want to
> engage in a conversation, you have to play fair and not use pejoratives. You
> have to ask questions because implicit in questions is choice.

PLAYING FAIR: USING WRITING CRITERIA

Establishing writing criteria can help eradicate vague or harsh feedback among students. Criteria—attributes a particular piece is expected to have—provide students with a common language for evaluating a piece. Unhelpful comments will fall by the wayside as students focus on helping one another write a strong title, or vary their sentence openings, or develop the voice, or achieve whatever else the criterion might be.

Criteria are a writing tool, a revision tool, and a grading tool all rolled into one. As Donald Graves points out, revision is happening just about every day. Thus, for students, it makes sense to give them guidelines from the get-go: Professional writers may find their way out of the murkiness of a rough draft to clarity without articulating criteria; for students, however, establishing criteria for a piece is enormously helpful in planning, writing, drafting, and editing. I like to think of criteria as one of those buoyed lines of rope holding a raft to the shore—they give students something to grab hold of as they swim into the deep waters of composition, providing them with a clear destination and clear markers for improving their writing. Following are a few solutions for common misunderstandings teachers often have concerning writing guidelines.

Make the list homegrown. To support students, teachers sometimes use premade rubrics which list the criteria for content, voice, style, organization, and writing conventions. This troubles me because premade grading standards might not adequately connect to what your students know or what they are learning in writing class. Writing criteria work best when they emerge from what students have absorbed and what they are learning and practicing.

I prefer involving students in the process by asking them to help me create content criteria (Boomer et al., 1992). I do the same collaborative process in creating editing criteria. I print the criteria we've agreed upon on a chart, and/or give students a copy to keep in their writing folders, so that they can have it as a reference. They often apply the criteria to their free-choice writing. Sure, you will have to help students adapt the criteria to other genres, but the payoff is that the process helps students become aware of the attributes that are common to good writing in any genre, as well as those that are genre-specific.

Keep revising for content and editing distinct. In some classrooms I've visited, teachers ask students to improve everything at once—asking them to revise and edit their entire piece. This is a daunting task that many professional writers wouldn't tackle. As one eighth grader told me, "When I know what I have to revise, I can do it. When the teacher just says 'revise,' I do nothing, because I don't know where to start."

Instead, I recommend negotiating a few simple criteria for content, a few for style and organization, and a few for writing conventions, then grading students on that basis (for more on editing, see pages 280–290; for more on grading, see pages 290–294). I usually combine the content and style criteria on one list; we develop a separate editing criteria list, building on skills students have practiced. We print our criteria on chart paper and add to the list throughout the year. I never ask students to edit for the entire list. Sometimes individuals choose two to four writing conventions. Other times, decisions students and I make emerge from mini-lessons and practice.

Avoid too much revision. I've also observed what I would call overuse of rubrics—teachers feel compelled to grade everything, and thus devise an elaborate rubric for each and every piece of writing students do. This is overwhelming for students and teachers alike. I have students rewrite only four to six long pieces during the school year. Revising every piece causes frustration and is an unrealistic goal, since the process can take up to four weeks, depending on the length of a piece.

NONFICTION GENRES: SOME CRITERIA TO CONSIDER

In this section I've listed criteria that can apply to a wide range of nonfiction genres. If you wish to articulate criteria that are genre-specific, such as criteria for paragraphs, essays, or writing a short biography, glance at the lessons on these genres in Chapters 5 and 6, and decide which attributes you want to include.

Use the information on pages 260–261 to establish guidelines for writing. Avoid overwhelming students with too many guidelines. For grades 4 to 6, include one to three items under each heading; for grades 7 and up, include two to four. You can also reflect on the sample criteria I have included in sidebars on pages 260 and 261.

Some Criteria to Use With Nonfiction Genres

Content

- The title is short and snappy.
- The lead paragraph or topic sentence grabs reader's attention and announces the topic.
- The topic, point, or purpose has been supported with specific details.
- Ideas are developed.
- The end leaves the reader pondering ideas.
- The purpose or point of the piece is clear.
- The topic has been narrowed and has a clear focus.
- A knowledge of the genre's structure is apparent.

Style and Organization

- The voice is strong.
- Sentences are varied.
- Verbs are strong.
- Nouns are specific.
- Dialogue and anecdote are effective.
- Changes in time are handled well.
- Ideas are in a logical order.
- Transitions between sentences are clear.
- Transitions between paragraphs are clear.

Writing Conventions: Mechanics and Usage

- Paragraphs have been marked.
- Sentences contain complete thoughts.
- Capitalization is used correctly.
- Correct punctuation (commas, apostrophes, semicolons, colons) make ideas clear.
- Correct spelling is appropriate for the student's development.
- English usage (agreement of subject and verb, pronouns and pronoun references, consistency of verb tense) is correct.

CRITERIA FOR FOURTH-GRADE BOOK REVIEW

Content

- The lead grabs attention.
- A short summary is included.
- Details from book support why you liked or disliked it.

Content & Style 70%

Style and Organization

- Sentence beginnings are varied.

Conventions

- Paragraphs are marked.
- Sentences are complete.

Writing conventions 30%

CRITERIA FOR SIXTH-GRADE HOW-TO PIECES

Content

- Title is short and catchy.
- The lead sentence states topic and grabs attention.
- Specific details are in logical order.
- Ending leaves reader thinking or laughing.

Content & Style 65%

Style and Organization

- Voice is active.
- Nouns are specific.

Conventions

- Paragraphs are marked.
- Commas set off introductory clauses.
- Sentences are complete.
- Capitalization is correct.

Writing conventions 35%

CRITERIA FOR EIGHTH-GRADE PERSUASIVE ESSAY

Content

- Title is short and catchy.
- Lead grabs attention and introduces position.
- Pros and cons are addressed.
- Essay includes statistics and/or experts' ideas or quotes.

Content & Style 70%

Style and Organization

- Voice is active and verbs are strong.
- Sentence openings are varied.
- Ideas are logically organized.

Conventions

- Paragraphs are marked.
- Commas separate compound sentences and follow introductory clauses, direct addresses, or adverbs at the start of a sentence.
- There are no run-on sentences.
- Pronoun references are correct.

Writing conventions 30%

HOW CRITERIA HELP TEACHERS

Specific criteria focus your lens for grading on the guidelines you and students have established. If I see loads of run-ons in students' writing and that was not a guideline, I don't take off for the run-ons. What I do is present mini-lessons that show students how to repair these (see pages 286–287). Then, they return to their papers and correct the run-ons. This is much more effective than your correcting all the errors on their papers. When students do the work, they are the ones who improve. I'll discuss using criteria for grading in more detail later in this chapter.

Criteria also arm me with specific ways to respond to students' writing at various points in their writing process. The sample sticky notes show my feedback on a first draft of a sixth grader's how-to piece and an eighth grader's persuasive essay. Notice that I comment on all that they are doing well, and then target areas that need improvement.

The feedback stage is crucial to students' progress. First, feedback arms students with specific suggestions for improving their piece. Second, if students struggle with revising from feedback, I know it's time for me to confer with them. For many teachers, however, the issue isn't just revision; it's selecting pieces to revise, an issue which we'll explore now.

- Your arguments for no homework on weekends are quite convincing.
- Using a student's quote in your lead and ending is effective.
- Excellent title.
- Can you reread and mark paragraphs – use ¶ symbol.
- Can you weave in 1 or 2 points that are against your position?

- You took the simple task of putting on a crew neck sweater and created clear steps.
- Strong verbs – stretch, slide, rummage – are effective
- Short anecdote makes a lead that grabs
- Can you add a conclusion?

My feedback on sixth grader's how-to piece.

Nonfiction Writing From the Inside Out

CHOOSING WHAT WRITING STUDENTS WILL REVISE

During a recent workshop I gave on revision, a seventh-grade teacher asked, "Who decides on what piece to revise? The teacher? The student? And how many pieces should students revise?" I hear questions like these often. They highlight an issue in middle and high school that teachers in self-contained classes don't usually experience. The amount of required writing increases in middle school. So a seventh-grade teacher might be required to teach students how to write three kinds of paragraphs, a personal and persuasive essay, a newspaper story, and a magazine article. Along with these escalated requirements, time for writing workshop has diminished in middle school. Writing daily and giving students their choice of genre are no longer options in a 45-minute English period.

In self-contained classes where writing workshop occurs daily or four times a week, there'll be times when students decide which piece to revise and times when the teacher and students confer to make this decision. The point to remember is that students cannot revise every piece and bring it to a publishable point. My strategy is to strike a balance between school-mandated writing requirements and the choices middle-grade and primary teachers can offer students.

The first piece of writing students complete in my class is a baseline piece (Graves 1983, 2004). The topic and genre are the students' choice. The piece remains in their folder as a sample to measure progress against. During the first two trimesters, I am teaching students how to write paragraphs, essays, short biographies, magazine articles, book reviews, and so on. In addition to letting students choose their topic, if they generate several paragraphs or two essays, I also allow them to select the one they want to revise. If they write one persuasive essay, then I might ask them all to revise that piece. Because writing book reviews occurs throughout the year, students can choose to revise one or two after they have written several.

The last twelve to fourteen weeks of school in my class is a writing workshop. Students generate several pieces, then choose two to revise and publish. If a chosen piece is long, then they may work on that one alone. Students and I find this time line satisfying because by March, they have internalized a broad range of writing genres to choose from, and they have learned a lot about craft. During this time mini-lessons on craft, revision, and editing continue. For students who have a tough time figuring out the criteria based on the genre they've chosen and the editing lists on charts, a short student-teacher conference can help them make choices.

REVISION: CLARIFY A COMPLEX PROCESS

To help you put into practice the revision ideas I've offered thus far, I think it's important to clarify significant moments in the revision process, and outline practices that support it.

- **Let the Writing Sit:** Before asking students to read a draft with an eye to revising it, follow Stephen R. Swinburne's advice: "Let the writing cool" for a few days or a week. The distance time offers can enable students to spot those clunky sentences and phrases they didn't notice while drafting.

- **Have Students Reread Their Notes:** Rereading and considering the notes taken while drafting can point writers to information they left out. It will also help them decide what details to add and where to add them. Encourage students to focus on meaning and what they are trying to say to readers.

- **Provide Feedback:** I offer feedback in addition to peer- and self-evaluation for at least half a year. Younger students will need more teacher feedback than those in grades 7 and up. This way, students experience the strategy of posing questions (see pages 267–269) to support revision.

- **Call for Self- and/or Peer-Evaluation:** Students study their early draft and measure it against content and style criteria. They can use questions you pose to support this process (see pages 267–271) and jot ideas on sticky notes, notebook paper, or on the revision reproducible on page 274.

- **Rewrite Parts:** Have students rewrite selected parts. You can read these and offer additional feedback on sticky notes. With large classes, this is more efficient than attempting to confer with everyone.

- **Confer:** You'll always need to identify those students who need more guidance. Have them sit by you to absorb a conversation and watch you respond to questions by showing them how you rewrite a lead or generate a list of alternate verbs.

- **Edit for Writing Conventions:** First, students read their piece to edit for one writing convention at a time—those conventions listed in the criteria. Next, a peer edits the piece. And finally—if the piece will be published—you edit the piece, as well.

- **Publish:** Students rewrite their piece incorporating the revisions and editing suggestions. Publishing can include displaying students' work on a class bulletin board or a bulletin board in the library or school office, or including the piece in a class or school literary magazine.

    As we continue, we'll look at three revisions strategies that I continually use.

Three Revision Strategies That Work

In this next section, I'll share three revision strategies that all serve to support young writers' craft—and confidence—as they plan, draft, and revise.

1. Build on Students' Strengths
2. Pose Questions
3. Encourage Independence

1. BUILD ON STUDENTS' STRENGTHS

Comments such as "A+, Beautiful" or "C, You Need to Work Harder" do not support writers. Students and professionals can best rewrite when they know specifically what *is* working and when they receive specific suggestions for improvement.

Here are some examples of feedback I give my students when they've turned in a draft of a piece for my feedback. These comments may come before or after they have received feedback from themselves or a peer. I write them on sticky notes so they can refer to them later:

You used a quote effectively in your lead.

The detailed anecdotes helped me understand your points.

The statistics supported your opinion and made your case credible.

Your strong voice celebrates the love for this topic you communicate.

Deserved praise builds writers' confidence, showcases their strengths, and makes students better able to handle your comments that call for revision.

Besides writing comments on sticky notes, I also emphasize students' strengths when I confer with them, especially those who require more guidance than I can offer in my notes. I try to keep a conference to a maximum of five minutes, so I can support six to ten students during a workshop period.

Generally speaking, in these brief meetings I'll recast my written feedback until I see the student gets it and is eager to act on it. For example, I might explain that the student's sentence "When my brother opened the box and saw the brown puppy, he was happy" has the potential for moving from telling to showing. First, I point out two passages where the student successfully showed. Next, I prompt the student with questions: What did your brother say? Do? Did the puppy do anything? As the student talks, I jot her words on a sticky note so she can fine-tune them on her own. Here's what the student dictates: "My brother opened the box. He gently picked up the puppy, held its fur against his cheek, and his grin widened every time the puppy licked his face."

Now I can build on this student's strength by saying, "Wow! Because you have begun to show feelings and reactions in your piece, and because you considered the questions, this rewrite helps me know your brother felt happy." What I'm doing is pointing to a successful moment in this piece or another piece in the student's folder. Then we work together to build on that success.

When students see what they have done, and when I can help them translate ideas into sentences, it empowers them. Suddenly, the process of rewriting doesn't seem so mysterious or impossible.

Building on students' strengths can be tricky. However, once students recognize, with your help, a strength they possess, then it's time to put those strong points to good use. If a student uses dialogue well, she can work with peers who need her support. A student who has a top-notch vocabulary can support classmates trying to find stronger verbs and specific nouns. The expert can also discuss his process with the class or a small group. Those who successfully use questions to drive them to think about revision can work with a peer and model the questioning process. Using student experts builds students' self-confidence and frees you to work one-on-one with those who need your expertise.

Scaffolding Idea: Helping Students Discover Their Strengths

There will be times when a student comes to the conference table with a very weak piece, making it tough for you to point to a strength. In such cases, I start by talking about the choice of topic and complimenting the student for her willingness to work with me. I can also point out strengths that come from the conversation. For example, a sixth grader needs help finding stronger verbs. First, I help him choose three verbs to improve. Then we discuss possibilities. Here I offer praise for the student's suggestions. If the student doesn't offer suggestions, then I offer an alternate verb. Next, I ask the student for one. I find that this give and take often enables the student to generate several possible verbs and provides me with the opportunity to give positive feedback. If this strategy doesn't work, I turn to a thesaurus and discuss possibilities with the student. I let the student choose the alternates he wishes to consider and offer positive feedback for his choices.

2. POSE QUESTIONS

Questions drive revision. Professional writers continually ask questions as they revise. Homer Hickam, Jr., told me: "I usually throw a book's worth of writing away by asking, Does this help the story? Is it necessary?"

In *On Writing Well*, William Zinsser advises: Reexamine each sentence you put on paper. Is every word doing new work? Can any thought be expressed with more economy? Is anything pompous or pretentious or faddish? Are you hanging on to something useless, just because you think it's beautiful? (page 17)

We can help students see that posing questions gives the task of rewriting a piece clear definition. With each question, they are asking about an idea, a word, a sentence to prove its worth. If it doesn't, it gets tossed. Arming students with questions such as: "Do I need this word?" "Does this section connect to my main point?" "Is this anecdote crucial to my reader's understanding?" gives them the language for effective revision. With this in mind, on pages 268–269, I've included some questions I ask students to provoke their thinking. Don't overwhelm students with too many questions at once. Choose questions that invite students to rethink sections of their piece based on a craft lesson you've presented or a few of the established criteria.

I find that these questions support students as they draft and revise a piece. When I circulate around the room and ask a student, "How's the writing going?" her response lets me know if she's having trouble crafting a lead that introduces the topic in a jazzy way. I select questions that are appropriate for the student's piece. For example, a fourth grader opened her essay this way: "I am not too good with grooming my horse." My first question was "Why?" She told me that she preferred riding in the field behind her house to washing and brushing her horse and mucking out the poop in stalls.

Once I asked, "Can you capture that feeling in your lead?' She began to write. A few minutes later, she proudly read this to me: "Sometimes I wash and brush my pony hastily and muck the poop from his stall after we've galloped around the field in back of my house. Caring for my pony is important, but riding him is what I love most." One or two questions can stimulate students' thinking and move them to continue a draft or successfully rewrite a section.

I find questions also help me provide written feedback on a draft or revisions students have made. These I write on sticky notes so students can mull over them and consider possibilities for rewrites. Focus on one or two areas—the lead and ending or verbs and showing. Stick to the criteria you and students have negotiated. Don't overwhelm students with too much feedback.

Content & Meaning	Questions

Title
- Does the title connect to the piece?
- Is the title short and energetic?
- Does the title grab the reader's attention and arouse curiosity?

Introduction/Lead
- Does the introduction grab the reader's attention?
- What details could be added to intrigue the reader?
- Does the introduction make the reader want to read on? Does it raise questions? Does it include fascinating information? Does it set a tone or mood that intrigues?
- Does the introduction let the reader know what the piece would be about?
- Does the introduction follow the criteria set by your teacher and class?

Text Content
- Can the reader state what the writer is saying?
- Does the reader need more details and information?
- Does the writer support his or her point?
- Are there stories and examples that hold the reader's interest?
- Do the details develop the point/position presented in the lead?
- Explain why the reader might find the arguments convincing.
- Are there sentences or sections that take the reader away from the topic? Should these be deleted?
- What ideas does the reader connect to? Explain why.
- Would changing the order of the paragraphs be helpful to the reader? Why?

Endings
- Did the ending just restate the lead?
- Did the writer stop at the right moment? Should the ending be shortened? Why?
- What thoughts did the writer leave the reader with in the ending?
- What ideas did the writer raise in the reader's mind?
- Will the reader think about the ending and the piece after he or she is finished reading it? Why or why not?

Second Reading	Questions
Verbs	• Are verbs strong? What images do these strong verbs create? Circle four to six verbs that could be stronger. • Are verbs in the active or passive voice? Circle verbs in the passive voice. • Point to the verbs that really helped the reader envision what the author was saying.
Nouns	• Are nouns specific? • Point out a few specific nouns and explain how they helped the reader better understand a point or idea. • Circle three or four general nouns that would be more effective if they were specific.
Adjectives	• Are there too many adjectives? • Circle three to six adjectives that could be omitted if the writer used more specific nouns.
Adverbs	• Are there too many adverbs? • Circle three to six adverbs that could be omitted if the writer used stronger verbs.
Descriptive Parts	• Does the author show instead of tell? • Find one place where the author shows, and explain how showing is effective. • Find a few places where the writer is telling and rewrite these so the writer is showing. • Are there enough specific details to help the reader picture a setting or time period?

POSING QUESTIONS IN ACTION

I often pose questions on sticky notes, which I hand back with students' drafts. Then when we confer about the piece, I'll take a moment to reread my notes—they're a handy memory refresher. As the student and I exchange ideas, I jot down further notes so the student can refer to these while revising.

To illustrate this process, here is an excerpt from a conversation with an eighth grader named Ted about his draft. To give you a bit more background, Ted has been diagnosed as learning disabled. He is an avid reader, but as a writer, he has difficulty elaborating ideas on paper, yet doesn't like to brainstorm ideas prior to writing.

I start the conference by asking Ted to read the positive statements from the sticky note. Then I probe with questions to encourage him to elaborate his ideas. As Ted talks, I jot down key points from our conference that he can use to add details to his piece.

ROBB: Can you choose two questions we can discuss? [If the student doesn't want to choose, then ask him if the two you select are okay with him.]

TED: Yeah. I think we should talk about what I see and hear.

ROBB: Tell me what you have seen.

TED: We always go on the beach on St. Thomas. My dad and I scuba together.

ROBB: Can you tell me what you saw? Can you give details so I can feel as if I'm with you?

TED: Yeah. [long pause] We saw sea anemones— they look like dozens of

> Ted
>
> I like to go scuba diving. It's so fun to go under water ~~tor~~ ~~together~~ and see whats there. I'm not crtafid yet because of ere problemsbut it wouldn't be long. And I'll be diving in the topices.
>
> - You really help me know how much you enjoy scuba diving and seeing what it's like underwater.
> - Wow! I never knew it's possible for a nonprofessional to become certified.
> - Can you help me be underwater with you?
>
> - Where do you scuba dive?
> - What kind of gear do you wear?
> - Do you go alone?
> - What have you seen that's fascinating?
> - Did you take lessons? Where? For how long? What did you practice?
> - What did you do to get certified?
> - Can you add your feelings to what you saw?
> - If you go with someone, what do you talk about before? after?
> - How do you communicate under water?

arms waving in the current. And coral. And schools of small fish swimming in front of me. Sometimes the fish look like a yellow or blue blur 'cause they go by so fast and so close together. Far off we saw a nurse shark, but it didn't come close to us. My dad found a bed of large clams with shells partly open. I saw crabs scuttling over the bottom.

ROBB: Wow! You know so much about the reef, and you describe it with precise, colorful words. I'm impressed. Can you tell me what kind of gear you were wearing?

TED: That day we had masks and oxygen tanks so we could go deeper. Sometimes I just wear a mask and snorkel and look down from the top of the water. I always wear rubber flippers. They make me move quickly when I kick.

ROBB: How did you feel swimming around the reef?

TED: It's weird. You're in a new world. So much goes on under the ocean and we don't know most of it.

ROBB: Here are the notes I jotted down based on what you told me. [I place them on Ted's piece.] Now, pick two more questions I posed, talk to yourself, and jot down ideas. Then you'll have great details to add to your piece.

When teachers ask questions while students draft and revise, they model a process students can absorb and internalize—a process that can lead to drafting and revising independently.

3. ENCOURAGE INDEPENDENCE

This third revision strategy is really a habit of mind that influences how you present the two previously discussed strategies. Everything you do with revision and editing works toward the ultimate goal of student independence. When you open a conference with a comment that celebrates what a student has done well, your goal is for students to know their own strengths and use these again and again. When you ask them questions about their piece, your goal is for them to eventually pose questions to themselves, just as the professional writers do as a matter of course. Being able to hold these inner conversations is the hallmark of independence in the practice of any art, whether painting, writing, composing music, or dancing, for with every art a thinking process is involved.

Getting students to this state of independence requires many scaffolds, large and small, from mini-lessons to teacher and peer feedback. For a first read, students focus on content and meaning.

PEER- AND SELF-REVISION: USING A REVISION REPRODUCIBLE

The reproducible on page 274 invites students to ferret out what worked, then ask questions that drive rewriting. Before setting students to revise peers' work or their own, it's crucial to discuss each item on the reproducible's list. You want to ensure that students understand the focus of their reading so the feedback is beneficial to writers. You'll need to reserve 15 to 25 minutes for peer- or self-revision, depending on the length of students' writing.

First, I review the revision process and note these steps on the chalkboard. The boldface sentences below are what I write on the board. Then, I discuss the explanations with students. Students' ability to discuss their revision tasks lets you know how much of your mini-lessons they have absorbed.

You can focus on three or four elements with older students. Younger students can evaluate two or three.

1. **Exchange papers in the group you sit with or with a partner so that you will read a peer's piece.** It's fine if the teachers assigns peer partners.

2. **Read the piece carefully.** I suggest students read the piece aloud in a very soft voice. As students read aloud they should consider the lead, the content, and the ending. At this point, I like to place a few questions on the chalkboard or chart paper to guide students. These questions can come from the ones on pages 268–269 or ones you create for students. Here's what the chart looks like for a personal essay in sixth grade:

Title:	Is it short and snappy? Does it arouse curiosity? Does it relate to the content?
Lead:	What technique does the author use? Is it effective? Why? Why not? Do you know the topic? Do you want to read on? Why?
Body:	Do the details relate to the topic? Does the author include anecdotes? Dialogue? Specific details? Is there too much information? What might be cut? If a personal essay: Does the author focus on one key event? If a persuasive essay: Does the author address opposing points? Are the arguments convincing? Any suggestions for improving this part?
Ending:	What thoughts does the writer leave you with? Should the ending be shortened or extended? Why? Does the ending leave you wanting more details in the body?

Nonfiction Writing From the Inside Out

3. **Think about each revision element on the sheet.** Provide positive feedback and try to use questions to point the writer to revision needs. For example: Can you shorten your title? Can you add the topic to your lead? Can you decide what details really support your essay and work with those? This is tough for students to do. However, my task is to always be kind and supportive.

4. **Return the writing to the author and discuss your suggestions.** Jot key points on a sticky note or on a blank piece of paper. Give these to the author.

5. **Ask students to set behavior guidelines for this task.** They all agree that they need to be silent while reading. Quiet conversations will occur if they have to ask a peer a question and as they review feedback.

6. **Invite students to use peer feedback to decide what they will rewrite.** Choice is important to writers. Ask students to consider the feedback they received and choose parts they feel will improve their piece.

The reproducible that follows focuses students on reading to evaluate content. After the reproducible, you'll find one completed by a student so you can see that with explanations and guidelines, peer evaluation works.

You can create similar reproducibles with different purposes. For example, you can ask students to test verbs to make sure they are strong and create images and check that nouns are specific. Or you might focus it on the

---

Self and Peer Revision For Content

Name Colleen   Date

Directions: Next to each item, celebrate what worked well. Pose one or two questions to point to an area you feel needs revision. Use the content criteria to focus on specific items such as including a quote or short dialogue or making transitions from one paragraph to the next.

Title: The Baby

Can You Summarize the Purpose of this Piece? To show its okay to have a baby and care for it and not be maried. The family gives support.

Lead: Made me want to know how family gave support. Used question - good. Having baby on April Fools is cool.

Content: Learn who Clare is. Learn about what family members were doing the day Clare goes in labor. This is good cause it brings in family and the essays also about family and how they feel.

Ending: Talks about family & friends supporting Clare. Maybe add a quote from clare or your mom. Make it more interesting.

Peer's Name (if peer evaluated) Katie D.

Self- and Peer-Revision for Content

Name _____ Date _____

Directions: Next to each item, celebrate what worked well. Pose one or two questions to point to an area you feel needs revision. Use the content criteria to focus on specific items, such as including a quote or short dialogue or making transitions from one paragraph to the next.

Title:

Can you summarize the purpose of this piece?

Lead:

Content:

Ending:

Peer's Name (if peer evaluated)_____

technique of showing, not telling by having them find two telling places to rewrite. The point to remember is not to overwhelm students with too many revision tasks. Always help students find verbs and telling places if this is too difficult for them.

TIPS THAT SUPPORT STUDENTS' REVISION PROCESS

Here are some tips for helping student writers read their own work to identify parts that need revising.

1. Reread your draft, looking for one craft element at a time.
2. Review the criteria one item at a time.
   - Reread your first sentence and write two to three alternates. Choose the best one.
   - Reread looking for places that are general and need more specific nouns. Rewrite.
   - Check that you shared feelings about the events you describe. Weave in feelings in places that need your take on the situation.
   - Write two to three alternate titles and choose the best one.

TWO MODEL REVISION LESSONS

You can present revision mini-lessons on leads, endings, specific details, throwaway words—virtually any aspect of writing—by following the directions for planning mini-lessons that are on page 316. Though I wish I could describe dozens of mini-lessons here, the page limits of this book prevent my doing so. However, I am confident that you can create effective mini-lessons that meet the unique needs of your students. Note, too, that the writer's craft mini-lessons earlier in the book (see Chapter 4) can be presented as revision mini-lessons as well.

SLOW DOWN:
REVISION
TAKES TIME

Donald Graves told me, "Writing is observing, waiting, having a sense of craft, not hurrying." To make this point, Graves often asks teachers and administrators he is advising about teaching writing to ponder these questions: "Do you make things? How do you go about making them? What time do you need?" The point is, if our students are to become better writers, we need to give them the time they need. A carpenter building a staircase doesn't rush the process—it takes the time it takes. Same with planting a garden, or knitting a sweater. So why is it that we think we can rush students through writing and still get good results?

So that you will have a couple of models to work from, here are two revision lessons that my students have found helpful: using active verbs and making transitions.

MODEL REVISION LESSON

Active Verbs Breathe Energy Into Writing

William Zinsser makes the case for active verbs: "Verbs are the strongest tools a writer is given, because they embody an action. Active verbs are stronger than passive verbs, because they propel a sentence forward. They also enable us to picture who did what, because they require a pronoun or noun: *I, we, she, you, boy, girl* (*Writing to Learn*, page 71).

Purpose

To transform verbs in the passive voice into the active voice so sentences have motion and energy.

Materials

Teacher's examples; student's writing

Guidelines

1. Explain how to identify verbs in the passive voice. These verbs—*was, were, are, is*— plus an action verb form the passive voice.

2. Provide examples for students to discuss and study. Here are some to share with your students.

    Passive Voice: My uncle Phil was taken to the train station. (Note that you don't learn who took the uncle and how they traveled.)

    Active Voice: Dad and I drove Uncle Phil to the train station. (Note how with the active voice you learn who drove Uncle Phil and how they traveled.)

3. Ask students to analyze the sentences that follow, explaining what they do and don't learn, following the sample analysis in number 2.

    Passive Voice: The beach cottage was flooded today.

    Active Voice: Strong winds and heavy rains flooded the beach cottage.

    Passive Voice: The lost puppy was seen in the park.

    Active Voice: Our neighbor spotted the lost puppy in the park.

4. Explain that to change passive to active voice requires some rewriting and rephrasing of a sentence.

5. Ask students to take a piece of writing from their folders and circle two to three verbs in the passive voice.

6. Circulate around the room, providing help in pinpointing passive-voice verbs. Teachers of fourth and fifth graders might want to start this revision process by circling passive-voice verbs for students.

7. Ask volunteers to write their passive-voice sentence and the rewrite on the chalkboard. Encourage students to add specific details and strong verbs to their rewrites. Here is an example from a fifth grader.

   Passive Voice: My brother, Angelo, was given a bike on his birthday.

   Active Voice: My grandparents presented my brother, Angelo, with a new bike on his tenth birthday.

8. Continue revising drafts, changing passive verbs to active verbs.

9. Remind students, once they understand passive and active voice, to use active verbs as they draft. It's one of the most important writing habits to cultivate.

MODEL REVISION LESSON

Paragraph-to-Paragraph Transitions

One of the most challenging writing techniques to teach middle-grade and middle-school students is how to transition from one paragraph to the next. In my classes students and I first study essays by professional writers. We also review nonfiction texts written by former students. I have learned, however, that most students require more than studying models.

My students understand the models I offer them. It's applying this knowledge to their own writing that proves so difficult. To move beyond this hurdle, I find that conferring with students can support their ability to build in transition sentences. During a conference, I think aloud to demonstrate how I develop a transition sentence. There are times when that's not enough, so I write a sample sentence on a sticky note. Either way, students and I discuss how the last sentence in the paragraph prepares readers for the content in the paragraph that follows.

Purpose

To create transitions between paragraphs in an essay

Materials

Samples from professional writers and student writers

Guidelines

On the First Day

1. Explain to students that transition sentences from paragraph to paragraph prepare readers for a switch in setting, time, topic, or event.

2. Model using an example from professional writers. I use the essay "A French Cat" by Jean Brody on pages 178–179. Students and I focus on transition sentences. Here are a few observations made by sixth graders:

   - The last sentence in paragraph one sort of gets you ready for the whole essay.
   - It also sets you up for the next two paragraphs.
   - The best transition is at the end of the third paragraph. The woman holds out her cat to Brody and the fourth paragraph starts with Brody taking him.

3. Continue using professional essays, newspaper editorials, and excerpts from informational chapter books. You can also use student work.

4. Study models until students can readily discuss how these transition sentences prepare them for the next paragraph.

On Another Day

1. Have students work on one of their essays and focus on transition sentences using these prompts:

   - Does my sentence make a connection to the next paragraph?
   - Have I adequately prepared the reader to read on?

2. Invite students to write transition sentences.

3. Collect them and read to discover students who need your support.

4. Sit side by side with students and model how you write a transition sentence. Then invite students to compose one.

   Though I continue trying to help students write transition sentences, believe me, there are always students who "don't get it." That's okay. I've planted the seed. Some will develop the skill this year from repeated lessons and conferences with me. Others will develop this skill as they continue their education.

WHEN MINI-LESSONS AREN'T ENOUGH

Like me, I'm sure you have students who are unable to revise a piece of writing. They don't seem to absorb mini-lessons and modeling during short conferences; they appear unable to apply craft lessons to their work. I try to carve out a longer chunk of time to show them how to improve a piece of writing.

You might have to take several 20 to 25 minute blocks from independent workshop time to support these writers. It's a worthwhile investment because you can forge the link between learning and application.

Luke, an eighth grader, struggled with drafting his biography. Because he lost his interview notes, the writing was tougher for him. When I read Luke's first draft, I realized he needed a long conference.

During the conference, I helped Luke create a list of questions about his friend that would give Luke the details needed to craft this piece. Next, I outlined our discussion of what should go in each paragraph. When Luke did not respond, I filled in the gaps for him. To support rewriting, I jotted on sticky notes what each paragraph should contain.

Though the revised draft needed a great deal of editing, Luke improved the content when I provided the structure.

Outline for Luke's biography.

The best advice I can offer you is not to expect a changeover after working on one piece. In fact, you might not see the progress you hope for even in one year. Communicate with students' upcoming teachers and explain the kinds of scaffolding that improve their writing. It can take several years to reverse entrenched patterns.

After Revision: Editing for Conventions

As much as students groan when invited to revise a piece, their protests escalate when they have to edit for writing conventions. "It was easier when the teacher marked my paper, and all I had to do was recopy it," a sixth grader tells me. It's tough and frustrating for students to edit for spelling, punctuation, usage, paragraphing, commas, and so on, all at once. Here are four strategies that "help the medicine go down."

STRATEGY ONE: READ YOUR PIECE ALOUD

The best writing lesson you can offer students is to develop the habit of reading their work aloud, listening for meaning (Calkins 1986, 1994, Graves 1983, 2003). Meaning drives organization, usage, and sentence structure, and reading aloud forces writers to attend to glitches in meaning that editing can repair.

Read aloud and edit for one writing convention at a time. (Most often, the writing conventions come from established criteria. Sometimes I refer students to a chart that contains a list of the conventions they've practiced and understand, and ask them to choose three or four and jot these on a sticky note.)

Rosalynn, an eighth grader, has a bubbly personality. She thinks aloud in long sentences to discover inferences and connections by hearing her ideas. Rosalynn's early drafts of essays have long, run-on sentences. When I confer with her, she says, "I always write that way—it's the way I talk."

"It's a great beginning," I tell her. "But you have to separate ideas so they are clear to the reader. The run-ons make it tough to filter the details that support your main point." I ask Rosalynn to read her paper aloud, slowly, listening for sentences that contain several ideas, then to place a check next to these passages and rewrite them. On page 281 are a before and a revised section from Rosalynn's first essay in eighth grade:

Nonfiction Writing From the Inside Out

Purely Pressured

Teenagers have many tough decisions to make concerning whom they hang out with. In Todd Strasser's "On the Bridge" the main character Seth hangs out with a boy named Adam, who loves to be a tough guy. Sometimes tough-guy friends like Adam, bring out the worst in their peers by pressuring them to do things they shouldn't.

Adam pressured Seth to smoke, and influenced him into thinking that fighting for no reason, and going far with girls were the coolest things ever. Seth tried to be just like Adam. Seth started to smoke, he wore a ripped jean jacket, and while he was hanging out with Adam on that bridge, he watched and tried to mimic Adam, as Adam waved to older girls, and signaled for a truck to honk. Seth did not however, flick his cigarette onto a car below, fearful that they would get in trouble. *[run-on 2 sentence]*

If Seth didn't idolize Adam, Seth probably wouldn't have been on the bridge when Adam tossed his cig. butt onto the truck. Little did Seth know, that Adam would soon act like the coward he was. When the furious men in the truck asked who flicked the cigarette, Seth didn't rat out Adam, but Adam lied to save his own skin, and

pointed to Seth. And even when the men were smashing his nose into the ash, Seth wouldn't tell them about Adam. Even though it took a total act of betrayal from Adam, his lying about the cigarette, and then lying about the guys pulling a knife on him, Adam's cowardice finally broke the spell over Seth. Now Seth was the cool one, who didn't act like a wuss; he was tougher than Adam.

Seth made a tough choice of throwing his bloody jacket and his friendship with Adam, in the garbage. I think he finally realized that he no longer needed to be cool, that even though the jacket looked awesome, it was exactly why he liked Adam's jacket, and Seth didn't need approval from Adam anymore. What would you have done? *[2 sentences]*

Before essay (left and above)

Edited essay (bottom left and below)

Purely Pressured

Rosalynn W

Teenagers have many tough decisions concerning who they hang out with. In Todd Strasser's "On the Bridge," the main character Seth hangs out with a boy named Adam who loves to be a tough guy. Sometimes tough-guy friends like Adam bring out the worst in their peers by pressuring them to do things they shouldn't.

Adam pressured Seth to smoke and influenced him into thinking that fighting for no reason and going far with girls were the coolest things ever. Seth tried to be just like Adam and started smoking and wearing a ripped jean jacket. On the bridge Seth watched and learned as Adam waved to older girls and got a truck honk. Seth did not however, flick his cigarette onto a car below fearful they'd get in trouble.

If Seth didn't idolize Adam, Seth probably wouldn't have been on the bridge when Adam tossed his Malboro® onto the truck. Little did Seth know that Adam would soon act like the coward he was. When the furious men in the truck asked who flicked the cigarette, Seth didn't rat out Adam. However, Adam lied to save his own skin and pointed to Seth. Even when the men were smashing ~~his nose into the~~ his ribs into the fender of the truck, Seth wouldn't tell them about Adam. It took a total act of betrayal and cowardice from Adam, lying about the cigarette and then lying about the guys pulling a knife on him, to break the spell over Seth. Now Seth was the cool one; he was tougher than Adam, and Adam knew it.

Seth made the tough choice to throw his bloody jacket and his friendship with Adam, in the garbage. I think Seth realized that he no longer needed to be cool by Adam's standards. Even though the jacket looked cool, it was just like Adam's, and Seth no longer needed approval from him. What would you have done?

Deuce Dooms Day at the Pool
Spencer B

Poodles are not the little prissy dogs that you might think they are. That's right, I've got a standard poodle that is rowdy and athletic and even swims! Unfortunately his doggy paddle is quite painful to those too close to him; I learned first hand last summer at the Stallard's pool, and it was not a fun way to learn.

~~If you have never met a poodle that is an athletic one and will chase after people while swimming then you just met your first.~~ This sultan of the swimming pool goes by the name of Deuce. His theory is "this swimming pool isn't big enough for the both of us."

It was warm Saturday around noon when my dad said, "Hey Spencer, what do you say we go over to Mr. Stallard's place and swim in the pool? It'll be a great for the dog." I agreed and within five minutes I found myself swimming in the pool that lye in the back yard of 644 West Bellview. The pool was surrounded by a light brown fence with woods behind it and the house looked exactly like a Pizza Hut. As Deuce sprinted around the perimeter of the pool, I swam in the clear blue water that was just the right temperature. When I wasn't gliding through the heavily chlorinated yet refreshing pool, I spent most of my time relaxing on a foam chair in the ~~deep~~ end that was eight feet deep. My dad sat on a chair that was on the concrete and read the paper taking advantage of the ~~joyful~~ sun. ~~As I took advantage of a little break from reality,~~ Deuce was eagerly awaiting the time when I would ~~get out of~~ leave the chair so he could get on and then ~~jump into~~ pounce it the water ~~from there~~. It was a perfect day to swim because it was a day of about 70 to 80 degrees and the pool was a perfect place to seek refuge from the glowing sun.

Spencer edits his essay.

Deuce ~~gets~~ grows rowdy ~~very easily~~ when he wants to play and I'm not playing ~~with~~ wrestling him. He was getting anxious and annoyed when I just sat on "his" chair. Within a short period of time, though, I ~~found out~~ discovered that he wanted to play. I opened my eyes after my short resting period and was scared to see Deuce in full pounce position! His head was low and his butt was high with his comb-like tail wagging furiously. ~~Before taking a second thought,~~ Immediately I bailed out of that chair ~~immediately~~ and into the water, ~~but~~ I didn't catch a full breath because the sight of a poodle about to jump is pretty darn funny. I swam to the bottom of the deep end right by the drain and all of a sudden I knew that Deuce was on the pool chair searching for me like a policeman searches a thief. I knew he was on it because he jumped just a bit too short of the chair and I saw his back legs slip into the water, ~~but~~ Deuce quickly recover. Because I can't hold my breath comfortably for over ~~forty~~ 40 seconds I started swimming towards the shallow end. I remember praying the whole time- please don't let him see me! He saw me. I not only heard but also felt a 45 pound poodle with sharp paws land in the water and also on me. on top of me

"Oooooowwwww!"

It felt like 10 knives were slashing my back and tearing it open. I have never felt so much pain in my life! I tried to go deeper in the water to get away from this relentless and horrible poodle, that seemed to be out to kill me, Unfortunately but I was already in the three foot area and couldn't go deep enough, so the knives just kept stabbing me unmercifully. I questioned, how am I even going to get out alive? Fortunately after about ten seconds of poodle abuse I had the power to push Deuce away or else be scratched even more. My lifeless body stumbled through the once relaxing water and up the steps, out of the pool.

I gave my dad an awkward look because I knew he had been watching the whole thing, and had been amused by it all.

"Wow, Spencer! What happened to your back?" he questioned sarcastically. "You have about ten red slash marks and a couple of paw prints on there."

"Oh nothing happened, I was just relaxing in the pool." I returned the sarcasm.

The best part was that my innocent little poodle didn't even know what was going on; he was just being a dog.

Spencer, another eighth grader, turns in a final draft that shows me he hasn't taken the time to read earlier drafts aloud. In a brief conference, I start him reading aloud and marking corrections. Some students will need to work closely with you to reap the benefits of this strategy.

Children's book editor Dianne Hess makes the case for content driving clarity:
Usually careful writing and good grammar go hand in hand. When you write, you are communicating with accuracy. And grammar helps you say things in the most accurate way. If someone takes the time to learn the craft of writing, they would most likely learn spelling and grammar as well—as they are tools of good writing. (Interview, 1994)

Nonfiction Writing From the Inside Out

STRATEGY TWO: POSE QUESTIONS

For students to do their "best proofreading," there are times that teachers need to provide them with some "how-to" suggestions. You can use the questions that follow to deepen students' understanding of ways to repair incorrect usage by presenting editing mini-lessons that relate to these questions (see pages 285–290). The best way for students to understand grammar is for them to apply grammar principles to their own writing (Robb 2001; Weaver, 1998).

Writing Convention	Questions/Prompts
Paragraphing	• Does the piece contain paragraphs? • Show the writer where to start a second paragraph and explain why. • Where did the writer change the time? place? event? topic?
Sentence Structure	• Can the writer combine ideas from two or three sentences into one sentence? Show, with a check, a place where the writer could do this. • Circle the openings of consecutive sentences that all start the same way. Suggest ways to vary the openings of these sentences. • Pinpoint any run-on sentences. • Find any places where the author needs to add an apostrophe, comma, or uppercase letter.
Punctuation	• Write editing symbols in the margin of a line that needs a comma, period, upper- or lowercase letter, apostrophe, and so on. (See page 284 or Appendix page 324 for editing symbols.)
Spelling	• Circle words that may be misspelled. • Try respelling the word by writing it above the circled word. • Ask a classmate to help respell words the writer may find tough to visualize.

STRATEGY THREE: TEACH STUDENTS EDITING SYMBOLS

Though your hands itch to edit students' papers, avoid correcting writing conventions that students can edit independently. Teach students the editing symbols (see mini-lesson below, and Appendix page 324). Use them when responding in the margins of a student's piece. Encourage students to use them while peer editing.

STRATEGY FOUR: MAKE IT COLLABORATIVE

The editing task becomes less tedious for students if they complete editing during class with the support of a peer. First, have students edit their own work. Then, have a peer partner edit the piece.

While students edit, circulate among them and provide support. Students will edit what they can find, and this means they won't find every error. For pieces that will be published, you can complete the editing just as copy editors comb through professional writers' manuscripts.

Editing Symbols

Meaning	Example
Insert	I am happy.
Upper Case (Capitalize)	leslie lopez
Lower Case	Car
Transpose	recieve
Remove, Delete	She is not here
Indent For A Paragraph	Once upon a time...
Add Period	Clean up
Add Comma	The sad, silent child wept.

In the next section you'll explore four mini-lessons that can help students become better at editing their writing. You'll have to repeat these throughout the year. But don't become discouraged; editing is a tough skill for this age group. Remember, however, the more students edit, the better at it they'll become.

Nonfiction Writing From the Inside Out

Mini-Lesson

Using Editing Symbols

Purpose

To use common editing symbols that signal the kind of punctuation that's needed on a line of text

Materials

Editing symbol sheet; students' own writing

Guidelines

On the First Day

1. Staple or tape into students' folders a copy of the editing symbols on Appendix page 324.

2. Review editing symbols and what each one signifies.

3. Invite pairs to discuss and practice writing the symbols.

On Another Day

1. Make an overhead transparency of a student's writing with your editing symbols in the margin. Select the work of a student no longer at the school or in that grade. (It is always a good practice to delete the student's name.)

2. Explain how each symbol pinpoints a need in a specific line.

3. Model how you read that line, incorporating the suggested change.

4. Encourage students to raise questions and discuss these.

On Another Day

1. Place the symbol on the line of a student's text that lacks specific punctuation. Mark only those editing needs that were in your "Mechanics Criteria."

2. Invite students to make corrections.

3. Circulate while students are proofreading and editing, offering support when necessary.

4. Hold a short conference and work one-on-one with students who are having difficulty editing.

5. Once students understand the process, you can invite them to peer-edit one another's papers. Make yourself available to students who need help.

Repairing Run-on Sentences

Purpose

To provide strategies that help students repair run-on sentences

Materials

Students' own writing

Guidelines

On the First Day

1. On large sheet of chart paper, write the following sentence, which is typical of the writing of middle-school students:

    Rosa bought a new dress she wore it to the dance.

2. Explain that this kind of run-on is really two complete thoughts written as one thought.

3. Tell students that there are four ways to repair this kind of run-on sentence. Write all four ways on chart paper and display on a wall or bulletin board so that students can refer to the suggestions.

    *   Create two complete sentences:
        Rosa bought a new dress. She wore it to the dance.
    *   Add a conjunction or connecting word and remove the subject of the second sentence:
        Rosa bought a new dress and wore it to the dance.
    *   Add a conjunction or connecting word and a comma, and keep the subject of the second sentence:
        Rosa bought a new dress, and she wore it to the dance.
    *   Use a semicolon instead of a conjunction:
        Rosa bought a new dress; she wore it to the dance.

4. Return a piece of writing to each student on which you've marked one or two run-on sentences.

5. Invite students in grades 4 and 5 to rewrite these sentences using the first three examples above.

6. Invite students in grades 6 and up to rewrite each sentence four different ways.

7. Continue to offer students practice using their own writing.

On Another Day

1. On a large sheet of chart paper, write this sentence, which is typical of the writing of

middle-school students:

> Kenny and Jake decided to go swimming at the pool 'cause it was a warm, sunny day and they stopped at Luis's house to see if he could swim and they packed bathing suits and towels and walked to the pool.

2. Explain that this kind of run-on has two or more sentences written as one sentence. Sometimes sentences contain ideas and details that do not relate to the main purpose of the sentence.

3. Tell students that there are two ways they can repair this kind of run-on:
   - Rearrange sentences that are too long and that contain ideas that don't relate to the main purpose of the sentence.
   - Create two or more sentences and organize them in a logical and clear sequence.

4. Here's one rewrite sixth graders composed:

> Because the day was warm and sunny, Kenny and Jake packed their bathing suits and towels and walked to the pool. On their way they stopped at Luis's house and invited him to swim with them.

5. Raise students' awareness of sentences that are a half-page to a page in length. Meet one-on-one with students who write with no punctuation. Here are some things you can do during these conferences:
   - Ask students to read the section aloud and listen for the places where they pause or take a breath. Students can use these pause points to decide on the kind of punctuation that's needed.
   - Have students circle all the *and's*, *but's*, *then's*, and *also's*. Students use these words to connect ideas. Help them see that they can eliminate these connectors with punctuation.

MINI-LESSON

Fix Sentence Fragments

Purpose

To show students that a group of words that does not express a complete thought is a fragment; to offer ways to turn fragments into sentences

Materials

Practice examples; students' writing

Guidelines

On the First Day

1. On the chalkboard or chart paper, write these examples of fragments that have been punctuated as sentences:

   a. Since our team won.

   b. Bitten by a rattlesnake.

   c. Near the stream in the woods.

2. For students with little to no grammar knowledge, discuss these fragments by showing how they raise the question "What happened next?" because each is an incomplete thought.

3. For students in grades 7 and up who have a knowledge of grammar, think aloud and discuss each fragment:

   For Fragment a:

   When a subordinate clause stands alone, it is a fragment. Complete the clause by telling what happened after your team won.

   For Fragment b:

   When a participial phrase stands alone, it is a fragment. Complete the participial phrase by explaining who the rattlesnake bit.

   For Fragment c:

   Two prepositional phrases constitute a fragment because they don't express a complete thought. Tell what occurred by the stream in the woods to change the fragment into sentences.

On Another Day

1. Invite students to rewrite the fragments.

   Here's what a pair of seventh graders wrote for Fragment a.:

   Since our team won our third game in a row, we have practiced basketball every day.

   Here's what an eighth grader wrote for Fragment b.:

   Bitten by a rattlesnake while hiking in the woods, the Boy Scout remained calm as he read the directions in his snake kit.

   Here's what a sixth grader wrote for Fragment c.:

   Near the stream in the woods a young doe gave birth and lovingly licked the newborn fawn.

2. Encourage discussion of the fragments and the sentences by asking students questions: Can you explain what kinds of phrases can cause fragments? Why do fragments confuse readers? Can you explain why the revisions are clearer?

MINI-LESSON

Paragraphing Your Piece

While drafting a piece, students are so intent on content that they often turn in a two-page letter or essay that's one long paragraph. Helping them understand when it's time to start a new paragraph, then asking them to paragraph a piece by placing the symbol [¶] next to the start of each new paragraph can develop students' awareness that paragraphing helps shape meaning.

Purpose
To develop some guidelines that help students know when to start a new paragraph

Materials
students' writing

Guidelines

On the First Day

1. On a large sheet of chart paper, write these revision tips for separating paragraphs in an essay.

   Revision Tips

   • Separate the introduction into its own paragraph.
   • Use the editing symbol (¶) to signal a new paragraph.
   • Start a new paragraph when:
     — you switch to another idea or topic
     — you change the setting or time
     — the speaker changes in a dialogue
     — you make a new point
   • Separate the ending into its own paragraph.

2. Think aloud, using a piece of student writing from someone no longer in the school or in that grade. Show how you use the paragraph symbol to mark the start of a new paragraph.

3. Repeat the modeling until you sense, from students' queries and reactions, that they understand the process.

On Another Day

1. Invite students to mark paragraphs using a piece of their own writing.
2. Invite pairs to share their work and offer feedback on paragraphing.
3. Work one-on-one with students who need your support to understand how to separate paragraphs.

Students' Errors Inform Teaching

As Connie Weaver noted (1996, 1998), students' errors are cause for celebration. Why? Because they are trying to use compound sentences or vary sentence openings with clauses and prepositional phrases, but they're not quite there yet. Offer students the mini-lessons they show you they need. That's a sure way to develop young writers' ability to express ideas clearly and creatively.

In fact, that's one of three primary purposes for reading and grading students' papers:

- to improve their writing;
- to build their confidence with editing and revision; and
- to inform you of the writing instruction they need.

Grade the Process, Not the Product

Grading writing is tough—even tougher if you don't have criteria or a rubric to guide you. Without criteria or a rubric, grading becomes subjective, and often it's the grade that stars and not the feedback that can support growth. From middle school through college, I had teachers who graded by instinct and the feelings a piece generated. So, when I received a paper with "B, good job" and asked the teacher how I could improve it, she would shrug her shoulders and say, "work harder." I can still recall the frustration I felt when I had no notion of what "Work harder" meant. Our students deserve better teaching. If students know the criteria or guidelines for a piece, then you can use these guidelines to provide feedback and assign a grade.

In my classes, when I establish a deadline—for a few students or for the entire class—so that I can grade a piece of writing, I ask students to place their final draft on top. Underneath, they include earlier drafts and revisions, peer- and/or self-evaluation sheets, feedback from me, a plan, and brainstorming lists. I'm looking for growth, improvement, and sustained effort on the pieces we bring to final draft.

For me, there are basically three situations when a student won't earn an A. The first is when a student who has natural writing ability puts little effort into improving a piece. The second is when a student neglects to file his plans and drafts in his writing folder and only turns in a final draft. The third scenario is when a student avoids the process, and then hastily composes a draft just before a deadline date. To prevent the second scenario, I set aside time to file papers, and I circulate to make sure students do this. Yet, there are always students who lose their papers because they have been stuffed into a notebook, then trashed. Since I frequently record where students are in the writing process (see page 30), and since I collect plans, and continually circulate while students draft, revise, edit, confer, and so on, I can identify and support students who avoid writing and using the process.

On the other hand, a student who works diligently to improve and shows steady progress can earn a B+ or an A. I'm up front with this standard because my goal is to accept the level of writing expertise that students bring to class, then help each one move forward.

WITH CRITERIA, GRADING IS FAIR

For final drafts, criteria enable me to grade fairly and offer specific reasons for the grade. I put two letter grades on students' work—one for content and style and the other for writing conventions. So a student who improved content and style greatly but did not repair run-ons might receive an A-/B-. I think it's beneficial for students to see two grades so they know their strengths and also what they need to improve in their next piece. You can establish the standards for A, B, C, and so on, and I encourage you to inform students of your standards to remove the mystery from grading.

Look at the first and final draft of an eighth-grade personal essay as well as my comments to see how this grading system works. Here are the criteria students and I negotiated:

Content: lead, focus is one event, anecdotes, dialogue

Style and Organization: active voice, strong verbs, show, don't tell

Conventions: punctuation of dialogue; repair fragments and run-ons; paragraphing;

comma to separate compound sentences and after introductory clause, direct address, or an adverb at the start of a sentence.

SELF-EVALUATION: INVOLVE STUDENTS IN GRADING

I am troubled when students tell me, "Thanks for giving me a good grade," or, "You gave me a low grade." Self-evaluation helps students understand to what extent they met the criteria. Not only do students self-evaluate at the revision stage, but sometimes I invite them to self-evaluate their process from start to finish and give themselves a grade. Students receive a self-evaluation guideline sheet that reflects some of the criteria for a piece.

The self-evaluations of Jeannette, Spencer, David and Lucy completed in January reveal how much

First Friendships

Every person, guaranteed, had a simple friendship at one point or another throughout their childhood which they still have fond memories of. The friend from that friendship was the kind who you can do anything with and tell everything to, no matter what. Whether you're still in contact with that person or not, you will probably remember them friend long after you have moved on to a newer, more complicated lifestyle. I have three such friendly memories, from a time predating kindergarten when I lived in the kind of neighborhood that no matter where you go or what you do, you are welcome.

All of the little girls in the neighborhood had pink, fluffy, white-walled rooms. In every one there were cute stuffed animals, fancy pillows, and, of course, lots of lace and frills. The biggest, brightest, and by far the coolest bedroom in my eyes was Page's, a girl who lived up the street and around a corner. She even had a skylight right over her bed! Page also had a walk-in closet, with a secret passageway from her stuffed animal-filled closet to who knows where. You entered it through a little door behind a projecting piece of wall, which only a small child could fit into. Once you entered and pulled that door shut, you could go anywhere you wanted, real or made-up. We had thousands of adventures through Page's little white door. The best by far was when we traveled by boat to Disney World and got to walk in a parade with Mickey and Minnie Mouse. Page also had a fluffy white dog. It was the kind of dog that is always named Muffin or Marshmallow or some such thing. This particular dog was the Muffin type, and lived up to its namesake one day by eating all of the blueberry muffins which Page's mom had just cooked for us. That was the only time anything was ever out of order in Page's perfect house.

On the first day of summer when I was four, a girl, her brother, and her mother from down the street appeared on our doorstep with a bucketful of freshly picked blackberries and raspberries. They grew wild all over the neighborhood and behind our house, but it was such a friendly deed that we invited them over that day, sealing our families' friendship. That girl was Rebecca Bacon. From then on, we would hang out, play together, and later, unbeknownst to us until we met there, go to school together. We are still friends today.

My best best friend in the old neighborhood was Abby Rogers. She lived a few doors down from me. One day, during the summer, we sold lemonade to the small handful of people

who passed by on their way to their various obligations. One of Abby's next door neighbors came over and chatted with her mother for a bit, then came over to us and gave us a fifty-cent piece for a cup of lemonade. When we split up the money afterwards, Abby tried to give me the fifty-cent piece. My eyes flew wide open and I told her in an astonished tone that she shouldn't give it to me because fifty cent pieces were worth more than ordinary money. I think I had learned this from my sister a few months earlier, when she gave me one and told me that, since it was a fifty cent piece, I should pay her back fifty cents and then some to make up for it.

During spring collection right after Easter one year, I remember walking down the street with Abby, Easter baskets and candy in hand. Stopping by everyone's piles, we picked out priceless treasures and giggled at how dumb people were for throwing out the things that they did. Our parents and neighbors were throwing out chairs, baskets, mattresses, and even a basketball hoop! We picked a basket out of a pile and put all of our Whoppers Easter Eggs in it, so that we could share all of the eggs instead of one of us having more. We soon found out why the basket was in the junk pile. The bottom fell through, spilling our precious sweets all over the damp ground around us. We ate them anyway.

Memories like these are always there, whether you want them or not. Even if they're tucked away in a dusty corner of your mind, you're bound to stumble across them one day. When you're stressed out or under a lot of pressure, they help you to recall a time when you had not a care in the world, because you didn't have to. If you're sad, being reminded of them will make you smile. The first buddies you remember having will always be the truest and closest as you remember them, No matter how many times you move or make how friends, you will always remember your first and best.

First draft of Christa's essay

Nonfiction Writing From the Inside Out

First Friendships

Did you have any really close friends when you were a child? Most people did, even if they don't remember now. I still remember mine, from my first neighborhood. We all lived within a few houses of each other, and were allowed to roam freely together all summer.

All of the little girls in the neighborhood had pink, fluffy, white-walled rooms. In every one there were cute stuffed animals, fancy pillows, and, of course, lots of lace and frills. The biggest, brightest, and by far the coolest bedroom in my eyes was Paige's, a girl who lived up the street and around a corner. She even had a skylight right over her bed! Paige also had a walk-in closet, with a secret passageway from her stuffed animal-filled closet to who knows where. You entered it through a little door behind a projecting piece of wall, which only a small child could fit into. Once you entered and pulled that door shut, you could go anywhere you wanted, real or made-up. We had thousands of adventures through Paige's little white door. The best by far was when we traveled by boat to Disney World and got to walk in a parade with Mickey and Minnie Mouse. Paige also had a fluffy white dog. It was the kind of dog that is always named Muffin or Marshmallow or some such thing. This particular dog was the Muffin type, and lived up to its namesake one day by eating all of the blueberry muffins which Paige's mom had just cooked for us. That was the only time anything was ever out of order in Paige's perfect house.

On the first day of summer when I was four, a girl, her brother, and her mother from down the street appeared on our doorstep with a bucketful of freshly picked blackberries and raspberries. They grew wild all over the neighborhood and behind our house, but it was such a friendly gesture that we invited them over that day, sealing our families' friendship. That girl was Rebecca Bacon. From then on, we would hang out, play together, and later, unbeknownst to us until we met there, go to school together. We are still friends today.

My best best friend in the old neighborhood was Abby Rogers. She lived a few doors down from me. One day, during the summer, we sold lemonade to the trickle of people passing by her house. One of Abby's next door neighbors came over and chatted with her mother for a bit, then came over to us and gave us a fifty-cent piece for a cup of lemonade. When we split up the money afterwards, Abby tried to give me the fifty-cent piece. My eyes flew wide open and I told her in an astonished tone that she shouldn't give it to me because fifty cent pieces were

these students understand about their process. Lucy separated her grade as she knows that's what I do. All three used terms such as "juicy" and "nosy"—terms from Kathleen Krull's advice to young biographers. Like Spencer, many students are uncomfortable grading themselves. However, once students understand how they used the writing process along with self-, peer, and teacher feedback to improve their writing, they not only accept responsibility for their grade but they also recognize that the power to rework a piece is in their hands.

Christa's final draft includes rewrites and edits.

worth more than ordinary money. I think I had learned this from my sister a few months earlier when she gave me one and told me that, since it was a fifty cent piece, I should pay her back fifty cents and then some to make up for it.

During spring collection right after Easter one year, I remember walking down the street with Abby, Easter baskets and candy in hand. Stopping by everyone's piles, we picked out priceless treasures and giggled at how dumb people were for throwing out the things that they did. Our parents and neighbors were throwing out chairs, baskets, mattresses, and even a basketball hoop! We picked a basket out of a pile and put all of our Whoppers Easter Eggs in it, so that we could share all of the eggs instead of one of us having more. We soon found out why the basket was in the junk pile. The bottom fell through, spilling our precious sweets all over the damp ground around us. We ate them anyway.

Memories like these are always there, whether you want them or not. Even if they're tucked away in a dusty corner of your mind, you're bound to stumble across them one day. When you're stressed out or under a lot of pressure, they help you to recall a time when you had not a care in the world. You'll smile when you think of having had such faithful friends. They will always be the truest and closest as you remember them, no matter who or where they are now. I know mine are.

SELF EVALUATION OF BIOGRAPHY

Name Jeannette _____ Date _____

Give yourself a grade on your biography and provide reasons that back up your decision.

In your discussion, comment on:

Were you nosy enough to collect some stories that grab the reader? Give one or two brief examples.

I think that I was nosy enough to collect some details, though I think that I should have asked for more lessons and stories from them. I collected: 1) she made her sister Christie smell pepper & 2) she made her own puppets & puppet theater.

Discuss the effectiveness of your title, lead, and ending.

I revised my title on the last draft which I believe made it more effective. Before it did not draw the reader in at all. I think my lead successfully pulled in the reader, though maybe I should have mentioned more about Cathie's adult life because only one paragraph had to do with her childhood. My ending was o.k. though I think I could have made it a little longer. Also, the last sentence was a bit cliche.

Did you carefully edit for punctuation and repairing run-on sentences? Did you add details? Briefly refer to these.

I think I could have edited a little more carefully. On some paragraphs I simply skimmed the sentences instead of detailed revising. I added some details and one more lesson that Cathie learned in college. I believe that I did not have any run-ons. (I think I would have caught them even by skimming.)

Grade: A

Eighth graders show how much they understand process.

SELF EVALUATION OF BIOGRAPHY

Name DAVID S _____ Date _____

Give yourself a grade on your biography and provide reasons that back up your decision.

In your discussion, comment on:

Were you nosy enough to collect some stories that grab the reader? Give one or two brief examples. Yes, I was nosey enough. I found a few stories that were funny or it was a bad judgement call on his part. For instance he crashed his dad's car & failed health class.

Discuss the effectiveness of your title, lead, and ending.

My title is effective because it makes the reader wonder about what was bad, good, & goofy times. My lead says some bad things he did & my ending & middle support my thesis.

Did you carefully edit for punctuation and repairing run-on sentences? Did you add details? Briefly refer to these.

Yes I did carefully edit. I read over it many times & made all the corrections Mrs. Robb told me to. I did add details. I even called my interviewy to ask follow up questions again. For instance how long they had known each other. (Jennifer & Josh)

Grade:

I would give myself an A as a grade.

Nonfiction Writing From the Inside Out

LET'S REVISIT THE REASONS WE GRADE STUDENTS' WRITING

The most obvious reason we grade is because schools require number or letter grades for report cards and students' permanent records. For me, grading students' work informs the decisions I make regarding what to teach, understanding what students have learned, and knowing who needs scaffolding to learn a planning, craft, revision, or editing lesson.

So, the challenges for teachers reach beyond the grade. What's tough is taking the time to use students' writing to determine what to teach or reteach, who requires longer conferences, who might benefit from working with a peer, and who can continue to work independently. When we use the process of grading to support our teaching and students' learning, the reasons for grading move beyond accountability to the heart and soul of teaching.

CONTINUE TO THINK ABOUT

"I'm done," Charlie tells me, holding out his writing for me to take.

"Did you read your piece aloud to hear the words and ideas?"

Charlie looks down, shuffles his feet, and mumbles, "No."

"Can you do that before I read it?" Dutifully, Charlie returns to his desk. As I circulate and help others, my eye flashes quickly in Charlie's direction. I note that his writing is on his desk, and he's reading a book slipped into his desk. I say nothing, but make a mental note to work one-on-one again with Charlie as he reads his piece aloud. Perhaps our meetings will create change—perhaps not. But I maintain my persistent stance, continually scaffolding and supporting student writers who view writing as a task to complete and put it out of their mind.

This support occurs during class time, when I can support peers and they can support one another. Hopefully, once students, like professional writers, see revision as an opportunity to improve writing rather than as punishment, they will look forward to rewriting.

I encourage you to share professional writers' thoughts on revision with your students so that they can see that revision is what writing is all about. Hudson Talbott's words, which follow, catch the writer's urgent need to continue improving a piece of writing. He asks teachers to "impress upon young writers" the points he makes.

I've learned to think of my work as being in flux . . . right up to press time—and rewriting can happen even after seeing galleys. My best work comes from looking at what I've just written and seeing what would make it better. That means the text goes through countless revisions before it's printed. It may be the tenth draft that finally reveals to the writer what the true essence of the work is, but you have to go through the previous nine to gain access to it.

CHAPTER EIGHT

WEAVING IDEAS TOGETHER

Final Reflections on Nonfiction Writing in the Classroom

In this final chapter, I have included ideas of professional writers that challenge you and me to continually reflect on our beliefs about writing and the writing lessons we offer our students. Share these quotes with colleagues, discuss them, and use them to inform your teaching and the writing environment you create for students.

While each professional writer celebrates the recursive nature of the writing process, each writer also develops this process in a way that is unique to that author. Our students are the same. They will embrace the recursive process but will also make adjustments that reflect their individual needs and writing style. Keep in mind that these needs will change with the demands of a project and as young writers mature.

I also want you to help your students realize that their daily lives, interests, and experiences contain worthwhile writing topics. To help students discover and explore their passions, invite them to talk to a partner or a small group. Observing the interest an idea stirs in others can be the springboard for students' mining a topic for a nonfiction piece.

As you read the selections that follow, consider what professional writers have to say as it relates to your workshop or class. Consider as well the notion of responding to your students' process adaptations positively, especially when they show you that their adjustments are supporting their thinking, planning, and composing. *My adaptations are in italics.*

In Their Own Words

Jean Craighead George

You have to enjoy being alone to be a writer. You have to enjoy reading and thinking about what's going on in your head. But my head seems to be peopled all the time. Kids should write at home—class is not a lone environment. I wrote at home as a child; I never wrote at school. I thought that all writers should be a little wacky, and I would write my stories on the roof. Then I decided it was more comfortable to come in and write. Go home and write in the privacy of your room.

In my classes, students who have difficulty writing in school write at home. During independent writing time, these students can sit on a comfortable pillow and think about their writing, read a book, listen to a peer's piece and offer feedback, talk to a peer to explore possible topics, or use the computer to complete a publishable draft. Some students are like Donald Graves and the other writers I interviewed. Graves notes: "I try to keep my [writing] study as simple as possible. Furniture is quite limited. I don't want a lot of distractions and lots of windows on the side and overhead." Some students crave similar quiet and minimal distractions.

The only restriction I place on students who choose to write at home is that they cannot disturb classmates who work at school. I'm always amazed at the number of students who can tune out the surrounding talk, as most writers I interviewed write in the silence of their office. The point is that every student won't respond to the same set of guidelines. Instead, if students are productive at home and meet deadlines, then we must respect the writing environment that suits them.

Joyce Hansen

Break down the wall of fear that students have about writing by creating the least stressful environment that you can muster in your classroom. One of the ways to do this is to encourage students to rewrite—let them know that they do not have to get it perfect the first go-round. Encourage journaling so that they have an opportunity to freely write down their thoughts, observations, ideas—these can be topics for essays and other kinds of nonfiction.

Like former teacher Joyce Hansen, I also believe that a large number of students fear writing. Stress levels rise in classrooms I've observed in which the recursive writing process has been reduced to five steps. Brainstorm on Monday, plan on Tuesday, draft on Wednesday, revise on Thursday, and publish on Friday. Just writing this list ties my stomach into knots, for its linear momentum has little relationship to the actual writing process. First, every piece of writing does not have to be revised and published. Second, we have to help students understand that revision, like a fairy godmother, awaits them, and that writing a perfect paper on a first draft is an unrealistic expectation—even for professional writers.

Homer Hickam, Jr.

I will often write down a very loose outline for the next few chapters after I've gotten started, just so I can better know where I'm going. Sometimes I'll throw the whole thing out and start over again. I have done that more than once.

Walter Dean Myers

How much does the nonfiction text change from the four sections to the final form? Sometimes a lot, sometimes a little. The first section is always the problem or question. The second section are the facts logically laid out, which I have used to derive an answer. The third section is the meat of the book or article and is the argument that the facts of the third section support my conclusions. If I write a one-page essay I will use this method. I'm not a slave to it. It's a tool.

What I think I'm doing is very much akin to what a sculptor does when he builds an armature on which to put the clay for a piece of work. The armature is the supporting structure which allows the artist to concentrate on what he wants to achieve without worrying about the piece falling over. I don't want my books to fall over.

Avoid the pitfall of having students plan a piece of writing, then rigidly adhering to that plan. Think of it like the side trips you take that move you away from your planned car route. Detours add zest and new experiences to your plans. My husband always tells me on car trips, "Plans are made to be changed." This is just as true for writers. A plan helps us start and envision the final destination. As we write, the plan changes because through writing we discover new ideas or find ways to improve upon those original thoughts.

Moreover, not all writers complete detailed plans, as Homer Hickam, Jr., points out. For some projects, students will understand the necessity of generating more details; in my classes, this usually occurs when students complete a great deal of research. For projects that build on personal experiences, a short list or a brief web is usually sufficient.

Pam Muñoz Ryan

Sometimes the impetus for an idea comes from a personal experience. Sometimes ideas come from something I read and about which I then become intrigued and subsequently research, which instigates a more complete inspiration. Other times I could be talking to my agent or editor and mention a project I'd been casually considering and one of them might say, "Write it today! That's a great idea." And their validation inspires me to continue. Other times, an idea just keeps nagging

at me until I succumb (from her Web site, www.PamMunozRyan.com).

Generating ideas for writing should always come from the student. That's the only way students will unearth ideas that intrigue and fascinate them. If your school district requires that you practice writing from a prompt to prepare students for state mandated tests, then explain why you have provided a prompt that day. Students will understand and work at the prompt as long as they can also explore their own topics. Learning to write well about their interests and passions will fortify students for writing to a prompt that holds little interest for them.

As much as Pam Muñoz Ryan appreciates validation from her editor and agent, my students desire validation of their ideas and their drafts from me and their peers. Always look for positive comments to offer students. It's no more than you want from administrators who observe your teaching. Growth comes from what students and adults can do well, not from continually focusing on negatives.

Throughout my education, teachers separated writing into creative writing and "the other kind of writing"—the boring nonfiction stuff. Content subject teachers often view nonfiction writing as "technical writing," and they invite students to present "just the facts" with monotonous clarity. Even today, the noncreative label sticks like flies to flypaper in educators' minds. High schools and universities have classes in "creative writing"—classes that dwell on fictional forms and ignore nonfiction.

Recently, I asked my sixth and eighth graders what advice they would offer other students and their teachers for writing nonfiction. The majority of the ideas that follow emerged from several discussions. I frequently ask my students for ideas and support. These exchanges show me what they have absorbed from Read Alouds, mini-lessons, and conferences, as well as how much they understand their writing process.

Sixteen Ideas to Integrate Into Your Workshop or Writing Class

1. **Read nonfiction aloud.** Read parts of informational texts and picture books. But also tune students' ears to essays by Bailey White, David Quammen, Lewis Thomas, and Barbara Kingsolver. Use passages from texts to model how to read like a writer and to learn about technique.

2. **Allow time.** For students to produce good writing, they need time. And each student's time needs will differ, just as the amount of time professional writers need for similar projects will differ. Moreover, writing that requires research takes more time than writing generated from personal experiences. Circulate among students as they work. Take note of where they are in the process, then establish a reasonable deadline date. I always offer my students the option of negotiating an extension, provided they discuss this request before the deadline date.

3. **Show that nonfiction is as creative as fiction.** Share selections from nonfiction texts that illustrate creativity. Present mini-lessons that show ways to start and end a piece,

Nonfiction Writing From the Inside Out

the importance of strong verbs and specific nouns, and so on. Then, with your support, have students apply what they have learned to their own writing.

4. **Set up different writing spaces.** Donald Graves points out that a classroom should have a quiet area, an area for talking, one for conferring, and one for reading and researching. Some students need the quiet that adult writers treasure and should be allowed to write at home.

5. **Know that ideas come from diverse places.** Offer students a rich array of experiences at school by reading aloud, letting them browse through books, and discussing their explorations with peers. Share what the pros have to say about finding topics, and encourage students to reflect on their outside-of-school lives.

6. **Encourage talk.** Peer talk and student-to-teacher talk can help students reclaim that one key event, that experience tinged with elation or deep pain, that's worth thinking and writing about. Show students how conversations with yourself—thinking aloud or with your inner voice—can also reclaim memories.

7. **Be flexible with plans.** Some students will plan an entire piece in their heads, while others will compose detailed written plans. The nature of the project can also determine the depth of planning. However, if the draft works, then be flexible and permit students to adapt the writing process.

8. **Encourage students to write with strong details.** Help them use specific nouns and verbs that paint images. Teach them to avoid adjectives and adverbs, to use them as sparingly as a cook uses herbs and spices. The details students offer can tap into readers' personal experiences and help them connect to the writing.

9. **Accept messy but readable drafts.** As Donald Murray advises, when students are ready to draft, encourage them to write quickly without referring to their notes. Writing at a furious pace can prevent the censorship genie from invading the writer's mind and derailing the drafting process. I accept messy first drafts as long as I can read them, and often messiness is no more than crossed-out words or phrases or additional writing in the margins.

10. **Provide different kinds of feedback.** Professional writers often have spouses or close friends read early drafts; all of them receive feedback from their editors. Provide opportunities for students to gather feedback from you and classmates. But also take the time to show students how self-evaluation can provide supportive feedback, as well.

11. **Let the writing rest.** I love Stephen R. Swinburne's image of cooling the writing—letting the heat and passion of the first draft settle. Returning to a draft or revised piece that has rested can enable the writer to self-evaluate more productively because he can read with more objectivity.

12. **Negotiate criteria.** Negotiate content and writing-convention criteria because these offer guidelines for revision and feedback.

13. **Point out what's working.** Always celebrate the positives you notice to build student writers' confidence and to give them areas that they can try to replicate in other parts of their piece. Next, limit your questions and suggestions to the given criteria; otherwise students feel like Tanya, a sixth grader who told me, "There's so much she [her teacher] wants me to fix. I can't do it." Let go of the notion that every piece has to be perfect and teach the student writer, not what the curriculum guide states.

14. **Encourage revision.** Donald Murray, in an article in *The Boston Globe* (June 25, 2002), celebrates the joys of revision. He notes: ". . . write it again—and again. Each time you will discover new information and new meaning. You will have the writer's thrill of writing what you didn't know you knew." Help students understand that they don't have to get it right on early drafts. Help them understand that writing is rewriting.

15. **Make editing reasonable.** Know that student writers will not be able to edit correctly for all writing conventions. The focus should be on content and writing conventions practiced in class. When students want to publish a piece, scaffold the editing by sitting side by side with them and walking them through corrections. If your classes have too many students to accomplish this, work with a few students each time you invite them to bring a piece to final draft. Become a copy editor for the rest of the students and mark, in pencil, the necessary corrections.

16. Respect differences in how students work through the process. My students were adamant about this suggestion. What professional writers say about their process supports what my students feel. I must confess that it took me time to accept the differences among my students. Abandon the idea of "I know how to do it and what will work." Instead, watch, listen, and talk to your students to discover what works for them. It will change as they grow as writers and readers; it will change with the topic they have chosen.

CONTINUE TO THINK ABOUT

I remember the day I arrived at school, walked into my eighth-grade reading-writing workshop, and Helen burst out laughing. Within seconds, all twenty-two students were laughing; they could hardly stop. The reason? Helen's mom was driving parallel to my car that morning. "You were talking and waving an arm—you looked so weird," blurted Helen, who, during homeroom, immediately reported my case of weirdness to her classmates.

What I had been doing was trying to decide on a literacy vignette to use in a book, and I wanted to hear and reflect on each one. When I told my students, Josh noted, "You shouldn't do that where everyone can see you." For an eighth grader conscious of what peers think, that was a natural comment. My response was that I wasn't concerned about what others would think. My primary goal was to find the best literacy vignette.

So what does this story help us understand? What thoughts should linger as we consider guiding a writing workshop and

A fifth grader reads her piece aloud.

writing nonfiction? First, our students might not be ready to receive specific strategies such as thinking aloud and conversing with oneself in front of peers. It's our job to respect where they are socially, emotionally, and with the writing process, as well.

We can toss out models and techniques for them to consider. We can present outstanding and thought-provoking mini-lessons. But our responsibility is to do what Donald Graves made clear when he said, "The child is more important than the writing." Our responsibility is to discover each student's emotional and writing needs, start where they are, and help them move forward. One prompt for all, one curriculum for all, will not support the fact that children's learning needs differ.

Posing questions supports responding to students' needs. How do they learn? What are their interests? What are their strengths? How do they feel about writing? How can I support them? Remember, my students always surprise me by learning, with nurturing support, what at first seemed impossible. Meeting each student's unique needs means that you will continually adjust your curriculum to meet students where they are and nudge them gently forward, all the time building the self-esteem and confidence they need to write willingly and well.

BIBLIOGRAPHY

PROFESSIONAL MATERIALS

Alvermann, D. E., Dillon, D. R., & O'Brien, D. G. (1987). *Using Discussion to Promote Reading Comprehension*. Newark, DE: The International Reading Association.

Alvermann, D. E. & Phelps, S. F. (1998). *Content Reading and Literacy: Succeeding in today's diverse classrooms* (2nd ed.). Boston: Allyn and Bacon.

Atwell, N. (1999). *In the Middle: New understanding about writing, reading, and learning.* Portsmouth, NH: Heinemann.

Bamford, R. A. & Kristo, J. V. (Eds.) (1998). *Making Facts Come Alive: Choosing quality nonfiction literature K–8*. Norwood, MA: Christopher-Gordon.

Baumann, J. F., Jones, L. A., & Seifert-Kessell, N. (1993). Using Think-Alouds to Enhance Children's Comprehension Monitoring Abilities. *The Reading Teacher.* 47, 184-193.

Beery, R. (2002). Hugs, Humor, Hankies, and History: Writing to bring social studies to life. In *Primary Voices*, 11(1), 18-23.

Boomer, G., Lester, N., Onore, C. S., & Cook, J. (Eds.). 1992. *Negotiating the Curriculum: Educating for the 21st century*. Washington, D.C.: Falmer Press.

Bronowski, J. (1980). The Reach of the Imagination. In A. M. Eastman et al. (Eds.), *The Norton Reader.* New York: W.W. Norton.

Calkins, L. M. (1986). *The Art of Teaching Writing* (2nd ed.). Portsmouth, NH: Heinemann.

Calkins, L. M. & Harwayne, S. (1991). *Living Between the Lines*. Portsmouth, NH: Heinemann.

Canfield, J., Hansen, M. V., & Gardner, B. (Eds.). (2000). *Chicken Soup for the Writer's Soul: Stories to open the heart and rekindle the spirit of writers*. Deerfield Beach, FL: Health Communications.

Dahl, K. L. & Farnan, N. (1998). *Children's Writing: Perspectives from research*. Newark, DE & Chicago: International Reading Association, National Reading Conference.

Duke, N. K & Bennett-Armistead, V. S. (2003). *Reading & Writing Informational Text in the Primary Grades: Research-based practices*. New York: Scholastic.

Elbow, P. (1998). *Writing With Power: Techniques for mastering the writing process*. New York: Oxford University Press.

Evans, K. S. (2001). *Literature Discussion Groups in the Intermediate Grades: Dilemmas and possibilities*. Newark, DE: International Reading Association.

Fiderer, A. (2002). *Paragraph Power: 50 engaging mini-lessons, activities, and student checklists for teaching paragraphing skills*. New York: Scholastic.

Fletcher, R. (1994). *What a Writer Needs.* Portsmouth, NH: Heinemann.

Fountas, I. C. and Pinnell, G. S. (2001). *Guiding Readers and Writers, Grades 3–6: Teaching comprehension, genre, and content literacy.* Portsmouth, NH: Heinemann.

Freeman, E. B. & Person, D. G. (1998). *Connecting Informational Children's Books With Content Area Learning.* Boston: Allyn and Bacon.

Furr, D. (2003). Struggling Readers Get Hooked on Writing. In *The Reading Teacher,* 56(6), 518–525.

Gambrell, L. B. (1996). What Research Reveals About Discussion. In L.B. Gambrell & J. F. Almasi (Eds.), *Lively Discussions! Fostering engaged reading.* Newark, DE: The International Reading Association.

Gillet, J. W. & Temple, C. (2000). *Understanding Reading Problems: Assessment and instruction.* New York: Longman.

Graves, D. H. (1994). *A Fresh Look at Writing.* Portsmouth, NH: Heinemann.

Graves, D. H. (1990). *Discover Your Own Literacy.* Portsmouth, NH: Heinemann.Graves, D. H. (1983, 2003). *Writing: Teachers and children at work.* Portsmouth, NH: Heinemann.

Hansen, J. (2001). *When Writers Read* (2nd ed.). Portsmouth, NH: Heinemann.

Harvey, S. (1998). *Nonfiction Matters: Reading, writing, and research in grades 3–8.* Portland, ME: Stenhouse.

Harwayne, S. (2000). *Lifetime Guarantees: Toward ambitious literacy teaching.* Portsmouth, NH: Heinemann.

Hauptman, L. M. (1995). *Between Two Fires: American Indians in the Civil War.* New York: The Free Press.

Hunter, M. (1976). *Talent Is Not Enough: Mollie Hunter on writing for children.* New York: Harper & Row.

Kletzien, S. B. & Dreher, M. J. (2003). *Informational Text in K–3 Classrooms: Helping children read and write.* Newark, DE: International Reading Association.

Laminack, L. & Bell, B. H. (2004). Stretching the Boundaries and Blurring the Lines of Genre. *Language Arts,* 81(3), 248–259.

Lamott, A. (1994). *Bird by Bird: Some instructions on writing and life.* New York: Anchor Books.

Lewin. T. (2003, April 26) Writing in schools is found both dismal and neglected. In *The New York Times,* section A, p. 13.

Macon, J. M., Bewell, D. & Vogt, M. (1991). *Responses to Literature: Grades K–8.* Newark, DE: International Reading Association.

Macrorie, K. (1985). *Telling Writing.* Upper Montclair, NJ: Boynton/Cook.

Mazzoni, S. A. & Gambrell, L. B. (1996). Text Talk: Using Discussion to Promote Comprehension of Informational Texts. In L. B. Gambrell & J. F. Amalsi (Eds.), *Lively Discussions! Fostering engaged reading.* Newark, DE: The International Reading Association.

McGee, L. M. & Richgels, D. J. (1985). Teaching Expository Text Structure to Elementary Students. *The Reading Teacher*, 38(8), April: 739–749.

Meltzer, M. & Saul, E. W. (1994). *Nonfiction for the Classroom: Milton Meltzer on writing, history, and social responsibility.* New York: Teachers College Press & Newark, DE: International Reading Association.

Moffett, J. (1999). *The Active Voice: A writing program across the curriculum* (2nd ed.). Portsmouth, NH: Heinemann.

Moffett, J. (1968). *Teaching the Universe of Discourse.* Boston: Houghton Mifflin.

Murray, D. M. (1996). *Crafting a Life in Essay, Story, Poem.* Portsmouth, NH: Boynton/Cook.

Murray, D. M. (1989). *Expecting the Unexpected: Teaching myself—and others—to read and write.* Portsmouth, NH: Boynton/Cook.

Murray, D. M. (1982). *Learning by Teaching.* Portsmouth, NH: Boynton/Cook.

Murray, D. M. (1990). *Shoptalk: Learning to write with writers.* Portsmouth, NH: Boynton/Cook.

Murray, D. M. (1984). *Write to Learn.* New York: Holt, Rinehart & Winston.

Murray, D. M. (2000). *Writing to Deadline: The journalist at work.* Portsmouth, NH: Heinemann.

Murphy, P. (2003). Discovering the Ending in the Beginning. *Language Arts*, July 80(6): 461–469.

Piccolo, J. (1987). Expository Text Structures: teaching and learning strategies. In *The Reading Teacher*, May: 838–847.

Portalupi, J. & Fletcher, R. (2001). *Nonfiction Craft Lessons: Teaching information writing K–8.* Portland, ME: Stenhouse.

Pressley, M. & Afflerbach, P. (1995). *Verbal Protocols of Reading: The nature of constructively responsive reading.* Hillsdale, NJ: Lawrence Erlbaum.

Ray, K. W. (1999). *Wondrous Words: Writers and writing in the elementary classroom.* Urbana, IL: National Council of Teachers of English.

Robb, L. (1998). *Easy-to-Manage Reading & Writing Conferences.* New York: Scholastic.

Robb, L. (2001). *Grammar Lessons & Strategies That Strengthen Students' Writing.* New York: Scholastic.

Robb, L. (2000). *Teaching Reading in Middle School: A strategic approach to teaching reading that improves comprehension and thinking.* New York: Scholastic.

Robb, L. (2003). *Teaching Reading in Social Studies, Science, and Math: Practical ways to weave comprehension strategies into your content area teaching.* New York: Scholastic.

Robb, L. (2002). Thinking About Books on Paper. In J. B. Elliott & M. M. Dupuis (Eds.), *Young Adult Literature in the Classroom: Reading it, teaching it, loving it.* Newark, DE: International Reading Association.

Rosenblatt, L. M. (1978). *The Reader, the Text, the Poem: The transactional theory of the literary work.* Carbondale, IL: Southern Illinois University Press.

Schuster, E. H. (2004). National and state writing tests: The writing process betrayed. In *Phi Delta Kappan*, 85(5), 375–382.

Self, J. (1987). *Plain Talk About Learning and Writing Across the Curriculum*. Urbana, IL: National Council of Teachers of English.

Tomlinson, C. M. & Lynch-Brown, C. (2002). *Essentials of Children's Literature* (4th ed.). Boston: Allyn & Bacon.

Vacca, R. T. & Vacca, J. A. (2000). *Content Area Reading: Literacy and learning across the curriculum* (6th ed.). New York: Longman.

Vaughan, J. L. & Estes, T. H. (1986). *Reading and Reasoning Beyond the Primary Grades*. Boston: Allyn & Bacon.

Weaver, C. (1996). *Teaching Grammar in Context*. Portsmouth, NH: Boynton/Cook.

Weaver, C. (1998). Teaching Grammar in the Context of Writing. In C. Weaver (Ed.), *Lessons to Share: On teaching grammar in context*. Portsmouth, NH: Boyton/Cook.

Welty, E. (1984). *One Writer's Beginnings*. Cambridge, MA: Harvard University Press.

Wigginton, E. (1985). *Sometimes a Shining Moment: The foxfire experience*. Garden City, NY: Anchor Books/Doubleday.

Wilhelm, J. D. (2001). *Improving Comprehension With Think-Aloud Strategies*. New York: Scholastic.

Winokur, J. (Ed.). (1999). *Advice to Writers: A compendium of quotes, anecdotes, and writerly wisdom from a dazzling array of literary lights*. New York: Vintage Books.

Yolen, J. (1983). *Writing Books for Children*. Boston: The Writer, Inc.

Zarnowski, M. (1998). It's More Than Dates and Places: How nonfiction contributes to understanding social studies. In R. A. Bamford and J. V. Kristo (Eds.), *Making Facts Come Alive: Choosing & using nonfiction literature K–8*. Morwood, MA: Christopher-Gordon.

Zinsser, W. (2001). *On Writing Well: The classic guide to writing nonfiction*. New York: Quill/HarperCollins.

Zinsser, W. (1988). *Writing to Learn*. New York: Harper & Row.

ESSAYS

Canfield, J., Hansen, M. V., Becker, M. & Kline, C. (Eds.). (1998). *Chicken Soup for the Pet Lover's Soul*. Deerfield Beach, FL: Health Communications.

Canfield, J., Hansen, M. V., Donnelly, M., Donnelly, C. & Tunney, J. (Eds.). (2000). *Chicken Soup for the Sports Fan's Soul*. Deerfield Beach, FL: Health Communications.

Canfield, J., Hansen, M. V. & Kirberger, K. (Eds.). (1997). *Chicken Soup for the Teenage Soul*. Deerfield Beach, FL: Health Communications.

Didion, J. (1969). *Slouching Towards Bethlehem*. New York: Farrar, Straus and Giroux.

Kingsolver, B. (1995). *High Tide in Tucson: Essays from now or never*. New York: HarperPerennial.

Kingsolver, B. (2002). *Small Wonder*. New York: HarperPerennial.

McLeod, A. S. (1994). *American Childhood: Essays on children's literature of the nineteenth and twentieth centuries*. Athens, GA: The University of Georgia Press.

Oates, J. C. & Atwan, R. (Eds.). (2000). *The Best American Essays of the Century*. Boston, MA: Houghton Mifflin.

Paterson, K. (1981). *Gates of Excellence: On reading and writing books for children*. New York: Elsevier/Nelson Books.

Quammen, D. (1988). *The Flight of the Iguana: A sidelong view of science and nature*. New York: Touchstone.

Quammen, D. (2003). *Monster of God: The man-eating predator in the jungles of history and the mind*. New York: Norton.

Quammen, D. (1996). *Song of the Dodo: Island biogeography in an age of extinctions*. New York: Touchstone.

Rooney, A. (2002). *Common Nonsense: Addressed to the reading public*. New York: Public Affairs.

Webster's New Universal Unabridged Dictionary (1979). Deluxe Second Edition. New York: Simon and Schuster.

White, B. (1993). *Mama Makes Up Her Mind: And other dangers of southern living*. New York: Vintage Books.

White, B. (1995). *Sleeping at the Starlite Motel: And other adventures on the way back home*. New York: Vintage Books.

The World Book Encyclopedia (1974). Chicago, IL: Field Enterprises Education Corporation. vol. 14, p. 674.

AUTHOR INTERVIEWS

Susan Bartoletti, March 2003

Bruce Brooks, August 1993

Pat Cummings, May 2003

Barbara Elleman, February 2003

Russell Freedman, may 2003

Jean Craighead George, January 2003

James Cross Giblin, March 2003

Donald Graves, January 2003

Joyce Hansen, January 2003

Homer Hickam, Jr., January 2003

Kathleen Krull, February 2003

Kathryn Lasky, February 2003

Julius Lester, April 2003

Lois Lowry, July 1993

Patricia McKissack, February 2003

Anne Scott McLeod, June 2003

Marissa Moss, March 2003

Donald Murray, January 2003

Walter Dean Myers, March 2003

Katherine Paterson, May 2003

David Quammen, June 2003

Stephen R. Swinburne, January 2003

Roger Sutton, January 2003

Hudson Talbott, April 2003

Michael O. Tunnell, February 2003

CHILDREN'S BOOKS CITED

Anderson, H.C. (1982). *The Snow Queen*, retold by Amy Ehrlich. New York: Dial.

Berger, M. & G. (1999). *Do Tarantulas Have Teeth? Questions and answers about poisonous creatures.* New York: Scholastic.

Berger, M. (2003). *Spinning Spiders.* New York: HarperTrophy.

Bridges, R. (1999). *Through My Eyes.* New York: Scholastic.

Burleigh, R. (2002). *Earth From Above for Young Readers*, photographs by Yann Arthus-Bertrand. New York: Abrams.

Byars, B. (1987). *The Pinballs.* New York: Harper & Row.

Frank, A. (1952). *The Diary of a Young Girl.* New York: Simon and Schuster.

Freedman, R. (2002). *Confucius: The golden rule.* New York: Scholastic.

Freedman R. (2000). *Give Me Liberty! The story of the Declaration of Independence.* New York: Holiday House.

Freedman, R. (1996). *The Life and Death of Crazy Horse.* New York: Scholastic.

Freedman, R. (1987). *Lincoln: A photobiography.* New York: Clarion.

Fritz, J. (1994). *Around the World in a Hundred Years: From Henry the navigator to Magellan.* New York: Putnam.

Fritz, J. (1987). *Early Thunder.* New York: Puffin.

George, J.C. (1991). *The Moon of the Mountain Lions.* New York: HarperCollins.

George, J.C. (1993). *The Moon of the Owls.* New York: HarperCollins.

George, J. C. (1992). *The Moon of the Wild Pigs.* New York: HarperCollins.

George, J.C. (2001). *Seasons of the Moon: Autumn moon.* New York: HarperTrophy.

George, J. C. (2001). *Seasons of the Moon: Winter moon.* New York: HarperTrophy.

Giblin, J.C. (1993). *Be Seated: A book about chairs.* New York: HarperCollins.

Giblin, J. C. (1999). *The Mystery of the Mammoth Bones.* New York: HarperCollins.

Giblin, J. C. (1995). *When Plague Strikes: The black death, smallpox, AIDS.* New York: HarperCollins.

Hansen, J. (1998). *Women of Hope: African Americans who made a difference.* New York: Scholastic.

Herman, J. (2001). *Labyrinth.* New York: Philomel.

Hirst, R. & Hirst, S. (1988). *My Place in Space.* New York: Orchard.

Jiang, Ji Li (1997). *Red Scarf Girl: A memoir of the cultural revolution.* New York: HarperCollins.

Krull, K. (2000). *Lives of Extraordinary Women: Rulers, rebels (and what the neighbors thought).* San Diego: Harcourt.

Krull, K. (1995). *Lives of the Artists: Masterpieces, messes (and what the neighbors thought).* San Diego: Harcourt.

Krull, K. (1997). *Lives of the Athletes: Thrills, spills (and what the neighbors thought)*. San Diego: Harcourt.

Krull, K. (1993). *Lives of the Musicians: Good times, bad times (and what the neighbors thought)*. San Diego: Harcourt.

Krull, K. (1994). *Lives of the Writers: Comedies, tragedies (and what the neighbors thought)*. San Diego: Harcourt.

Krull, K. (1996). *Wilma Unlimited: How Wilma Rudolph became the world's fastest woman*. San Diego: Harcourt.

Lasky, K. (1994). *Days of the Dead*. New York: Hyperion.

Lasky, K. (1994). *The Librarian Who Measured the Earth*. Boston: Little, Brown.

Lasky, K. (1997). *Marven of the Great North Woods*. San Diego: Harcourt.

Lasky, K. (1998). *Shadows in the Dawn: The lemurs of Madagascar*. San Diego: Harcourt.

Lavies, B. (1993). *A Gathering of Garter Snakes*. New York: Dutton.

Lester, J. (1998). *Black Cowboy Wild Horses: A true story*. New York: Dial

Lester, J. (1998). *From Slave Ship to Freedom Road*. New York: Dial.

Levinson, N. S. (1998). *...If You Lived in the Alaska Territory*. New York: Scholastic.

Levy, E. (1987). *...If You Were There When They Signed the Constitution*. New York: Scholastic.

Lewin, T. (2003). *Tooth and Claw: Animal adventures in the wild*. New York: HarperCollins.

Macaulay, D. (1973). *Cathedral: The story of its construction*. Boston: Houghton Mifflin.

McKissack, P. C. & McKissack, F. L. (1999). *Black Hands, White Sails: The Story of African-American whalers*. New York: Scholastic.

McKissack, P. C. & McKissack, F. L. (2003). *Days of Jubilee: The end of slavery in the United States*. New York: Scholastic.

McKissack, P. C. & McKissack, F. L. (1996). *Rebels Against Slavery: American slave revolts*. New York: Scholastic.

McKissack, P. C. & McKissack, F. L. (1995). *Red-Tail Angels: The story of the Tuskegee airmen of World War II*. New York: Walker.

McKissack, P. C. & McKissack, F. L. (1998). *Young, Black, and Determined: A biography of Lorraine Hansberry*. New York: Holiday House.

Meltzer, M. (1996). *Weapons & Warfare: From the stone age to the space age*. New York: HarperCollins.

Moss, M. (1999). *Emma's Journal: The story of a colonial girl*. San Diego: Harcourt.

Moss, M. (2000). *Hannah's Journal: The story of an immigrant girl*. San Diego: Harcourt.

Moss, M. (1998). *Rachel's Journal: The story of a pioneer girl*. San Diego: Harcourt.

Moss, M. (2001). *Rose's Journal: The story of a girl in the Great Depression*. San Diego: Harcourt.

Murphy, J. (2000). *Blizzard! The storm that changed America*. New York: Scholastic.

Murphy, J. (1995). *The Great Fire*. New York: Scholastic.

Myers, W. D. (2001). *Bad Boy: A memoir*. New York: HarperCollins.

Myers, W.D. (2001). *The Greatest: Muhammad Ali*. New York: Scholastic.

Myers, W. D. (1993). *Malcolm X: By any means necessary*. New York: Scholastic.

Myers, W. D. (1991). *Now Is Your Time! The African-American struggle for freedom*. New York: HarperCollins.

Nelson, M. (2001). *Carver: A Life in Poems*. Asheville, NC: Front Street.

Parker, S. *High in the Sky*. (1997). Cambridge, MA: Candlewick.

Pinkney, A. D. (1993). *Alvin Ailey*. New York: Hyperion.

Pinkney, A. D. (1998). *Duke Ellington*. New York: Hyperion.

Ryan, P. M. (2002). *When Marian Sang: The true recital of Marian Anderson*. New York: Scholastic.

Smith, C. R., Jr. (2003). *Hoop Queens*. Cambridge, MA: Candlewick.

Swinburne, S. R. (2003). *Black Bear: North America's bear*. Honesdale, PA: Boyds Mill Press.

Swinburne, S. R. *Bobcat: North America's cat*. Honesdale, PA: Boyds Mill Press.

Swinburne, S. R. (1999). *Coyote: North America's dog*. Honesdale, PA: Boyds Mill Press.

Talbott, H. (2000). *Forging Freedom: A true story of heroism during the Holocaust*. New York: Putnam.

Talbott, H. (2003). *Safari Journal*. San Diego: Harcourt.

Tanaka, S. (2003). *The Alamo: A day that changed America*. New York: Hyperion.

Tolkien, J.R.R. (1965). *The Return of the King (The Lord of the Rings, Part 3)*. New York: Ballentine Books.

Tunnell, M. O. & Chilcoat, G. W. (1996). *The Children of Topaz: The story of a Japanese-American internment camp*. New York: Holiday House.

Tunnell, M. O. (1993). *The Joke's on George*. New York: Tambourine.

APPENDICES

Tips For Developing
Your Own Mini-Lessons

This book does not include every mini-lesson your students will need. You will want to design your own lessons, based on the knowledge of writing nonfiction your students walk into your class with, and based on what they show you they need as you explore nonfiction together. My goal in this section is to share my thinking process so you can plan mini-lessons.

MAKE THE STRUCTURE OF YOUR MINI-LESSONS CONSISTENT

You'll notice that the mini-lessons in this book follow a consistent pattern that you can adapt and implement in your classes. Each lesson includes these four elements:

- Topic
- Purpose
- Materials
- Guidelines

I find that the consistent structure helps me map out a new mini-lesson, and the predictability is good for students, too.

Let me model how I plan a mini-lesson on helping eighth graders write a title for their informative articles. Even though the guidelines students and I established included a short title, most turned in first drafts with "Information Article" for their title. Students' writing showed me what they needed.

So I began using the four parts to plan my mini-lesson. I had my topic, now I had to consider my purpose. Having a clear purpose can make it easier to decide whether to offer students materials for the first lesson so they can try the strategy themselves, or whether I model the entire lesson. Knowing your purpose can help you decide the materials you need and how to use them.

MAKE THE PURPOSE OF THE MINI-LESSON CLEAR

My purpose was to enable students to write short titles that pulled readers into the article and introduced the topic. I decided to collect informational picture and chapter books and magazines from our classroom and school libraries. I felt that students could learn a great deal about titles by studying these three genres after I completed a think-aloud using a title I considered tops and one I felt was uninteresting. Now the guidelines were clear because I understood my role and students' role.

KNOW THE GUIDELINES AND SHARE THESE WITH STUDENTS

Take the time to jot down your mini-lesson plans. You can keep your mini-lesson notes in a three-ring binder, a file folder, or a notebook. I've expanded my notes for guidelines, which I jot down in short phrases to make the ideas clearer:

1. *Organize students into groups of four.*
2. *For two to three minutes, have partners discuss what makes a good title. Collect their ideas on chart paper.*
3. *Think aloud to share your ideas on what makes one title top-notch and what makes another ordinary and uninteresting.*
4. *Give each group a picture book, a chapter book, and a magazine article.*
5. *Have groups evaluate titles, discuss which ones they liked and disliked, and explain why.*
6. *Ask groups to choose a spokesperson to present the group's findings.*
7. *Wrap up by asking students to adjust and add to their list of ideas of what makes a terrific title, using their experiences.*

RECAP OF SUGGESTIONS FOR CREATING A MINI-LESSON

- Identify the **topic**.
- State the mini-lesson's **purpose**.
- Decide whether you will involve students.
- Consider what kinds of **materials** students need or the materials you need.
- Frame the **guidelines** based on your purpose and topic.
- **Think aloud** and show students how you interpret and/or understand the materials—this provides them with a mental model of what to do to accomplish the task.
- Jot down the **guidelines** so you know how to proceed.
- Prepare the chart so it contains the title and purpose of the mini-lesson.
- Under guidelines, collect students' ideas before and after they study sample titles from informational texts and articles

Tips for Guiding Students with Brief Conferences

Because students in your class will be at different points in the writing process, you need a teaching tool that can support individual needs. The brief conference is that tool, for it allows you to respond to students' questions and support them if the writing has derailed.

Like a gardener checking flowers beds to see if snapdragons need water or roses need plant food, I move around the room as students read, collect ideas, think, plan, draft, revise, or edit to discover their needs. In my hand are sticky notes and a pencil so I can jot down suggestions and give students the key points we discussed. Here are some points students might receive:

• Can you circle verbs in this paragraph and find stronger ones?

• The lead contains important details. Try two or three and consider opening with a quote or a short anecdote.

• Reread and use the symbol for paragraph to mark them.

As you read on you'll explore the three kinds of conferences my students experience: impromptu and longer planned encounters that I lead, and peer conferences that students run.

IMPROMPTU ENCOUNTERS: SHORT AND FOCUSED

These unplanned meetings occur as you support students while you move around the room. They are effective because you can spot students who require support on a single issue such as where to mark paragraphs or how to start the essay and respond to them immediately. Here are some suggestions for productive impromptu conferences.

Watch your student. Open by stating what you observe. For example, I might start with, "You have two pages of super ideas about dogs. Do you want to talk about which ideas you will include in your How-to-Care-for-a Dog piece?"

Wait at least one minute for the student to say something. That minute can feel like an eternity, but the purpose of these mini-meetings is to lead students to solving their own writing problems. In a safe class environment, students will ask for help. Even so, I always try to pose questions or offer a suggestion that starts the student thinking instead of me doing the work.

Help the student find possible solutions. In addition to asking a question that provokes thinking, you can suggest that students obtain peer feedback.

Intervene if you believe that the student would benefit from your support. Start the conversation with a question that includes what you observe. I pause next to Anita who has been fidgeting and say, "Wow! That's a great list of ideas for gymnastics. Would you like to discuss these so you can decide which items to include in your piece?"

Sometimes, I think a student needs help when in fact, that student is thinking and simply needs more time. Questions offer students choice. I never want to intervene unless students agree. If your intervention will take more than four minutes, schedule a planned conference later in the period or the next day.

PLANNED CONFERENCES: PROVIDE MORE TIME

When students are stuck and need more than a short encounter, try a planned conference that takes from five to seven minutes. Planned conferences provide the time for you to coach, then observe the student's attempts.

Sit next to the student. When you're nearby, you help a student look at her work through a zoom lens. If a student has difficulty brainstorming or paragraphing, I coach by generating a few ideas with the student's help or by thinking aloud as I mark one or two paragraphs. Then I invite the student to practice while I am there to build confidence and ask questions that can develop independence.

Record the highlights of conferences using the reproducible on page 320. Students keep these conference forms in their writing folders, using them like road maps during the process.

Planned Conference Form

Name _____ Date _____

Conference topic:

Key points of discussion:

Student's plan of action:

Does student need to schedule another conference?

List time for next conference:

Nonfiction Writing From the Inside Out

Resources to Help You Select Nonfiction

If your school library does not subscribe to these resources, encourage your librarian to reserve funds for some of these. Many schools have parent-teacher organizations that raise money for books, and local public libraries often have many of these resources.

- *The Best in Children's Nonfiction: Reading, Writing, and Teaching Orbis Pictus Award Books,* J. M. Jensen, R.M. Kerper, & M. Zarnowski, (Eds.), National Council of Teachers of English, 2001.
- *Book Links: Connecting Books, Libraries, and Classrooms.* A bimonthly magazine that explores themes, many in science and social studies. Includes annotated books lists and teaching ideas. (American Library Association, 50 East Huron, Chicago, IL 60611.)
- *Eyeopeners II* by Beverly Kobrin: Includes an introduction to nonfiction for children and an annotated list of 800 recommended books. New York: Scholastic, 1995.
- *The Horn Book Guide,* published by The Horn Book, Inc., is a biannual publication that organizes books by genre, subject, and age appropriateness. Reviewers rate books from 1 to 6. I urge teachers to order books with ratings of 1, 2, or 3, but the best books are those rated 1 and 2. (The Horn Book, Inc., 56 Roald St., Suite 200, Boston, MA 02129.)
- *It's the Story That Counts: More Children's Books for Mathematical Learning K–6,* by Whitin and Wilde, Portsmouth, NH: Heinemann.
- *The Kobrin Letter: Concerning Children's Books About Real People, Places, and Things.* Uses a newsletter format to review new and top-notch old information books on selected topics. (732 Greer Rd., Palo Alto, CA 94303.)

- "Notable Children's Trade Books for a Global Society" is an annual annotated list published in *The Dragon Lode,* the magazine for the international Reading Association's Special Interest Group on Reading and Literature. This biannual magazine contains annotated lists of outstanding fiction and nonfiction on various topics. (Obtain the name and address of the current Membership Chair from IRA, 800 Barksdale Rd., P.O. Box 8139, Newark, DE 19714.)
- "Notable Social Studies Trade Books for Young Readers" is annotated and published annually in the May/June issue of *Social Education,* 3501 Newark St. N.W., Washington, D.C. 20016.
- "Outstanding Science Trade Books for Children" is an annual annotated list of science books published in the March issue of *Science and Children,* NSTA, 1840 Wilson Blvd., Arlington, VA 22201.
- "Orbis Pictus Award-Winners, Honor Books, and Notables" is published annually in *Language Arts.*
- *Read Any Good Math Lately? Children's Books for Mathematical Learning K–6* by Whitin and Wilde, Portsmouth, NH: Heinemann, 1992.
- *Searchit.heinemann.com.* A Web site that contains the newest and best science trade books.
- *The Wonderful World of Mathematics,* edited by Thiessen and Matthias, Reston, VA: National Council of Teachers of Mathematics, 1992.

Some Excellent Magazines and Newspapers

Students enjoy magazines because articles are usually short and contain many interesting photographs, illustrations, maps, puzzles, diagrams, and charts. Here are some excellent resources:

Calliope is a 48-page, themed magazine about people and events of the past. *Cobblestone Publishing, 7 School St., Peterborough, NH 03458*

Cobblestone is a 48-page, theme-related magazine. It offers an imaginative approach to teaching history and those people, events, and ideas that have shaped the American experience. *Cobblestone Publishing, 7 School St., Peterborough, NH 03458*

Field & Stream, Jr. has articles on conservation, hunting, fishing, sporting ethics, and nature. *Times Mirror Magazines, 2 Park Ave., New York, NY*

Ranger Rick helps deepen children's understanding of nature. *National Wildlife Federation, 8925 Leesburg Pike, Vienna, VA 22184-001*

Scholastic Dynamath contains 16 pages of word problems, test prep ideas, and computation for grades 5 and 6. *Scholastic, 557 Broadway, New York, NY 10012*

Scholastic Math has articles that offer strategies for problem solving, computation, statistics, test prep, consumer math, and real-life math applications for grades 7 to 9. *Scholastic, 557 Broadway, New York, NY 10012*

Scholastic News is a weekly classroom newspaper for students in grades 3 to 6. *Scholastic, 557 Broadway, New York, NY 10012*

Scholastic Scope is a language arts magazine that presents plays, interviews, poetry, fiction, and nonfiction for students in grades 6 to 10. *Scholastic, 557 Broadway, New York, NY 10012*

Science Weekly motivates students to learn about their world and develops science and technology awareness. Available for grades 3 to 8. *Science Weekly, 2141 Industrial Parkway, Suite 202, Silver Spring, MD 20904*

Science World is published biweekly and has several feature articles and brief newsworthy items based on current research in all the sciences. It is ideal for grades 7 to 10. *Scholastic, 557 Broadway, New York, NY 10012*

The Wall Street Journal, Classroom Edition is for students in grades 7 to 12 and tries to improve their business and economic literacy. *The Wall Street Journal, Classroom Edition, P.O. Box JJ, Sonoma, CA 95476*

Zoobooks offer entertaining and informative full-color articles about wildlife and are ideal for students in grades 3 to 8. *Wildlife Education Limited, 3590 Kettner Blvd., San Diego, CA 92101*

Transition Words and Phrases
Help Make Writing Clear

Like tour guides, transition words make connections between ideas in sentences; they provide links from the end of one paragraph to the start of the next one, making reasoning logical and clear. Have students staple or tape the reproducible that follows on the inside of their writing folders. This way, while drafting and revising, students can easily refer to the page.

TRANSITION WORDS AND PHRASES
Location or Place

above	across	among	along	behind
below	beneath	nearby	in back of	outside
under	to the right/left	between	inside	over
throughout	beside	near	on top of	around

Time

after	during	until	then	before
first	second	third	yesterday	tomorrow
next	later	soon	when	as soon as
today	meanwhile	finally	at last	

TO EMPHASIZE A POINT

again	repeatedly	for this reason	in fact

To Add More Information

again	also	another	and	in addition
as well	besides	moreover	along with	for example

FOR CONCLUSIONS

as a result	therefore	finally

Comparison Words

like	also	in the same way

Contrast Words

but	however	yet	although	otherwise

Ready to Edit

Once students understand a mini-lesson and can successfully complete the student practice activities, have them edit their own work. To call their attention to editing needs, place a check in the margin next to the line that requires repairs, or use the editing symbols below.

Remember: Always have students edit for one item at a time. Structure this for them by listing on the chalkboard the order of items they should edit.

Symbol	Meaning	Example
∧	Insert	I ∧happy. (am)
≡	Uppercase (Capitalize)	leslie lopez
/	Lowercase	Car
∿	Transpose	recieve
℈	Remove, Delete	She is ~~not~~ here.
¶	Indent for a Paragraph	¶ Once upon a time...
⊙	Add Period	Clean up⊙
⋀	Add Comma	The sad silent child wept

Figurative Language: The Writer's Tools

Here are explanations and examples of the figurative language student writers can use while crafting paragraphs. Photocopy this page and have students keep one in their writing folders. Encourage students to refer to this resource when they are drafting and rewriting.

Simile: compares two unlike things that have one thing in common; uses *like* or *as*.

Example: Toby let loose on his sleek brass sax, curling his notes *like a kite tail in the wind*.
— *Duke Ellington* by Andrea Davis Pinkney

Metaphor: compares two unlike things that have one thing in common without using *like* or *as*.

Example: Their [bear cubs] claws are grappling hooks.
— *Black Bear: North America's Bear* by Stephen R. Swinburne, page 14

Personification: gives human emotions and abilities to places, things, ideas, animals, etc.

Example: Across the marsh, cattails *shiver* in a gust of wind.
— *Bobcat: North America's Cat* by Stephen R. Swinburne, page 19

Alliteration: the repetition of a beginning consonant sound

Example: Numerous damaged ships were being towed in by tugs, while *b*roken and *b*attered *b*oats could be seen in all directions.
— *Blizzard!* by Jim Murphy, page 110

Onomatopoeia: a word or phrase that creates a sound

Example: At the *crack* of the starting gun, she [Wilma Rudolph] surged into the humid air like a tornado.
— *Wilma Unlimited: How Wilma Rudolph Became the World's Fastest Woman* by Kathleen Krull

Example of a Status of the Class Form

P= Planning
D= Drafting
R= Revising
E= Editing
C= Peer Conference
c= Teacher Conference
D= Final Draft

Status of Class Dates

	4/12	4/14	4/15	4/20	4/22	4/24	4/26	4/27		
William Bayliss	P	P	D	D	P	P	P	D		
Spencer Burkholder	D	D	D	PC	R	R	E			
Garland Caldwell	R	R	TC	PC	R	E	E	FD		
Lee Carter	P	P	D	D	P	P	D	D		
Tyler Crowe	TC	TC	PC	PC	R	R	E	E		
Marina de Medici	PC	R	R	PC	E	E	FD	FD		
Eleanor Hamman	P	D	D	D	PC	D	PC	R		
Dylan Harry	D	D	D	TC	PC	R	R	PC		
Katheryne Lawson	P	P	P	D	D	TC	D	TC		
Emily Levi	P	D	D	TC	PC	R	E	FD		
Nick Marfing	P	P	D	D	D	PC	R	R		
Avery McIntosh	TC	PC	P	P	PC	D	D	D		

Nonfiction Writing From the Inside Out

Index

Nonfiction Writing From the Inside Out